The World's Great
REGIMENTS

The World's Great REGIMENTS

Vezio Melegari

Spring Books

London · New York · Sydney · Toronto

© Copyright 1968 by Rizzoli Editore, Milano
© Copyright 1969 by Weidenfeld and Nicolson, London
Translated from the Italian by Ronald Strom
Published in Italian under the title *I Grandi Reggimenti*

This edition published 1972 by
The Hamlyn Publishing Group Limited
London · New York · Sydney · Toronto
Hamlyn House, Feltham, Middlesex, England

Printed in Holland by Senefelder, Purmerend

ISBN 0 600 33899 1

To my father

Valour:

Valour is not a futile,
heedless and impassioned courage,
seeking out danger for danger's sake, flaunting
itself in vain, aiming only
for glory and the hollow praise of men.
The courage I speak of is a wise
and measured one, inspired by the sight
of its foes, taking command
in the midst of danger, letting no opportunity slip by,
yet never overestimating
its strength; a courage which undertakes
hazardous tasks yet never attempts
the impossible, which leaves nothing to chance that
might be accomplished by fortitude, which,
when counsel fails, is ready to brave all,
prepared in the name of duty
to die in victory or to survive in defeat.

ESPRIT FLÉCHIER

Funeral oration for
Henri de la Tour d'Auvergne,
Vicomte de Turenne,
Maréchal de France.

International Advisory-Board

CONTENTS

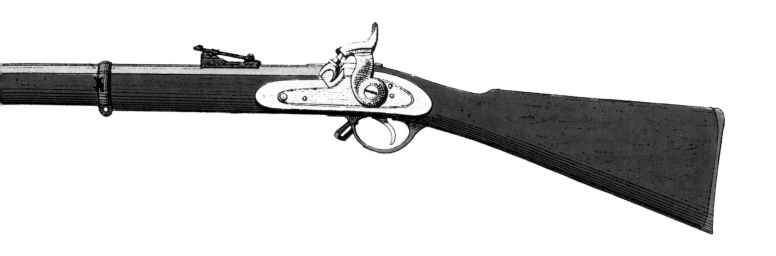

PREFACE

'I love the brisk drilling of soldiers on parade grounds, the uniform beauty of soldiers and horsemen in their harmoniously moving formations, with their indomitable frayed banners, the sheen of shot-scored bronze helmets...'

These are verses from Pushkin's Bronze horseman but they might well be, at first sight, the words of a diligent schoolboy out of the past or an excerpt from some old book of adventure. They might go on to describe a parade with the unfailing mention of the blare of trumpets, the roll of drums, the clatter of horses' hooves, and the clicking of bayonets being fixed on rifles.

The scene is both ancient and modern, changing and timeless. The years go by, one generation succeeds another, times change, and political regimes are altered; but regiments, however altered in the faces of their men and the style of their uniforms, march towards the future with their old cadence. Their goal is outside time and their step has lost none of its assurance.

People watch them pass with varying and sometimes conflicting emotions, but never with indifference. Like it or not, the regiments have made history. Many of them are history.

Some among many are described in this book, in which they appear not only as the protagonists of the age-old tragedy of war but, more importantly, as the source and impulse of new emotions.

Let the reader not be misled by the motto Suum cuique at the beginning of this volume. Not a few readers will search for their 'own' regiment in vain. In fact, this book does not and could not include 'everyone's own.' Vezio Melegari must have been tempted to provide a complete and systematic work. As often happens with popularisers, from Comenius on, Melegari must have hoped to 'say everything for everyone', to encompass the subject of famous units within the limits of a certain number of pages and a certain approach.

It is no accident that he began with the Curetes and ended with the Paras. But the physical limits of a single volume prohibit, and must always prohibit, such an ambitious and, I would even say impossible goal. The author could not but realise that all regiments have their own fame and history - a fame and history that often require treatment battalion by battalion, company by company, platoon by platoon, squad by squad, and even man by man. It is just as well then that the author has made his own selection and followed his own inclinations, his own bent, even his own prejudices and preferences. In this way he has produced a book that is lively and new, entertaining and true, and not a punctilious compendium of data. He has written a book that will appeal to readers interested in the beautiful and lasting, not a pedantically arranged review but a free excursus from episode to episode.

Nevertheless the book has its fixed centre, the definitive element, the basic contribution. And it is doubly satisfying me to acknowledge this, both out of gratitude towards the author and because of my personal interest in the subject as a collector and as an organiser of collectors and students of military uniforms. One rarely encounters a publishing venture of such importance in the field of military uniforms and models. The illustrations in this book are outstanding, and one can only hope that similar enterprises will be undertaken in future. For despite the immense wealth of painted, engraved, and drawn soldiers executed by artists of diverse skills, it was no easy task to discover the unpublished or little known and at the same time present them attractively and assimilate them into a text that ranged from the era of myth to that of the atom bomb and required illustrations of historic fidelity and artistic quality.

Although this book disavows concern with scientific systematisation, it must still command the admiration of all of us who for years have dedicated ourselves to the valuable task of gathering and organising the evidence of mankind's military glories. I am pleased to commend this book in the certainty that it will invite the reader to find in the asperities of the past the promise of a serene future.

INTRODUCTION

A name, a number, a badge, a colour, a flag — for most people the term 'regiment' suggests an organic unit that is distinct and different from every other, beyond its precise and scientific military definition. A history of regiments from this point of view would no doubt be extremely fascinating, but in my opinion it would limit the subject matter and perhaps also detract from the attraction of the great panorama of military history, to which the regiment has made a decisive contribution but of which it still remains only a part.

Since I wished to present a colourful and honest picture of the long road traversed by the soldiers of all time, including the mythical and legendary period at the very beginning, I could not neglect some units that were larger and smaller than the regiment together with units radically different from the regiment, units like the phalanx, and the *turma*, the battalion and the battery, the squadron and the brigade — all names that are as well known as that of the regiment, and sometimes dearer to the heart and more evocative.

The illustrations have been chosen with the criteria of setting no rigid limits and refusing to make arbitrary value judgments. I have intentionally allowed the technical and documentary illustrations of uniforms to take second place to the poetic flavour of paper soldiers and have preferred to complement the text with famous prints

and contemporary photographs rather than with historic relics. Certainly, in the selection of single illustrations, I have tried above all to do full justice to the subject and to considerations of artistic merit. The so-called paper soldier — sought after and collected with passionate and tenacious care by no small number of collectors — sometimes discloses surprising and exciting aspects and always reveals evocative and pleasant features.

Many of the illustrations in these pages have never been published before. The originals are often preserved in collections that are not easily accessible and in others that are all but unknown. The most characteristic example may be that of 'Achille Bertarelli' Civic Print Collection in Milan. I thank them here first of all, not only because of the assistance given me but also to indicate the value and quantity of this military history section, in large part still to be discovered. The help of the Centro Internazionale di Uniformologia in Rome, and its Secretary General, Lt. Col. Alessandro Gasparinetti, the help of Col. Frederick P. Todd, former director of the West Point Museum, and that of other institutions and individuals mentioned elsewhere in the book has been equally important.

Where it has not been possible to find contemporary illustrations, reconstructions have been used. Recourse has been made to the most probable sources and the most likely interpretations.

This refers especially to the earlier plates illustrating military units of antiquity. But some very modern uniforms have also forced the author and illustrator to fall back on hypothesis: there are wars now being waged in the world, and certain details of uniform, though apparently insignificant, that are nevertheless covered by military secrecy.

On the other hand, this book is not intended as a treatise on uniforms nor is it intended as an organic summary of military history. Undoubtedly it is more evocative than scientific, more episodic than systematic. But it can be considered, and this is its chief ambition, an introduction to the history of military honour, sometimes hypothetical, never complete, atrociously abused by modern man but fortunately intact in the eternal pages of history.

PART ONE

From Myth
to the Middle Ages

From the Heavens to the Praetorium

The Sword of Light

The Curetes may be the oldest military unit in Greek mythology. They (how many we do not know) took part in the fearful affair of Cronus. Tormented by the prophecy of the dying Uranus (whom he had mutilated with a sickle, still the traditional weapon of certain Galla tribes), Cronus, the youngest of the seven Titans born from the earth, eliminated one by one the children that Rhea, his wife and sister, regularly produced, every nine months. According to the prophecy, one of his children would snatch the crown of king of the world from Cronus' head. Thus Cronus devoured them as soon as they were born. Such was the fate of Hestia, Demeter, Hera, Hades and Poseidon. But Rhea saved the sixth child by hiding him in a cave in Crete and putting in his cradle a common stone wrapped in swaddling clothes, which Cronus unsuspectingly swallowed. But to prevent the unnatural father from finding the child anywhere in the sky, on the earth or in the sea, the infant's cradle was hung on the branches of a tree. Around the tree a guard was mounted by the Curetes, who beat their swords against their shields to drown the infant's cries. This child was called Zeus and, as everyone knows, he did in fact succeed to the throne of the universe.

The Curetes, or 'shaven-headed youths' (such as we were when we were army recruits), are often confused with the Gorybantes, a heavenly company of nine armed dancers. In the Museo Nazionale Romano there is a fragment of a relief showing three dancers with the infant Zeus. But the mythological Curetes must have had their origins in the reality of history and ancient customs. One can see in them the bodyguard of the sacred king, who in the ritual ceremonies of the Pelasgian era must have paraded before him, beating their weapons to drive away spirits. And in remotest times, according to Porphyry of Tyre, it was their task to cut the throats of children offered on the bloody altar of Cronus.

The angelic hosts of Jehovah, the biblical God of battle, were purely heavenly. From *Joshua* to *Isaiah* and from *Judges* to *Revelation*, the angels are always clearly distinguished from the other forces of Jehovah, be they terrestrial (the people of Israel) or sky-borne (the winds, storms, thunder and lightning).

Certainly Judaism created the most satisfying idea of an angel. The celestial messengers of the Bible - more numerous than the stars and scattered namelessly (with certain exceptions, as in the list given by Enoch) in the infinite spaces of light - represent a compendium of the most ancient angelology, Persian and Babylonian, faithful to the model of the heavenly spirit as an omnipresent guardian of human life.

Above: *An armed angel in an 18th-century illustration.* Opposite: *The assembly of the warrior angels in an engraving from a 19th-century edition of Milton's* Paradise Lost. *Notice that armour is limited to certain units only, while all have a spear and shield.*

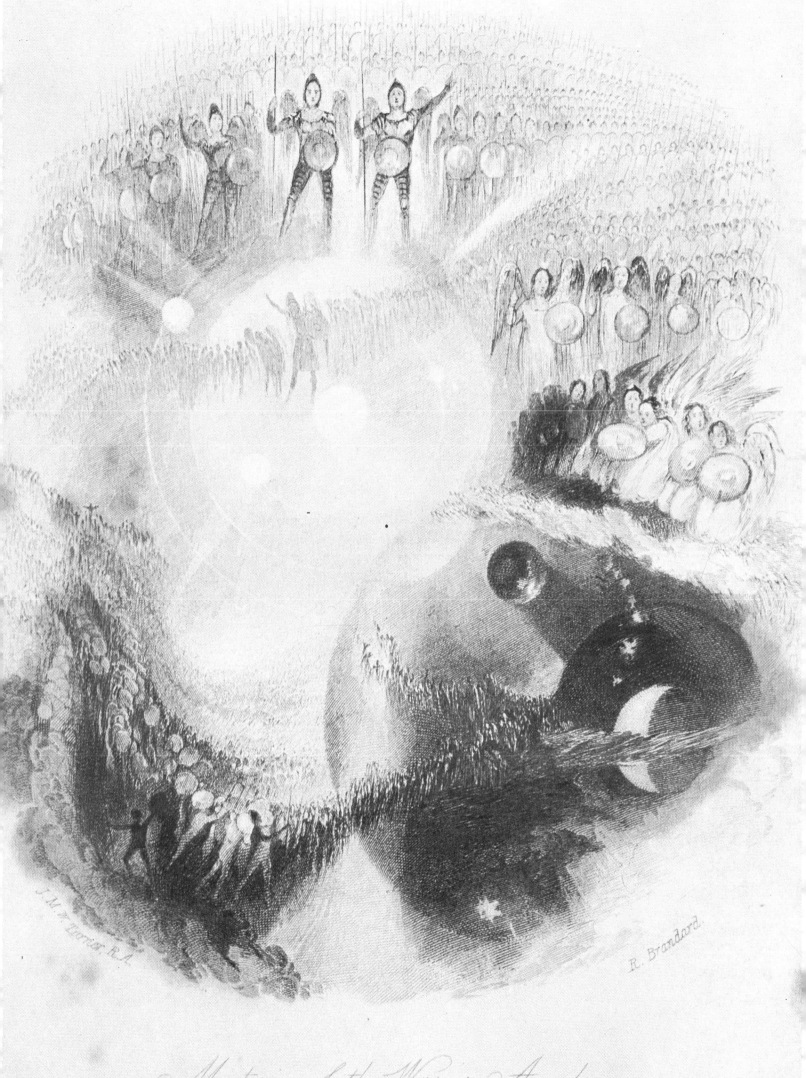

Mustering of the Warrior Angels.

The Kiss of the Valkyries

In the most ancient Mediterranean mythology appears the figure of the Libyan goddess Neith. She belongs to that Pelasgian complex of religious beliefs in which the universe was believed to be dominated by a universal goddess and her priestesses. It was believed that woman was made pregnant by the wind or by having swallowed something, usually insects or beans. Frightened man obeyed her and worshipped her. The goddess Neith had a temple at Sais which was guarded by armed virgin priestesses who engaged in combat every year to compete for the title of high priestess. And it was in Libya, according to Pelasgian myth, that Athena was born. In playful combat she accidentally killed her companion Pallas, and out of grief she took her friend's name. What makes this legend interesting is that it shows there were, even in ancient times, bands of armed women. The priestesses of the Libyan Syrtes were not alone. As a matter of fact, the moon priestesses who held sway on the south-eastern banks of the Black Sea also bore arms. And they may have been the originals, by way of travellers' accounts, of the mythical Amazons, of whom more will be said later on.

The Libyan origin of Athena seems to be confirmed by the fact that even in classical times the triumphal 'Ololu! Ololu!' was still shouted in honour of the goddess. It seems that this cry represents a very ancient Libyan expression.

There is more variety and evocative power in the cry of other mythical warrior women. Or so it would seem from the Wagnerian opera named after these women, the Valkyries:

> Hojotoho! Hojotoho!
> Hejaha! Hejaha!
> Hahej! Hahej! Hejaho!

This is the song of Brunhilde ('leaping joyously from rock to rock') at the beginning of the second act of the *Valkyrie*. Grimgerda and Rossweise, the other Wagnerian Valkyries (though these are literary names) take up the cry later, when they appear on horseback in the lightning, each bearing a dead warrior across her saddle. Evidently their lips have not touched the cold lips of the warriors. For Wotan (Odin) had given his virgin daughters the power of restoring the dead war-

riors with a kiss, so that they could be brought to the great paradise of heroes, Valhalla. Here the heroes fought amongst themselves every day until they fell, only to revive and return the next day to the fray fighting from dawn to dusk. Between golden walls and under a roof of bronze shields there were six hundred and forty doors, each one large enough to allow eight hundred warriors to enter and leave in review formation, to charge out on to the field of eternal battle and eternal glory.

As there have been those who tried to count the number of angels in the Bible, there have also been those who have tried to count the number of heroes in the Valhall. Their calculations would suggest that the heroic company consisted of six hundred and fourteen thousand souls, but it is impossible that the ancient creators of the myth could have used such large numbers, and one must consider the figures cited in the poetic texts (the primary source of Nordic mythology) as a mere indication, an invitation to think of the Valhall as an immense barracks.

According to modern scholars, the Valhall, as it is described in the *Edda* for example, is a reflection of the Colosseum, which may have been seen by some Scandinavian traveller at the time it still preserved its many portals and when gladiators were still engaged in their battles to the death.

In the Valhall Odin lived on wine, but the fallen warriors ate the flesh of a boar that was stewed every day. In the evening the boar was recomposed and prepared to provide sustenance again the next day. Heidrun the goat ate the leaves of a particular tree and then provided an alcoholic milk for the warriors.

One corner of the heavenly barracks, the Wingolf, was the seat of the Valkyries, who distributed meat and brew (as well as kisses) to the valiant warriors.

Surprisingly enough, Nordic mythology envisaged an end to this resort of strong delights. One day the boar would not be recomposed and Heidrun's tree would have produced its leaves. Then giants would push through the six hundred and forty doors and in a few seconds the paradise of heroes would crumble beneath their blows. Eternity was not for the Valhall.

In the four theatrical sketches reproduced below are depicted Valkyries according to the traditional iconography. Such may have been the appearance of the 'Gothic Amazons', the lady warriors who followed the triumphal chariot of Aurelian on his way back from Syria after defeating Tetricus and Zenobia.

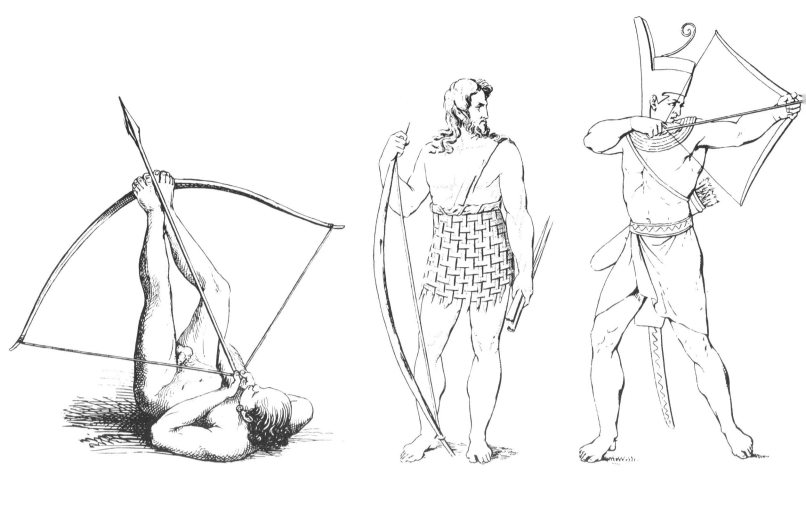

Amazons and Archers

The offensive weapon is nothing more than an extension of the arm, a supplement to strength and human effort that overcomes the limits imposed by nature.

Raimondo Montecuccoli (1609-80), who knew a great deal about such matters, considered the lance the most beautiful and effective weapon of offence, but surely the arrow has a truer nobility and is dearer to mankind's martial memories. Along with the bow and crossbow it survived to the dawn of modern times.

The bow and arrow were so much a part of ancient man that one can trace them back beyond the dawn of history to the darkness of myth. The legendary company of the Amazons, to which reference has already been made, illuminates one aspect of this history.

Sources are unanimous in saying that the bow was the primary weapon of these intrepid warrior women. An uncertain etymological reading of their name, altogether erroneous according to some scholars, led to the suggestion that for greater ease in drawing back the cord of the bow, an Amazon cut or burnt off her right breast. But there is no confirmation of this in any ancient works of art depicting Amazons. On the contrary, there is a bas-relief preserved in Rome depicting the beautiful Penthesilea among a group of Amazons rushing to help Priam. Penthesilea, doomed to die by the hand of Achilles, is shown, in fact, with the right breast uncovered.

Archaeology has not succeeded in establishing the date and place of origin of the bow. It was probably invented by a people of northern Africa in the Mesolithic period, about nine thousand years ago. Ash branches stretched with animal tendons were used to shoot and hurl flint-headed arrows or, when the prey was to be stunned rather than killed, blunt wood-headed arrows. For ninety centuries, until the invention of the rifle, man was to have no more efficient portable weapon. The bow was also assimilated into religion, and divinities appeared who were expert archers, such as Apollo and Diana. Even today, among the pigmies of Gabon a hymn is sung to the most beautiful and mysterious bow of all:

> Rainbow! Rainbow!
> Powerful bow of the Hunter up there,
> Of the Hunter who pursues the cloudy herd
> Like a drove of frightened elephants,
> Rainbow, thank him for us ....

The Dorians, a spear-hurling people, destroyed Mycenean civilisation and caused the decline of the bow when that weapon had already become a tradition. The consequent Greek scorn for the bow is reflected in the *Iliad*. But this scorn did not extend to the east, so that the collision between Greece and Asia was described as the collision of the spear and the bow. In any case, Polycrates of Samos (sixth century BC) maintained a permanent corps of one thousand archers, and the Athenian ships at the battle of Salamis had foot soldiers aboard armed with bows, with duties comparable to those of the modern marines.

Among Italic peoples, companies of archers were kept chiefly by the Umbrians, the Lucanians, the Sardinians and the Etruscans. Rome adopted the bow only after the Second Punic War. Livy mentions archers aboard the ships of Marcellus at Syracuse. But like the Greeks, the Romans did not have great esteem for the bow, their archers generally coming from the armies of their *socii* or allies, in particular from Crete and Syria.

The archer's equipment was almost always very light (an exception were the Assyrians, who employed fully armoured archers; but more of them later). The Cretan archers carried a quiver on their backs and defended themselves with a small shield. In the Mycenean age the archer's headgear was usually the skin of a wild animal. In ancient tactics the archers often represented the breaching force; the enemy forces, disarrayed by their arrows, would then be crushed by the subsequent charge of the cavalry.

Among the most famous units of archers in antiquity were those recruited by Ramses III among the Negroes of Numidia. After meticulous training (they could hit a moving target at three hundred feet) they went into action at the battle of the Delta. It was in this battle, (towards the end of the thirteenth century BC) that Pharaoh halted the advance of the Peoples of the Sea.

Above, left to right: *South American native archer, prehistoric archer, Egyptian archer, Roman archer. All 19th-century illustrations. Opposite: Persian bronze quiver (from Luristan), 7th-8th century* BC. *It is 60 cm. long and 14 cm. wide. Preserved in Teheran, Archaelogical Museum.*

A Monster Called Phalanx

The phalanx was the first true formation used by the Greek infantry. The Hellenic peoples frequently had to face the Persian hordes, which were by far superior numerically and were extremely mobile, and to meet this challenge the Greeks evolved that particular formation which has come to be known as the phalanx. Originally the Greek phalanx (whose etymological root indicates something extremely tight and compact) was an essentially defensive formation, designed to absorb the particular impact, enormous but disordered, of the Persian cavalry, which quite often was accompanied by assaults of scythe-chariots, i.e. chariots with wheels equipped with cutting blades. Later, as its inner structure was developed, the phalanx was capable of a wide range of tactical manoeuvres. Masters of the phalanx were first Epamimondas the Theban and then Alexander the Great.

The structure of the Macedonian phalanx, the most famous of all, was no less rigorously geometric than its predecessors, but it was more agile and hence more easily manoeuvred. It was composed of sixteen units, called *syntagmata*, lined up with each other, and each syntagma consisted of a square of men sixteen deep and sixteen wide. The soldiers forming the phalanx, the *pezetaeri*, were heavily armed. Each wore a helmet, cuirass and greaves and carried a short sword and a long pike called a *sarisa* (or *sarissa*). Sources do not agree on the length of the sarisa, the most spectacular element of the phalanx structure, but it was between twelve and perhaps twenty feet long. Finally these soldiers bore a large oval shield or *hoplon* - hence the name of hoplite, which was applied to these soldiers.

The form of combat of the phalanx was simple. In defence or when absorbing the enemy onslaught, the first six ranks lowered their sarisae and pointed them at the enemy, while the other ten rows raised theirs to protect the forward rows from enemy arrows. In attack, the phalanx advanced slowly, in compact order and with the same disposition of the *sarisae* used in defence. It was a monster bristling with iron which advanced irresistibly, so as to arouse terror in any enemy.

At first both Philip II and Alexander the Great employed the Greek phalanx without any substantial alterations, and when change did come, it was rather of a psychological order. The two Macedonian warriors fully realised that final victory on the field of battle could not be achieved by the phalanx as such; it was particularly ill-suited for sudden rapid manoeuvres especially on rough terrain. The destructive force of the Macedonian army was concentrated in the powerful cavalry, and in particular in the eight squadrons of *Hetaeri*, two thousand strong in all, recruited among the Macedonian nobility and heavily armed. One of these squadrons served as the emperor's bodyguard.

Noteworthy among the other special units created by Alexander was that of the *Argyraspides*, apparently consisting of three thousand infantrymen distinguished for their strength and valour. As their name indicates, their distinguishing feature was a silver shield - an emblem that enjoyed much popularity in later centuries. There were even Argyraspides in the Roman army under Caracalla.

Among the adversaries that Alexander came up against were the romantic Theban youths of the sacred battalion, the three hundred 'Young Lovers' who constituted the last bulwark of Greek freedom at Chaeronea (338 BC), where they all died with their weapons in their hands. Other 'sacred battalions' (or 'sacred legions' or 'sacred troops') were part of later armies (for example, there was one with Hannibal at Zama, consisting of the cream of the Carthaginian army), but the Theban troop remains a unique example in military history, albeit a much discussed example.

Other Greek units included specialist mercenaries, like the Cretan archers, Rhodian slingers and the Thracian peltasts. It is also worth mentioning the three hundred Spartan *Hippeis* who comprised the royal guard at the beginning of the fifth century BC. They were hoplites, i.e. foot soldiers, but as their name indicates, officially they were part of the cavalry. This was an honorary association, as they never used horses. This indicates that the cavalry were socially pre-eminent in Greece: chivalry and nobility were loosely equated.

Alexander the Great and the Queen of the Amazons, in an engraving by Pinelli. Among the Macedonian emperor's innovations (aside from the reordering of the phalanx) was the so-called 'Iranisation' of the army, i.e. the assimilation of 30,000 Iranians (called Epigones) into the army when he went to Bactric and defeated Bexus, the slayer of Darius (329 BC)

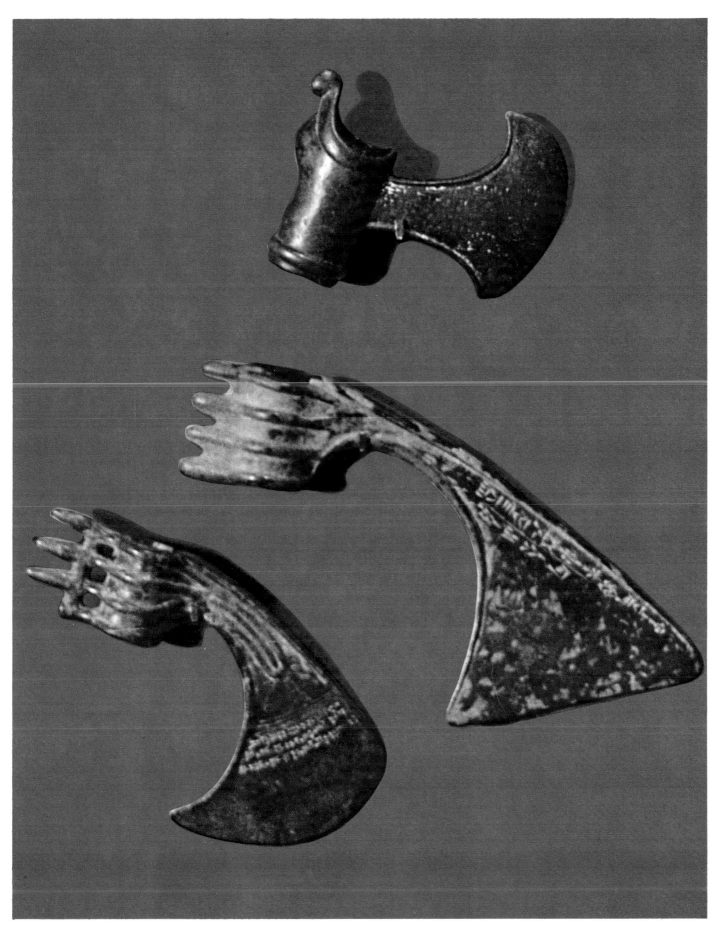

From top to bottom: *Bronze axe, in the shape of a halberd, 10.5 cm. wide. It bears a six-line inscription mentioning the name of Addapaksu-Sukkal of Susa. From Luristan (Iran), 18th century* BC. *Bronze axe with the name of Shilnak-Inshushinak, King of Susa. It is 22 cm. long and dates to the 12th century* BC. *Bronze axe; the blade is covered with decorations in relief and carved. It bears the name of Nebuchadnezzar I, King of Babylonia. It is 16 cm. long and comes from Luristan, dating from the 12th century* BC. *These axes borne by Medes, Persians, Cimmerians, and Scythians, who penetrated Iran in succession, laying the base of that Persian empire which only the Macedonian phalanx would succeed in mortally wounding and destroying eight centuries later.*

Salisburgum
Buda
Danubius fl.
D A C I A
Brixino
Forum Iulij
Aquileia
Altinum
Patavium
Guastalla
Ferraria
Padus fl.
MARE ADRIATICUM
DALMATIA
Sirmium
Singedunum
Danubius fl.
Ladera
Spalatum
ILLYRICUM
Ravenna
Ariminum
Vrbinum
Firmum
Spoletum
Sena
ROMA
ITALIA
Sutrium
Lateranum
Troia
Capua
Tiberis fl.
Sinuessa
Beneventu
Nola
Melphia
Salernu
Neapolis
Amalphis
Sipontum
Manfredonia
Barium
Hydrus
Dioclea
Sardica
THRAC
MACEDONIA
EPIRUS VETUS
Cosentia
Cephaloedium
Panormus
Mons Regalis
SICILIA I.
Corynthus
ACHAIA
Melita I
Cebarsussa
M E D I T E
Ptolemais

SPECIAL UNITS OF THE HELLENIC ARMY
AND THEIR CHIEF PROVENANCE

Peltasts
(Thrace)

Cavalry
(Macedonia)

Foreign Hoplite
Infantry
(Italy)

Archers
(Crete)

Slingers
(Sicily and
Rhodes)

Greek
Hoplite Infantry
(Peloponnese)

Armour and War Chariots

Among many ancient peoples, the Persians, Parthians and Sarmatians in particular, and among the Romans and Byzantines and in the Middle Ages as well, the armed forces included a heavy cavalry wearing a full suit of armour. The horse and rider were fully covered with scales, or small plates of metal, horn or stiffened leather. On Trajan's Column in Rome horsemen in cataphracts are depicted alongside cuirassed legionaries. It was a heavy, indeed a very heavy cavalry whose efficiency, however, never matched the wealth and grandeur of its equipment. Nevertheless they were attributed an importance equal to that of the pezetaeri, the hoplites of the Macedonian phalanx.

This heavy cavalry included several units distinguished by their armour, which might consist of metallic plates of bronze or iron mail for both man and horse. The horses had to be particularly strong and a special breed was developed by crossing an Asian horse known as a Neseus with others from Libya.

The sarisa was the cataphract's main weapon, as it had been the hoplite's. This made them a really fearful foe for the infantry, at least as long as they remained in the saddle.

In the *Aethiopica* Heliodorus speaks at length of the cataphracts as they must have been in the army of the eastern Roman empire. 'The cataphract,' he says, 'is

an outstanding man extremely strong in body. He wears a solid helmet with a single opening, made in the form of a man's face, and this covers everything from the top of his head to the nape of his neck, except for the eyes.' He then goes on to describe the suit 'of square copper or iron plates, a palm long and a palm wide,' that reaches to the knees and is 'necessarily open at the hips'. There were shin guards and iron shoes as well, and similar armour for the horse ('a covering of iron mail'), on which the cataphract, 'because of his weight, had to be lifted by others'. At the call to battle, horse and rider went forth 'against the enemy' with the lance at rest, like 'moving statues hammered out of iron'.

On the Gallic front the Romans had to face a very heavily armoured cavalry. Here too the texts speak of *cataphractari*, soldiers covered in iron from head to foot in the manner of the Greek and Roman cataphracts. Each cataphractarius was followed by two other horsemen ready to help him or exchange horses when his was wounded. These two attendants were less heavily armoured than the cataphractarius but they, too, wore a helmet and cuirass.

The organisation of certain units of the Assyrian army, equipped with bows, was not much different. In fact, the Assyrians had two kinds of archers: those with light armour who fought barefoot and bareheaded, and those who were fully armoured, with conical helmets, scale armour or perhaps iron mail. Archaeologists at Nineveh have uncovered what appears to be remains of this fabric, if it can be called such. Bas-relief sculptures confirm the use of mail.

The typical Assyrian weapon was not the bow but the chariot, at least at the beginning of Assyrian history. The charioteers - if one can apply that name to men who were trained to fight on those chariots - comprised selected men who were assigned to special units.

At least two types of Assyrian war chariot are known: a light chariot manned by a driver and an archer, and a heavy chariot manned by a driver, an archer and two equerries. In bas-reliefs men and horses are depicted covered with armour and trappings which were clearly intended for protection. The chariots were drawn by two or occasionally three horses. The third horse, when there was one, ran alongside the chariot as a reserve to replace one of the others in case of injury. In the Bible Isiah compares the wheels of the Assyrian chariots to the whirlwind, their horses' hoofs to flints.

The Egyptians came in contact with war chariots when their land was invaded by the Hyksos in about 1750 BC, but they did not employ them extensively except as a means of transporting infantry. Finally, at the time of Thutmos III, there appeared units of light

Opposite: *A horseman wearing the cataphractus, from a 19th-century drawing.* Above: *A 19th-century depiction of two ancient horsemen. The one on the left is about to mount with the aid of a support attached to his spear. The other wears the cataphractus, a coat of copper scales, reconstructed after Roman sources. The Parthians also protected horse and rider with a metal coat of overlapping plates. They had such confidence in this type of cuirass that they did without a shield. The horsemen went into action armed only with a spear and a bow. Their skill was such that the 'Parthian arrow' became proverbial as a 'parting shot'.*

chariots mounted by a driver and an archer or, more frequently, by a single man who served both as driver and archer. These units were thrown into battle in the same way that the cavalry, then unknown in Egypt, could be used. When the Hyksos were invading Egypt the Shang dynasty was beginning in China (a period when the people questioned the oracles by writing their questions on tortoise shells and who in the course of six centuries founded the China we know today). It was a dynasty which created an extraordinary civilisation and remarkable institutions of war. Their war chariots' two wheels had a diameter of five feet and were drawn by a team of two or four horses. The chariot had a driver, an archer and a third man armed with a *ko*. This was a kind of axe with a blade about six inches long.

The Hour of the Elephant

The impact of a running elephant is equivalent to that of a fully loaded armoured truck at top speed: a missile weighing about nine thousand pounds. And if one considers the terrifying appearance of a charging elephant, one can understand why man in remote antiquity made use of that animal on the battlefield. Thus elephants were attached to special units and provided a means of transport in battle for archers, slingers and lancers, who rode in small towers set on the elephants' backs.

All historians agree that the 'good Lucans' of Pyrrhus who - at least at their first appearance on the battlefield of Heraclea (280 BC) - terrorised the Roman troops, were nothing but Asian, or more properly Indian elephants.

In their legendary march across Asia, the troops of Alexander the Great suffered a serious defeat at the hands of Porus, the giant king of the region beyond the Hydaspes (the modern River Jhelum, a tributary of the Indus), mainly because of Porus' elephants. Porus was the ablest warrior that Alexander ever faced. His army of about forty thousand infantry and four thousand cavalry was supported by two hundred war elephants bearing archers on their backs, who rained arrows down on to the enemy while the infantry advanced behind them.

Nevertheless it was clear to Alexander that the effectiveness of the elepant was due chiefly to their appearance, which still terrified long after it had become a common sight. Alexander's recovery was not long in coming, and the elephants were routed by a bombardment of shouts and other noises supported by a solid rain of arrows.

More or less similar was the Roman reaction - after the initial shock - at Maleventum (modern Benevento), when in 275 BC under the command of Curius Dentatus, the Romans defeated Pyrrhus and met the threat of the elephants with flaming arrows, and daring Velites risked being crushed to death when they ran between the enormous feet of the elephants to cut their tendons with a sword.

During the Punic wars the Carthaginians did not obtain the expected results from their elephants. They used African elephants, which are larger than the Indian elephants but have a much more unpredictable temperament. It was enough for the Romans to overcome the fright their appearance caused and then frighten them in turn for them to career away in mad flight, creating havoc in the Carthaginian army as well.

During the First Punic War, Hasdrubal in Sicily had to destroy the elephants in his army because they had become too dangerous, or at least of dubious utility. Thirty years later, in 218 BC, Hannibal crossed the

Alps and inflicted severe defeats on the Roman army at Ticinus, Trebbia, Lake Trasimenus and Cannae. The elephants had crossed the Pyrenees and the Alps with him, but it seems that in the descents they had given no end of trouble to their drivers. Later the Romans also used elephants in their Asian campaigns. Caesar seems

to have used one to frighten Cassivellaunus and to cross the Thames during the campaign in Britain.

Throughout the Middle Ages and even in modern times, some middle eastern armies continued to have elephant units, but they were almost exclusively pack animals for provisions.

An engraving by Cornelius Cort (from a drawing attributed to Raphael) depicting the meeting at Beneventum of Pyrrhus and the Romans (275 BC). Pyrrhus had landed at Tarentum with 35,000 men and twenty war elephants in 280 BC. He had defeated the Romans at Heraclea, a battle important not only because of the elephants but because it represented the first encounter of the Roman legion and the Greek phalanx.

The Roman Legion

According to Vegetius it was a god that inspired the Romans to create the legion. From earliest Roman times, from the period of Romulus to the republic, the army was composed of several legions, but each legion was a small select army in itself. This is not surprising when one recalls that the verb *deligere*, from which the word legion is derived, means 'to select' in Latin.

Three thousand selected foot-soldiers, then, formed the original legion. The legionaries were selected from among men between the ages of seventeen and forty-six, preferably peasants, smiths, woodcutters and hunters.

The Roman preference for infantry over cavalry has been attributed to the fact that the Seven Hills produced little fodder for the horses. The Romans did in fact prefer infantry, but for another reason. Infantry can fight on any terrain and can be moved with method and constancy. And where it arrives it stays. It is the foot soldier who conquers and maintains empires. Thus even the cavalry in the Roman army was trained to fight on foot. The cavalry consisted of noblemen, who did not feel that their rank was demeaned by fighting side by side with plebeians. Battle levelled all distinctions, and thus the miracle of an army which represented all classes was achieved.

The legion consisted of three thousand men from the period of Romulus to that of Servius Tullius, four thousand from Servius to the Second Punic War, reaching its maximum under Marius with six thousand men. During the empire the legion was subdivided into cohorts, *centuriae* and *manipuli*. One centurion of the first cohort, comprising about eleven hundred foot soldiers and one hundred and thirty-six horsemen, was entrusted with the golden eagle that represented the supreme insignia of the legion. (At the time of Romulus a crown of vines bound to a pole sufficed.) The other cohorts consisted of five hundred and forty-five foot soldiers and sixty-six horsemen, except the fourth and the seventh which counted six hundred foot soldiers. Such was Gibbon's estimate, and he added that there were seven hundred and twenty-six horses in the legion.

When on the march the Roman foot soldier carried, in addition to his weapons, a spit, a bowl, a spoon, a basket, a sickle, a saw, a rope and other tools, as well as provisions for several days; a load that Josephus called fit for a beast of burden and one that attracted Cicero's admiration.

The first cohort seem to have been the most select as well as the largest. During an encounter in Britain, Caesar sent the first cohorts of two legions to the aid of his guard. Crastinus, the hero of Pharsalus, was the *primipilum*, or leader, of the first century of the first cohort of the famous Tenth Legion.

But the legion too was to decline, and this was mainly due to corruption. There were scandalous dealings under Marius and Silla and things became still worse under Augustus, who opened the ranks of the legion to foreign mercenaries. Caracalla, notwithstanding his mad prodigality to the army, tried in his own way to save a situation that was threatening to become tragic. (Two centuries earlier, Tiberius had complained that disciplined volunteers could not be found.) Caracalla created a phalanx of sixteen thousand select Roman infantry, armed in the Macedonia fashion and organised on the model of Alexander's army. The idea of imitating Alexander was not merely one of Caracalla's manias. Alexander Severus Teo created a corps of *Argyraspides* and a phalanx of thirty thousand men.

Nevertheless the legions continued to survive and fight. Those composed of Europeans were always, it appears, superior to those formed of Easterners (it was Montesquieu who drew attention to this fact), and it is understandable that Vespasian, when he was proclaimed emperor by the Syrian legions, did not want to face Vitellius except with legions recruited in Mesia, Pannonia and Dalmatia.

Above are illustrated Roman standards and legionaries, after a reasonably accurate late-Renaissance source. The Roman insignia became more complicated with the passing of time and lost its original simplicity. The first emblem of the Romulean era was, in fact, a bunch of fronds attached to the top of a pole or spear.

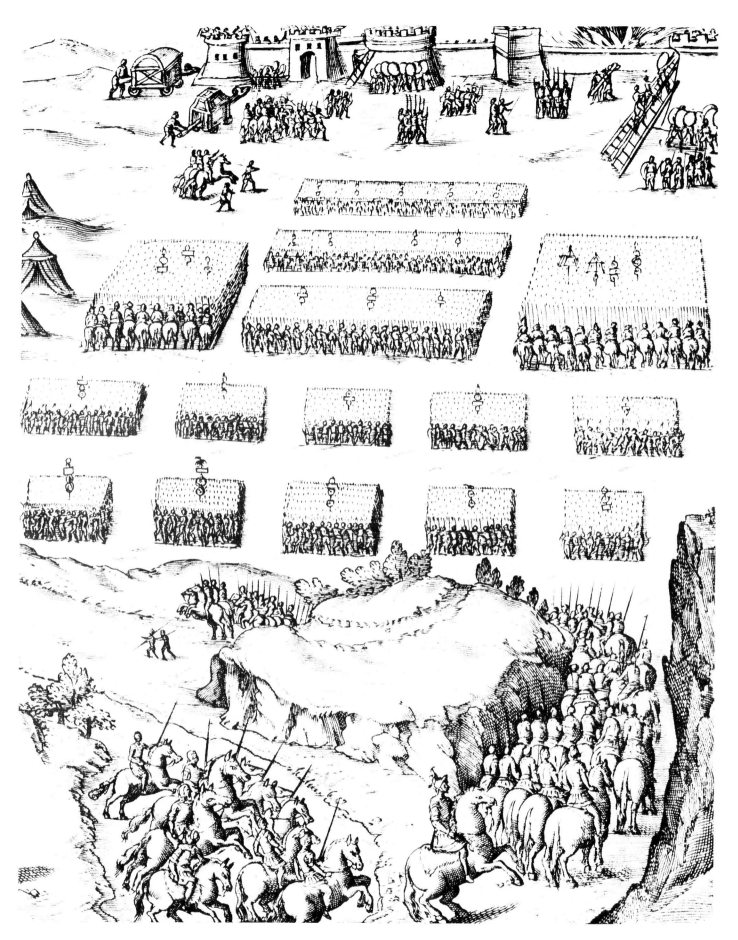

Roman soldiers marching toward a besieged city, in a 16th-century print. In the background a legion in its typical battle formation, with the turmae of the cavalry on the flanks. The legion formation was basically that of the phalanx, i.e., a single mass of soldiers drawn up behind a front rank. The formation was later modified (after the Gallic invasions of the 4th century BC) *into the so-called 'maniple' formation, whose development is credited to Furius Camillus. It fought on three lines (hastati, principes, triarii), each of which was composed in turn of minor units, the centuries (60-80 men), the maniples (two or three centuries), and, after the time of Marius, the cohorts (consisting of three maniples each).*

Roman soldiers of the Imperial period (1st-2nd centuries AD) as illustrated in a page of the famous series of illustrations of the Münchener Bilderbogen *published by Braun und Schneider. From left to right: a standard bearer, an imperator, and two soldiers. The legionaries generally marched in a column of ten carrying all their arms and baggabe (impedimenta) with them.*

From the Praetorians to the Barbarian Hordes

In Roman times the term *praetorium* was applied to the tent of the commander-in-chief in the *castra* or military camps, to the residence of the governor of a province and, in Rome, to the barracks of the Praetorian Guards.

From the time of the republic the best soldiers of the legion were gathered into the so-called 'Praetorian cohort', which was entrusted with protecting and escorting the legion's commandant. When he became emperor Augustus kept the name of Praetorian cohort but entrusted the unit with the functions of a royal guard. He fixed the number of Praetorian cohorts at nine, or a total of nine thousand men.

The number of Praetorians was not always the same. Each emperor increased or decreased their numbers depending on the circumstances. There were sixteen cohorts under Vitellius and only three under Vespasian. The Praetorians' term of enlistment was shorter than that of ordinary legionaries (sixteen instead of twenty

years), they were paid considerably more and their prospects of promotion and advancement were good. Among other things, they also served as training cadres for legionary officers. As long as the empire was sound, Praetorians were only recruited among Italian peoples, preferably Latins, Etruscans and Umbrians.

According to Suetonius, Claudius who owed his throne to the Praetorians, was the first emperor to buy the loyalty of the Praetorians with a donation of money. Then began the most shameful 'auction' in history; it was the venality of the Praetorians that decided who would wear the purple. Septimius Severus restored temporary order but he made the same error which finally ruined the legions: he ordered that the ranks of the Praetorians be opened not only to Italian people but to the strongest and most valiant men throughout the empire. And he increased their number to fifty thousand. Their strength became uncontrollable and the extreme power of their commander-in-chief unchecked.

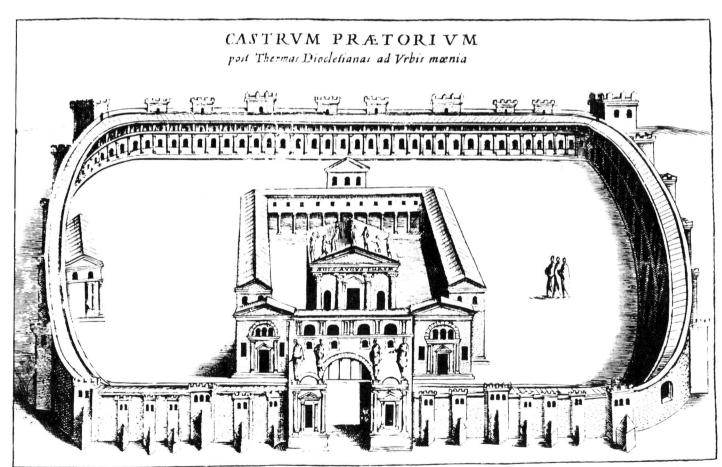

CASTRVM PRÆTORIVM
post Thermas Diocletianas ad Vrbis mœnia

Castrumprætoriu teste Suetonio locus erat celebratissimus à Tiberio Cæsare Prætorianis cohortibus quæ à custodijs Imperatoris erant constitutus, ne uagarentur, ac per hospitia ut mos erat diuerterentur. Scriptores qui antiquitati student, uarie de huiusmodi situ opinatur, qui eum uia Appia nó procul ab æde S.Sebastiani collocat. Qui in extrema Vrbis parte ex Plinio fuisse comemorat, inter uias Nomentana et Tiburtina ut hodie uestigia urbis mœnib'adiuncta in eo latere, quo Oriente respiciunt, ostenditur. Scriptores 2ª sententia qua rum inuentor ac delineator diligés est Pyrrhus Ligorius uerisimiliter, immo et efficacius probare contendut, et ex ibide ruinis, et ex fuga Neronis qui cu infundu Pharontis liberti sui pro: penaret iter faciens p uias salaria et Nomentana ex prætorio quod prope erat Prætorianor, clamore cótra se concitatu audiuit et expauit ut refert ide Suetonius. Huic equide sententia sponte subscribo, quia fundametis innititur erat hoc castrú ex lateré pulcherrimo opere reticulato costructu ubi mansiones eleganter depictæ erant et porticus columnis suffultate menhtijs, maltha desuper sumo cu artisicio coopertis Intus ædicula teste Herrodiano in gratia Cæsaris, siue Augustor. fabricata ut ex tegulis ibi repertis uidere est cu hac inscriptione ex æde Augustor, p fistulas plubeas aqua in huic locu deducebatur ut scribit Capitolinus quas P.op: Rom" in iurgio cu Prætorianis inito, quod ipsi loca et tepla cópilare uolebat abscidit unde co: adsi Pretoriani pace cu Pepulo cossi mure coacti ... huius casu uinen hodie sccupatur quauis priscis serorib'ut ide Pyr Ligorius testatur in suis paradoxis extitit teplu a Xpianis extructu

38

The commander of the Praetorians, or Prefect of the Praetorium, took on ever greater political importance with the progressive decline of imperial authority, and the Praetorian Guard played an active and often decisive role in the dramatic and tragic history of the imperial period. They were present at every important event - the murder of Caligula, the battles between Vitellius and Vespasian, the murder of Pertinax. The popularity of the Praetorians - or perhaps it was their notoriety - is confirmed by the numerous depictions of them that have survived in works of art. They were simultaneously the protectors and arbiters of imperial authority, particularly when weak and inept successors had ascended the throne of Augustus.

In the struggle between Maxentius and Constantine the Praetorians sided with Maxentius and fought valiantly at the battle of Milvian Bridge (AD 312). Constantine did not have the temperament to tolerate an imperial guard such as the Praetorians had become; he dissolved the corps, and it was never reformed. He replaced it with a guard of *Praesentes*, who were subdivided into *Palatini* (those who escorted military commanders in the provinces).

The barbarians, like the Romans, had special units even in the earliest times when their attitude to Rome was primarily defensive. They marched and fought in throngs or *catervae*, about the organisation of which there is no certain information. We do know, however, that the Gauls, for instance, had special corps even in ancient times. According to an ancient Celtic custom, the most valiant chiefs were always surrounded by young warriors known as *Hambacti* or *Solduri*, who constituted a bodyguard sworn and faithful unto death. In fact, the Solduri considered it an infamy to return alive to camp once the chief had fallen. The chief, in turn, protected them in every possible way, covering them with honours and dividing his booty with them. They fought on horseback, and contributed to the development of that long contempt into which the infantry soon fell, and, to the formation of the equestrian order, which was to lord it over civil assemblies as well as battlefields. From Martial we learn that the Gauls favoured the colours golden-yellow and red and that their cloaks only covered half of their buttocks:

> *Roma magis fuscis, vestitur Gallia russis,*
> *Et placet hic pueris, militibusque color.*
> *Dimidiasque nates gallica pulla tegit.*

Actually, before they came in contact with the Romans, the Gauls had fought stark naked. It was only as they became familiar with the garb of the Quirites that the Gauls began to dress their own warriors.

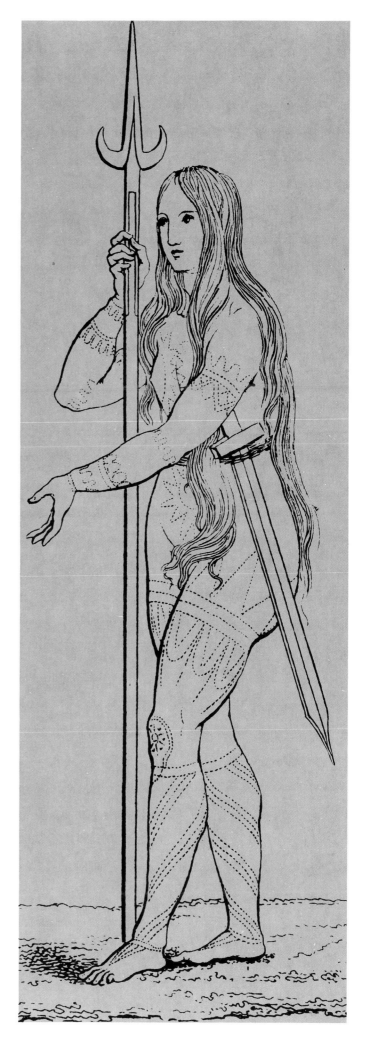

Opposite left: *The Castrum Praetorium, the famous camp of the Praetorian Guard.* Opposite right: *One of the warrior virgins of the Britons who resisted the Roman advance (from a 19th-century drawing). The Monotapa Amazons of Mozambique, seen by Pigafetta and other explorers must have been similar.*

PART TWO

The Dawn
of the Colonels

From Company to Regiment

The Carroccio Guards

With the end of the domination of the Countess Mathilda, civic militias arose in Tuscany. In 1250 Florence had a military ordinance that provided for twenty companies of militia men, each under the command of a captain and all subject to the *Capitano del popolo*. His emblem was a white standard with a red cross. These twenty companies of soldiers, recruited among those citizens most practised in arms in the various quarters of the city, were supported by the 'subsidiaries', also organised in companies, two of crossbowmen, two of shield bearers, one of pioneers and one of sappers and explosive experts. There was also a 'market company' for provisions and a baggage train for transport. The so-called *palvesaria* bore a large wooden shield called a *palvese,* about four feet long and half as broad, which when set on the ground served to protect the crossbowmen, while the *guastatori*, together with the *marraioli* and the *pallaioli*, functioned as veritable engineering units that looked after communications, fortification, defence and so on. The Florentine militia had a horse-drawn waggon on which a wooden castle was erected. This structure was surmounted by the *Martinella*, the bell that called the citizens to arms in case of external attack and, in battle, signalled the various units. There was also the *carroccio*, an implement of war that was typical of the Middle Ages, not just in Florence but throughout Europe.

The Milanese carroccio was a four-wheeled waggon in the centre of which stood a tall solid pole with a cross or a golden orb at the top and the flag of the commune lower down. At the foot of the pole was an altar at which a priest celebrated the mass and administered extreme unction to the dying and dead. The platform round the pole was large enough to hold fifty guardsmen and a dozen trumpeters, who during the march or in battle, played military hymns. The waggon was drawn by three or four pairs of heavy oxen covered with rich saddle-cloths. The carroccio was an invention of Aribertus, bishop of Milan, who in 1039 was in conflict with the emperor and instituted the device to provide a symbol and a rallying point for the city's troops, in the same way that the Ark of the Covenant served the ancient Jews. The use of the carroccio spread throughout Lombardy, so that by the time of the Lombard League almost all the civil militias had their own carroccio and special guards. The carroccio, of Bologna, for example, was protected by fifteen hundred foot soldiers and by two groups of horses.

On 29 May 1176, the Lombard League faced the army of Frederick Barbarossa at the battle of Legnano. The imperial army, composed of cavalry and well-trained troops, seemed about to win a victory over the citizens' militias when the situation was reversed by the charge of the Carroccio Guards known as the 'Company of Death', composed of three hundred young men from the leading Milanese families.

The carroccio was used in France and England. In 1138 in the Battle of The Standard at which the English beat the Scots under David I, the victors had a waggon surmounted by a ship's mast with a silver crucifix.

Opposite, above: *A medieval depiction of the god Mars, from a 15th-century German manuscript.* Above: *The Carroccio of Treviso, 14th century. The Carroccio was a Lombard institution, established by Aribertus, the archbishop of Milano, in the first decades of the 11th century. It was the symbol of the freedom of the cities during the struggle against feudalism.* Below: *Norman warriors accoutred after the portrayals of the famous Bayeux tapestries. Note the variety of ornaments, from the bow to the cudgel. In the background is an axe-bearer. The axe had been the typical weapon of the Vikings, whose descendants were the Normans.*

The Carroccio of the Milanese, guarded by the Death Company, dominates the scene of the battle of Legnano, in this fine picture by Amos Cassioli. The Death Company was commanded by Alberto da Giussano and consisted of nine hundred citizens of Milan. It fought by the side of the Carroccio at Legnano in 1176 during the decisive engagement between the civic militias of the Lombard League and the forces of Barbarossa.

The Teutonic Knights

The horse, 'man's noblest conquest' according to Buffon, was domesticated at a very early date. The Babylonians rode and the Hyksos introduced the horse to Egypt. It at once became a prized object and a privilege of the nobility, anticipating certain consequences of a social nature that have survived to modern times. Even for the Greeks and Romans, being a knight meant not only belonging to a special military order but membership of a social and political class as well. In Rome membership of the equestrian order was based on wealthy and personal nobility, in contrast to the senatorial class, which was a hereditary nobility.

But knighthood as a social institution had its great period in the feudal Middle Ages. Although there was never a total identification of knighthood with the feudal lord, fighting on horseback was an irrefutable sign of nobility and power. To win knighthood was an aspiration that ennobled the manly and adventurous spirit of many feudal lords, especially when the barbarian violence that followed the collapse of Roman institutions had abated and the human soul once more felt the need to restore justice, to put an end to the abuses and brutalities of the past and give the use of arms a just and holy purpose. The Crusades, with their religious inspiration, represent the most concrete result of this evolution. In fact, the knightly Orders which were formed during the Crusades codified the rules and norms of chivalrous behaviour, which until that time

had been merely a matter of convention. From a military point of view, the formation of the Orders did not do much to alter the concept of 'single combat' so dear to feudal times. Throughout the Middle Ages, the heavily armed knight went into battle flanked by pages and equerries to seek out his personal adversary, whom he engaged amidst a tremendous clanking of iron.

Nevertheless there occasionally appeared on the battlefield a wall of iron formed by knights riding abreast with lances lowered in phalanx fashion. A scene like this must have faced the Russians, on 5 April 1242, when they faced the Teutonic Knights on the frozen waters of Lake Peipus. The great Russian film director Eisenstein, in his *Alexander Nevsky*, recreated a magnificent version of this battle, which has come to be known as the 'Ice Battle.' The Teutonic Knights sank in the frozen waters, weighed down by their pride and iron equipment, as if symbolising the end of a world that had come to replace its original ideals with an insatiable thirst for power and its pure heart with a vain show of pretentious crests and white cloaks with black crosses.

The origin of the Order of St Mary of the Teutons is still debated. Some attribute its foundation to Barbarossa, others to a German living in Ptolemais. In any case, the most probable date is 1190. Only German knights were admitted to the Order.

Like the other Orders established to defend the Christian kingdom of Jerusalem, such as the Hospitalers the Teutonic Knights soon left Palestine. They went back to Germany, where they devoted themselves to a rather energetic Christianisation of the pagan peoples of the Baltic coast, from the mouth of the Vistula to the gulf of Finland, meeting strenuous resistance. In 1236 the Order assimilated the Order of the Knights of the Sword, and thus reinforced finally achieved victory and the consequent Germanisation of the peoples of Prussia, Livonia, Courland and Estonia. Having reached the borders of Russia, the Order now looked to the east, but as we have seen their hopes were drowned forever in the Peipus.

The Order of the Teutonic Knights was suppressed by Napoleon in 1809. But the white mantle with a black cross outlined in silver, given to them by Pope Celestine at the time of the Crusades, had already become a permanent German symbol which was to inspire the colours of the Prussian flag and the medal of the Iron Cross.

Hofmeister des deutschen Ordens.　　　　　Schwertbruder.

Ordo domus Sanctae Mariae Teutonicorum *in Jerusalem. This was the name of the knightly order restricted to German nobles during the Third Crusade. Depicted above is the Hofmeister, or Grand Master, with another knight. He wears on his chest the black cross intersected by a golden cross, after the stipulations of Pope Celestine III, who approved the order. The ordinary horsemen wore a silver-edged black cross, as illustrated in the ornament reproduced overleaf, taken from a history of knightly orders by Bernardo Giustiniano, published in Venice in 1672. The Teutonic Knights were largely responsible for the Germanisation of the lands facing the Baltic. The Russians defeated the Teutonic Knights at the famous Battle on the Ice (1242).*

Genoese Arbalesters and Francs Archers

The arbalest, a crossbow, was a most fearful hand weapon of the Middle Ages, which could kill a man at more than two hundred paces. This is why the Church, at the Second Lateran Council, forbade its use in wars between Christians. It consisted essentially of a bow, of wood or metal, a long stick and a cord or sinew. Arbalests are first mentioned in Italy in a treaty of alliance between the citizens of Genoa and Alessandria.

Men armed with arbalests, (arbalesters), fought on foot or on horseback. Italian arbalesters, especially the Pisans and even more the Genoese, were held in high esteem. The kings of France employed Genoese arbalesters, and Philip VI recruited fifteen thousand during the Hundred Years War.

At the battle of Crecy, 26 August 1346, the Genoese fatigued by a too rapid advance, reached the battlefield physically weakened and with their morale low. And a violent storm soaked their weapons. The sun came out too late to dry them but, shining in the eyes of the arbalesters, obstructed their aim. Under the attack of the English archers they fell back in disorder on the infantry and cavalry. The cavalry charged, ho-

ping to save the situation, but failed. It was a devastating defeat with enormous losses. But the Genoese arbalesters continued to serve in France. In the first years of the fifteenth century, many of their companies garrisoned the major cities of the realm. Paris, for example, had a guard of two thousand arbalesters in 1416. But two years later the city militia rose in favour of the duke of Burgundy, and the Genoese arbalesters were massacred by the rebels.

The rivals and successors of the arbalesters were the *francs archers* or longbowmen. The long bows of these soldiers were made of wood, shot long arrows and required particular skill from the bowmen. Often this skill was passed from father to son, and children were instructed from the age of seven to use the bow, which required a special balance of the torso and arms. The English long bow was superior to the arbalest both in the rapidity of its shot and in its power of penetration. It could shoot twelve arrows; a distance of almost six hundred feet in the time an arbalest took to shoot two.

The francs archers were created in France by Charles VII between 1448 and 1451. He ordered every parish and every fifty households in the realm to provide a fully equipped bowman. The bowman was selected by the aldermen of the parish from among those skilled in the use of the bow, and he was obliged to practise on all holidays. On service he was paid four francs per month and was exempt from certain *tailles*, both feudal and royal. He had to be ready to depart at a moment's notice at the king's command.

The exemption from taxes caused these soldiers to be called *francs*, or 'free'. They did not have a proper uniform and assembled in companies of four hundred or five hundred men under the command of a nobleman. They fought in the later stages of the Hundred Years War, at Formigny (1450) and Castillon (1453). But they did not comport themselves with distinction at the battle of Guinegatte, 4 August 1479, when they faced, among the other troops of Maximilian I, the first Lansquenets.

Louis XI disbanded these bowmen in the same year. But his successors, Charles VII and Louis XII, used them again. Francis I reorganised them and, in 1552, established them in a legion. They were finally suppressed during the reign of Charles IX.

Two medieval crossbowmen. The one in black is stretching the bow with a hand winch. Later this is replaced by the more practical lever jack. Opposite: *Burgundian soldiers of the late 15th century in an illustration from Braun and Schneider's 19th-century history of costume.*

Soldiers of Fortune

Huomo d'arme.

The long war between the monarchies of France and England in the late Middle Ages and the introduction of payment to militias in the thirteenth century gave rise to those companies of mercenaries known as soldiers of fortune or Free Companies.

The first such companies of any note were formed by English captains who went to France to fight alongside the regulars of Edward II. Some of these were Jacques Wyn, Frank Hennequin, Garciot de Castro and the famous John Hawkwood, who later won fame in Italy under the name Giovanni Acuto. But there were also genuine companies led by bandits known by such evocative nicknames as 'Petit Meschin', 'Brisebarre' and others. They sacked and looted and kidnapped women and children - not to mention priests, in case they required the last Sacrament in the event of mortal injury.

A company known as the Tards-Venus captured the papal property of Pont-Saint-Esprit on 28 December 1360. The pope had to proclaim a veritable crusade against them and appealed to the sovereigns of Eu-

rope. But their response was so half-hearted that the Tards-Venus abandoned the papal territory only when the pope persuaded them to go off and fight the Viscontis of Milan.

The number of troops varied greatly from band to band, but they must usually have been about five hundred, judging from the company of Arnaud de Cervole, which numbered two hundred lances and four hundred bows, a total of six hundred warriors in all, which was considered 'large' by contemporary chroniclers. With camp followers and auxiliaries, these companies must have amounted to two thousand people. So the fantastic figures mentioned by some chroniclers must be the fruit of the terror aroused by these companies.

The first companies of soldiers of fortune appeared in Italy during the period when the communes were being transformed into seignories. These companies consisted of foreign troops commanded by foreign chiefs. Apparently the seigneurs had little trust in the militias of the communes which they had subjected or were in the process of subjecting. Almost all the bands and companies were formed from troops that had come to Italy with the armies of the German Roman Empire. From condotta, the agreement by which these troops were paid, came the term condottiero, which was applied to their leaders. Their first undertaking that can be dated goes back to 1329, when eight hundred Germans who had entered Italy in the entourage of Louis the Bavarian assembled near Fucecchio and elected Marco Visconti as their condottiero, who led them in the sack of Lucca.

Other Germans, who had fought for the League in various Italian cities against Mastino della Scala, formed the Company of St George, and in 1342 the Grand Company of Werner von Urslingen, who named himself duke and boasted that he was the 'enemy of God, of pity and of mercy'. They ravaged central Italy until they were forced to withdraw to Germany by a coalition of the Estes of Ferrara, the Gonzagas of Mantua, the Scaligers of Verona, the pope and the Viscontis of Milan. But Werner, notorious in Italy as 'Duke Guarnieri', returned, this time in the service of Louis of Hungary, in his offensive against Naples. Dismissed by this sovereign he entered the service of Joanna of Naples and then, attracted by more tempting offers, returned to the service of Louis of Hungary. He joined forces with Montreal d'Albarno, an ex-Francis-

Above: *An armed man of the Renaissance, from an engraving attributed to Titian or his school.* Opposite: *Halberdiers of the feudal bands* (above) *and the royal harquebusiers* (below) *of the time of Isabella and Ferdinand, from a sheet of paper cut-out soldiers published in Spain at the beginning of the 20th century.*

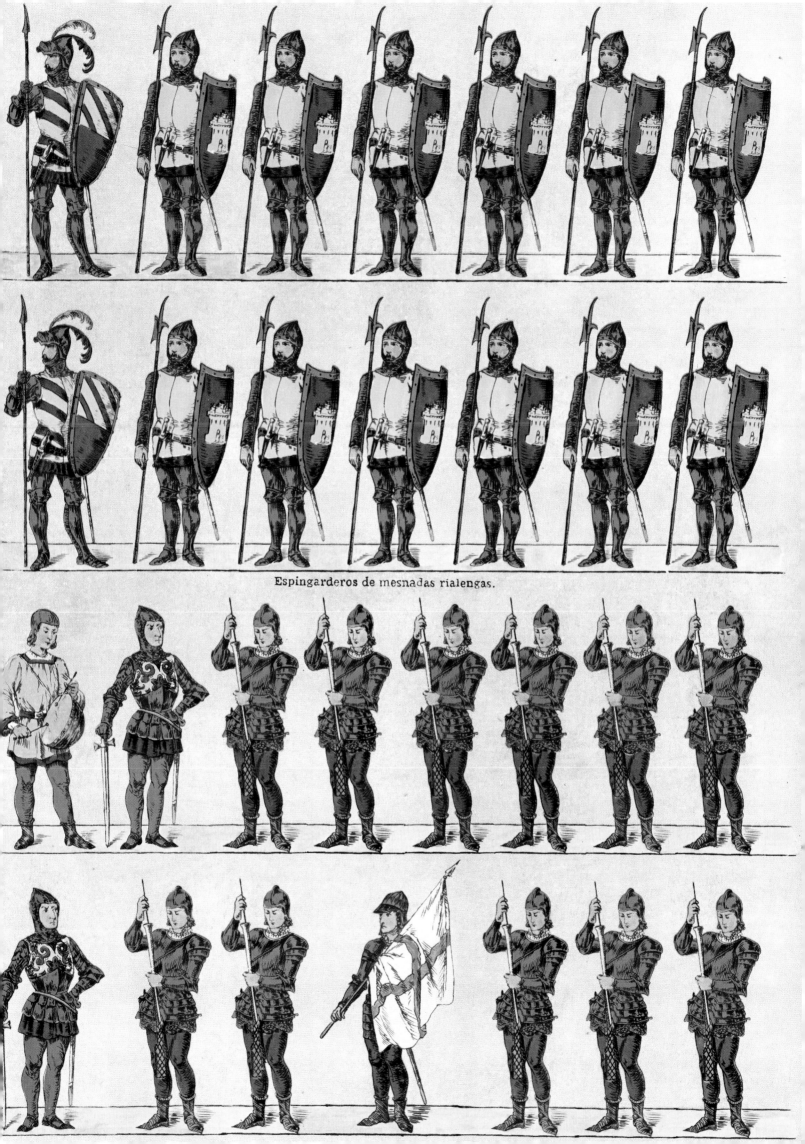

Espingarderos de mesnadas rialengas.

can from Provence who styled himself 'captain in battle and standard-bearer of the Church', and reconstituted the Grand Company in 1350, again ravaging central Italy, and alternating allegiance between Pope Clement VI and his adversaries, the lords of Romagna.

After serving in Campania, Latium and the Marches, Montreal d'Albarno went to Lombardy, where he was in the pay of Giovanni Visconti, archbishop of Milan. He went to Rome to recruit soldiers but was captured by Cola di Rienzo and beheaded in 1354. Conrad of Landau took his place, and joining forces with another condottiero, Hans von Baumgarten, these bands joined in the wars that the Viscontis were waging against their many adversaries. In 1363, during the war between Florence and Pisa, mercenaries in the service of Florence, dissatisfied with their pay, placed a hat on top of a high pole as a symbol of their rebellion and rioted around it. Dismissed by the signoria of Florence, they formed the Company of the Cappelletto ('Little Hat'),

which devastated the territory of Arezzo and papal lands until they were destroyed by the Siennese in 1364.

After 1380, foreign mercenaries began to disappear from the Italian scene and the warrior bands assumed local character. This was the period of the great Italian condottieri, which was to last until the expedition of Charles VIII in 1494 and only began its slow decline in the first twenty years of the sixteenth century. The history of the fifteeth century was dominated by the figures of Pandolfo Malatesta, Brancaccio da Montone, Francesco Bussone (known as Carmagnola), and Francesco Sforza, who became duke of Milan in 1450.

Unlike the great companies of foreign mercenaries, the Italian bands were often strictly regional. The chief was usually a minor lord who recruited his troops among his subjects and vassals. He won political benefits, and his mercenaries received payment and a share of the booty. Enrolment was for a fixed period, and the companies numbered about three hundred horse and

two hundred foot, in addition to auxiliaries, who brought the total to about a thousand men. Machiavelli's remark that the battles between these companies were 'farces' and that the adversaries agreed in advance is refuted by consideration of the wars in which such condottieri as Nicolò Piccinino, Alberico da Barbiano, Braccio Fortebraccio da Montone and Bartolomeo Colleoni figured.

One of the noblest condottieri was Giovanni dalle Bande Nere (Giovanni of the Black Bands), the son of Giovanni de' Medici and Caterina Sforza. He was in the service of Francis I, king of France, at Pavia, where he was wounded. But he achieved greater distinction in the service of Pope Leo X, another Medici, against the lords of the Marches and against the Franco-Venetian League. When the Lansquenets descended on Italy, he led a kind of guerilla warfare which effectively slowed their advance. Near Mantua he was wounded above the knee by a small cannonball, and later died.

This splendid picture of a feudal army on the march comes from a 15th-century German manuscript. It gives a striking idea of what a company of soldiers of fortune must have looked like. They travelled with their families and complete households.

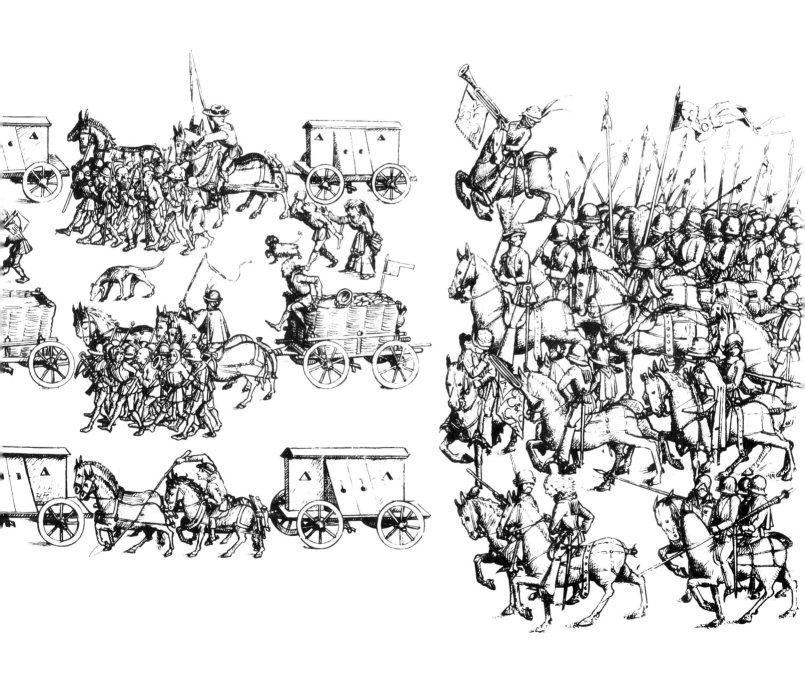

Pikemen and Halberdiers

Pikes and halberds, shafted weapons derived from the spear, were extremely popular in the fifteenth and sixteenth centuries. But they had already been used in battle by the soldiers of fortune led by John Hawkwood. Entrusting their horses to the equerries, the soldiers would form a square and hold their pikes in front of them, thus forming a wall of blades to resist enemy attack. This technique of battle was nothing new (suffice it to recall the phalanx), but it demonstrates the effectiveness of that simple weapon, which differed from the spear and lance only in length of shaft, which exceeded fifteen feet. It is true that the length and consequent weight of the weapon made manoeuvering difficult, and because the formation was static, pikemen were particularly vulnerable on the flanks. It was natural, therefore, after the invention of firearms, to supplement pike units with a number of harquebusiers.

Spain was famous for its 'Dry Pikes', units of soldiers that went to battle armed only with pikes. In the Piedmontese army, pikemen made up one third of a regiment, while in the Swiss militias they represented two-thirds. The Swiss were extremely proficient in the use of the pike.

As firearms were improved throughout the latter half of the seventeeth century, pike units became less common, and in 1703, when a way was found of attaching a bayonet to a rifle barrel without interfering with the shot, they were no longer required.

Units armed with the halberd, another shafted weapon derived from the lance and battle-axe, were always divided into two branches: one for the special personal guard of the prince or commander, the other for combat units which used the halberd as a cutting or spearing weapon. The Lansquenets were the most famous halberdiers. Francis I of France absorbed them into his legions, but by the end of the sixteenth century they were serving only as royal guards, performing this function until 1756, when they were finally abolished. The Swiss halberdiers, however, survived and served as guards at royal residences, though their services were chiefly decorative. In 1564 the hereditary prince Charles Emmanuel of Savoy was given a special guard of halberdiers known as the *Guardia Alabardieri del Serenissimo Principe*.

A Swiss halberdier. Opposite: *Louis XI, King of France (1423-1483) with his court and soldiers, in a 19th-century illustration by Pellerin d'Epinal. There are* pikemen, francs archeurs, *and* tireurs, *the elements of the first permanent French army.*

PELLERIN & Cie, imp.-edit.

SOLDATS SOUS LOUIS XI

IMAGERIE D'ÉPINAL N° 400

Dame de la Cour.   La Reine.   Le Cardinal la Balue.   Le Roi Louis XI.   Le duc de Bourgogne.   Page.   Chevalier de St Michel.   Seigneur Français.   Seigneur Bourguignon.

PIQUIERS.

COULÉVRINIERS A MAIN.

PIQUIERS.

FRANCS ARCHERS.

PIQUIERS.

Lansquenets

The Lansquenets, from the German *Landsknecht* (lit. men of the plains), were a militia of foot soldiers formed in the late fifteenth century by Maximilian of Austria. The soldiers were selected for strength and courage. This militia was created to replace the Swiss infantry.

The sword borne by these troops was also called a *lansquenet* and bore some resemblance to the Roman gladius. It had a very broad two-edged blade about thirty-two inches long. The grip had a pommel in the form of a truncated cone and the guard was a metal loop twisted into the shape of a figure eight. Later, the name lansquenet was also applied to a *dagger* less than twenty-six inches long, another two-edged blade used by those soldiers.

In Maximilian's Germany the Lansquenets were organised into regiments of four thousand or six thousand men, divided into large companies of four hundred men each. They had various uniforms, depending on the countries and the armies in which they fought. Towards the end they wore navy-style trousers.

Strong and courageous troops, the Lansquenets were very demanding about money and were not always well disciplined. Like all mercenaries, for that matter, they easily transferred their allegiance from one camp to another, sometimes in whole units complete with officers and insignia. They fought only for booty and represented a terrible calamity for the lands they passed through.

Like the Swiss infantry, the Lansquenets fought in large battalions arrayed in compact masses of men. Those in the outer ranks were armed with pikes thirteen feet long to contain cavalry assaults. Those in the inner ranks (the battalion was twenty men deep) were armed with halberds and swords. The flanks were protected by crossbowmen as well as by pikemen and, later, by harquebusiers. Sufficient space between men was left so that the halberdiers and swordsmen could move easily in and out of the ranks. But the entire battalion closed tight to withstand cavalry attacks. During the Thirty Years War, the Lansquenets provided the backbone of both Gustavus Adolphus' forces and of the imperial armies. The end of that war saw their decline.

In the splendid engravings of Goltzius reproduced here, two lansquenets are depicted. The standard bearer may be Captain Gerrit Pietersz of Haarlem. Opposite: German lansquenets. They are armed with the typical lansquenet sword with a double-edged broad blade.

Colonels and Regiments

The term 'colonel', derived from the column (or *colonna*) of soldiers, seems to have come into use in Italy in the time of Charles V. More precisely, the commander of an infantry regiment then began to be called a 'colonel'.

In Piedmont the rank of colonel appeared at the time of Emanuel Philibert, about 1560, and was conferred on the officer who commanded a *colonnellato*, a territorial area from which units of country infantry militia were drawn. The colonel supervised the recruitment and training of the companies and was sometimes the military governor of the area. In 1556 Emmanuel Philibert reorganised the infantry and divided its forces into colonelcies, each of which consisted of six companies. The companies were subdivided into four centuries, and the centuries into four squads.

The colonelcies, which later became regiments, included a colonelcy company, a sort of command company, consisting of forty halberdiers and three hundred and fifty harquebusiers with sixteen corporals. The regimental colours were entrusted to a unit of soldiers known as the *confidenti*.

The rank of colonel was applied to regimental commanders of infantry under Henry II, but the new title did not totally replace the older title of field master. The colonels temporarily disappeared during the French revolution, when the regiments were called 'demi-brigades' and their commanders 'demi-brigade commanders'. But in 1803 Napoleon Bonaparte restored the regiment and the rank. A curiosity of the *ancien régime* was the rank of 'honorary colonel'. In return for the payment of a modest sum one could become the 'owner' of a regiment.

In addition to the rank of colonel, that of colonel-general was created (by Francis I) for the commander-in-chief of infantry. Later Henry IV also created the rank of colonel-general of cavalry, and Napoleon created colonel-generals of curassiers, artillery and light cavalry. These titles fell into disuse in France after the fall of Charles X in 1830, just when the rank of colonel-general was acquiring particular importance in Germany, where it was applied to army commanders.

To return to the rank - or, more accurately, to the title - of honorary colonel, it should be noted that it still exists in England. These colonels do not actually direct battalions, which are tactically organised in brigades. Royal princes and field-marshals are honorary regimental colonels in the guards.

Finally, until the end of the eighteenth century, the colonels enjoyed the privilege of giving their names to the regiments and having their own regimental colours.

Opposite: *17th-century uniforms on an imaginary battlefield.* Above: *The colours of the* Cent Suisses *and a light cavalry guardsman during the reign of Louis XIII of France. The* Chevalégers de la Garde *were founded in 1588 and dissolved in 1787. Henry IV wanted to call them* Gendarmes *when he ascended the throne in 1589, but they preferred to keep their original name. The* Hundred Swiss *were established by Charles VIII in 1496 and were the first permanent Swiss unit outside Switzerland. They were augmented in 1616, under Louis XIII, by the Swiss Guards. They were massacred while defending the palace and the royal family when the populace of Paris invaded the Tuileries in 1792. The French soldiers jokingly called the Swiss troops* les culs rouges.

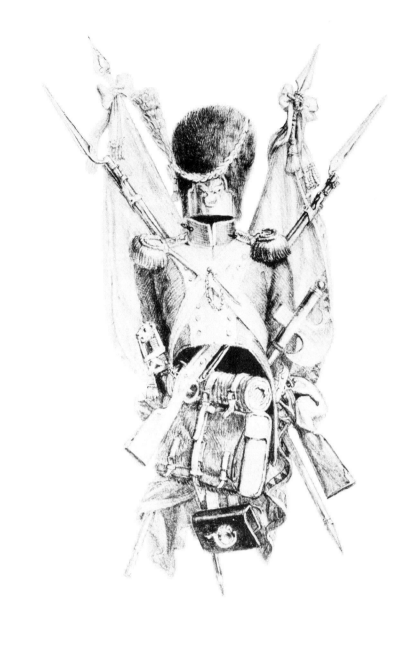

PART THREE

The Best Blood
in Europe

England and Scotland

Drums and Shillings

It is hard to establish which is the oldest surviving military unit. We are pretty certain, however, that it must be British and, in particular, Scottish. Some would date the origin of the Royal Scots to 882 AD. If this is true, then the Royal Scots represent the oldest infantry regiment in the world. Nor is their claim diminished by the fact that in the Middle Ages they served French kings. More than once the Scots and the French have been allies. The most faithful knights of Joan of Arc were in fact Scots, and a Scots Guard was still in the service of the French throne in the eighteenth century.

The Royal Scots also served other sovereigns. They were with Gustavus Adolphus of Sweden when he died on the battlefield at Lützen, 16 November 1632. At that time, units were still called by the names of their colonels. Thus they were called 'the Douglas' when Charles II finally assimilated them into the English army and 'lent' them to Louis XIV. Some time later their colonel was made Earl of Dumbarton, and from that time the regiment marched to the beat of the famous 'Dumbarton drums' - at Tangier against the barbarised soldiers, at Sedgemoor in 1685, on the side of James II against the rebels, and at Steinkirk in 1692 against the French (Colonel Douglas lost his life trying to rescue a colour.) Later they fought in Canada, Havana, Spain and Portugal. At Waterloo one of their four battalions (the Third) astonished Marshal Ney, *le brave des braves*, resisting in square formation seven awesome charges of the French heavy cavalry and leaving four hundred comrades dead on the field.

The seniority of the Royal Scots is challenged by the popular 'Beefeaters'. This is the name given to the Yeomen Warders of Her Majesty's Tower of London and to the members of the Queen's Bodyguard of the Yeomen of the Guard. They are two separate units, though the similarity of uniform makes it easy to confuse them. The only difference is that the Tower Guards do not wear the bronze-buckled sash that once held the harquebus.

The Yeomen of the Guard were established in 1485 by Henry VII and were armed with bows and halberds. They numbered one hundred, half horse and half foot. During the reign of Henry VIII, who had a passion for the army, their pay was increased to four shillings a day, a large sum in those days. There was some protest against this liberality and thus was coined the name of 'Beefeater', indicating an expensive diet.

Above: *The Victoria Cross, the decoration established by Queen Victoria on 29 January 1856. It is most prized by English soldiers. The first Victoria Crosses were cast from the bronze of the Russian cannons taken at Sebastopol in 1855.* Opposite: *A Yeoman of the Guard, from a 19th-century illustration.*

Ironsides, Guards and Grenadiers

It is said that Oliver Cromwell was a country gentleman and an ordinary Parliamentarian until the age of forty-four. Then came the stroke of genius and luck, unlimited power and his military masterpiece - the heavy cavalry known as the Ironsides. In the civil war that broke out when Parliament resisted the king's attempt to establish absolute power, Colonel Cromwell's Ironsides wrote some of the most stirring pages. In the battle of Marston Moor, 2 August 1644, they sang a Puritan psalm before they charged with their long straight swords and dispersed the regiments of their adversaries. A visor attached to their steel helmets protected their eyes from the sun's rays, and a cuirass covered their leather jerkins. They began with their typical knee-to-knee charge, spurring their heavy horses against those of the royal cavalry commanded by Prince Rupert. It was Rupert, in fact, who coined the term 'Ironsides'.

Marston Moor was not the first defeat the Royalists suffered at the hands of the bourgeois army of Cromwell, nor was it the last. Less than a year later, on 4 June 1645, Prince Rupert again saw those awesome soldiers advance and rout his forces at Naseby.

The Ironsides were Cromwell's faithful followers. During the last years of the Lord Protector's government, they were sent to fight alongside the French against the Spanish and shared the victory of the Dunes. They silently disappeared after the dissolution of Cromwell's Commonwealth. And their great adversary, Prince Rupert, withdrew to study mezzotint engraving and a way to make the glass pendants of Restoration chandeliers look like diamonds.

The Restoration managed to preserve something from the Commonwealth period. More than one English regiment today can trace its foundation to the time of Cromwell. The most famous example, perhaps, are the Blues, of whom more will be said later.

There was an important new development in those years, the birth of the grenadiers. The hand grenade, a typical explosive weapon used by the infantry in the two wars of the twentieth century, had its first period of glory in the late seventeenth-early eighteenth century. In 1678 men were chosen to form a company of grenadiers for every infantry regiment. Their uniforms were modified to suit this new weapon, and their headgear eventually became a distinguishing feature. The broadbrimmed feathered hat of the period was abandoned in favour of a kind of elongated bishop's mitre, adorned with symbols, decorations and mottoes, often in Latin. Thus the hand could be easily raised above the head to throw the grenade without being obstructed in any way. In 1768 a bearskin was added to this hat, and the symbols, mottoes and decorations were brought together on a metal badge on the front of the hat. Such a mitre-cap was worn by the 23rd Infantry Grenadiers who attacked Bunker Hill on that terrible 17 June 1775, when revolutionary America began firing at the Red Coats of George III. There were seventy-five of them when (at 2.30 p.m.) the order was given to attack. Only five escaped unharmed. The 23rd Infantry has some illustrious forebearers. In Shakespeare's *Henry V* there is a mention of the Welsh soldiers' habit of wearing a leek on their hats on St David's Day (1 March). And the men of the 23rd, now the Royal Welsh Fusiliers, do so to this day.

Turning back to the grenadiers, mention must be made of the Grenadier Guards, who, together with the Coldstreams, the Scots, the Irish and the Welsh make up the Foot Guards. The Grenadier Guards are descendants of the First Regiment of Foot Guards. At the battle of Waterloo, it was they who had to repulse and counter attack Napoleon's *Vieille Garde*. Having defeated the Old Guard, they received the prestigious title of Grenadier Guards from the crown.

AN "IRONSIDE" 1644

One of Oliver Cromwell's Ironsides. These heavy cavalrymen were recruited among the followers of the Lord Protector. They performed many feats of valour. Their characteristic helmet had a visor and a neckpiece called a lobster tail.

Uniforms of the Foot Infantry Guards Regiment in 1745. From left to right: *officer, grenadier drummer, sergeant, grenadier fifer, grenadier, and infantryman. The regiment was founded in 1660 as the Life Guards. It took part in many memorable battles, including Blenheim, Ramillies, Oudenard, Malphaquet, Dettingen and Waterloo. At Waterloo the regiment faced the veterans of the Napoleonic* Vieille Garde *in hand-to-hand combat. When the battle was over, by way of perpetual celebration of their victory over the most famous soldiers in the world, they were given the title of Grenadiers, the title that their brave adversaries had borne so nobly. The present uniform of the Grenadier Guards is quite different from the one illustrated. From the time they became grenadiers, they received a large black bearskin decorated with a white feather.*

The Horse Guards

Any consideration of the uniforms of the British army usually begins with the Life Guards. They wear the most spectacular military uniform, and not just in modern times. Anyone who has glanced at a tourist brochure of the British Isles has seen the red-coated trooper, with his high boots, cuirass and feathered helmet, sitting like a statue on his black mount. The unit dates back to 1660, the year in which Charles II, restored to the throne, began to reorganise the army. The Horse Guards (as they were then called) originally comprised three units of two hunderd 'carabineers' recruited among those gentlemen who had followed the king into exile during the Civil War. The shining cuirass (which was sometimes given a coat of rust-resistant black paint during wartime) was not always a prerogative of the Life Guards. It has been part of the regulation uniform for officers and men, except for musicians and trumpeters, since 1621. Three centuries ago the trumpeters were often called upon to negotiate surrenders and armistices (a relic of the Middle Ages, when this function was performed by the herald). Consequently they bore sabres with broken tips.

From their beginnings the Life Guards rarely left English soil except with the king. But in 1808 they were in Spain against Napoleon and then at Waterloo in the Heavy Cavalry Brigade, in the Sudan in the re-

bellion of 1882 and in South Africa against the Boers.

The two regiments of Life Guards, the First and Second, commonly called the 'Tins', were consolidated in 1922, and together with the Royal Horse Guards or 'Blues', joined in 1939 to form the First Household Cavalry Regiment. Soon after that they dismounted from their horses for armoured vehicles, to fight in the middle east, Italy and north-western Europe.

After the war, the 'Tins' and 'Blues' separated as units but kept their armoured cars. Only one squadron from each regiment is mounted on horseback, for official ceremonies. These two squadrons have resumed their old traditions: the bandoleer with the red braid (in the eighteenth century the powder flask hung on the right from this braid); the chin strap passing just under the lower lip; braid on the right shoulder for officers and on the left for non-commissioned officers; the horses' manes brushed to the left for the 'Tins' and the right for the 'Blues'; and the farriers (with black plumes for the 'Tins' and red for the 'Blues') armed with an axe reminiscent of those used two centuries ago to deliver the *coup de grace* to fallen horses.

From time to time these regiments attracted the particular attention of the people and the sovereign. George II considered the 'Blues' his favourite regiment and kept them permanently at Windsor Castle. He became their colonel and had a unit named after him. In 1805 he gave them a pair of silver kettledrums which are still in service.

In 1831 the last of the Hanoverians, William IV, established that the Life Guards and the Royal Horse Guards should wear as part of their dress uniform a Roman-style helmet crested with black fur. With their normal uniform they wore a grenadier's busby, fourteen inches high (in 1822 it had been twenty inches high), and adorned with a plume of swan feathers, white for the 'Tins' and red for the 'Blues'. Ten years later the busby was the official headgear of the Household Cavalry, except for evening parade.

Under Queen Victoria a German type of headgear, the Albert helmet, was introduced. It is still worn on parade, but trimmed now of most of its earlier ornaments. The immobility that can be achieved by the Guards and their horses has always been a source of admiration to the English.

There is a picture in an 1882 issue of the *Graphic* showing a Life Guard on sentinel duty at Whitehall, unperturbed by the cloud of smoke pouring from a cauldron of tar that a group of workmen are using to asphalt the road. The caption, affectionately witty, reads: 'Under fire again'. At that time the regiment had just returned from the severe trials of the rebellion in the Sudan.

A guard of the 2nd Life Guards Regiment, dressed in the uniform of 1914. The helmet with the hanging plume is still worn. The helmet, like the cuirass, is of polished steel.

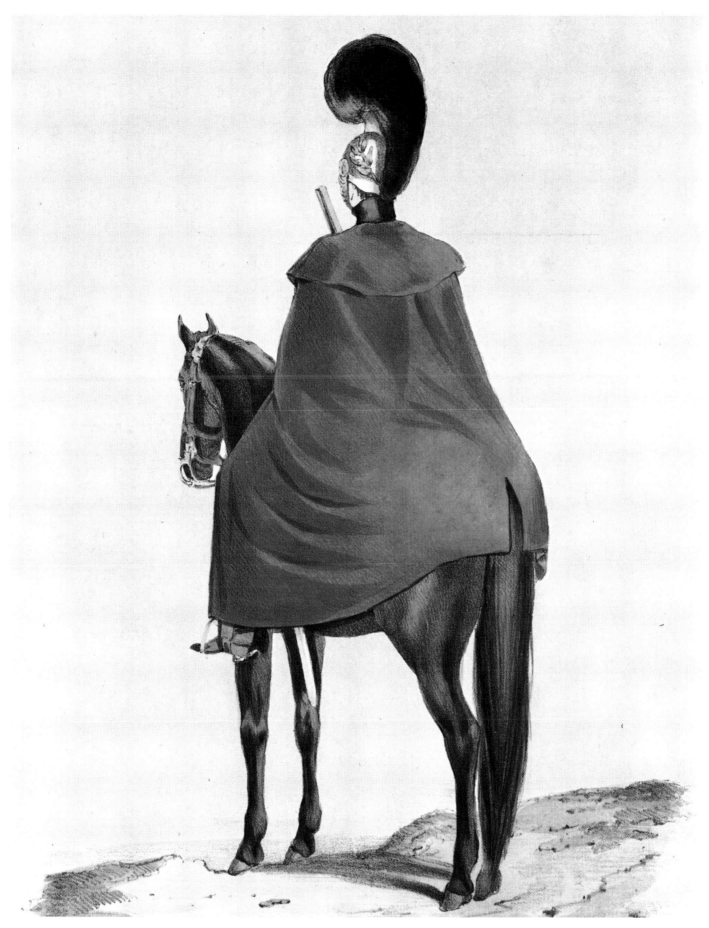

Soldier of the 1st Life Guards. The so-called Roman style helmet is adorned with a bearskin and was first worn between 1827 and 1832. The 1st Life Guards, founded by Charles II in 1660, is the oldest surviving cavalry regiment of the British Army. Its original name was His Majesty's Own Troop of Life Guards. Gentlemen of rank paid a fee in order to join the troop. The Life Guards numbered two regiments until 1922; in that year they were made a single unit. During the Second World War, they abandoned their horses for armoured vehicles. This was not the first time that they dismounted from their horses. In 1884, during the Nile Campaign, they rode dromedaries.

In 1831 the uniforms of the British Army reached a peak of extravagance. The water-colour print reproduced here dates from that time and shows part of the General Staff at a solemn ceremony. Note in the centre the Hussar officer with his large dark feather, probably a member of the 10th Royal Hussars, famous for the privileges that King George IV showered on it. He was Prince of Wales when he was made their colonel. When he came to the throne the price of the officer's uniform of the 10th rose to £400. The cost in other regiments did not exceed £300. Noteworthy too is the uniform of the last officer. His helmet, the famous Polish czapka, indicates that he belonged to a Lancer Regiment.

The Men of Balaclava

'C'est magnifique, mais ce n'est pas la guerre.' These were the words in which the French general Bosquet described the Charge of the Light Brigade, which he witnessed in all its tragic glory. It was because of that charge that the day of Balaclava represents one of the best-known events of the Crimean War.

With fatal uncertainty the charge was ordered when the battle to defend Balaclava, which had begun at 6 p.m. on 25 October 1854, seemed to be going badly. The six hundred men of the Light Brigade were not the only cavalrymen at the disposal of the Franco-English forces. There was also the Heavy Brigade (which, together with the Light Brigade, composed the cavalry division commanded by Major-General Lord Lucan), and the Fourth Regiment of French *Chasseurs d'Afrique*. The infantry included a battalion of Scots of the 93rd Highlanders and a detachment of the Royal Marines. There were sixteen thousand men in all, under the command of Marshal Lord Raglan, to resist the twenty-five thousand Russians under Count Liprandi.

The Heavy Brigade, under the command of Sir James Scarlett, was composed of dragoons of the 1st Royal Dragoons, the famous Royal Scot Greys (2nd Dragoons), the 5th Royal Inniskilling Dragoon Guards and two other regiments, the 4th and 5th Dragoon Guards. The Light Brigade, under Lord Cardigan, comprised the 4th, 8th, 13th and the 11th Hussars (Prince Albert's Own 11th Hussars, the only regiment of the British army that still wears, as it did then, crimson trousers) and the 17th Lancers, the Death or Glory Boys.

The Heavy Brigade had the honour of the first action, and with less than half its strength it managed to stop the Russian cavalry, which had captured several redoubts guarded by the Turks and was trying to turn to the right of the Allied troops. This charge which has passed into history as the 'Charge of the Three Hundred', lasted eight minutes. The Russians fell back and withdrew to reform their ranks behind the artillery that had advanced into the valley which the cartographers had named North Valley. But that valley, barely a mile of plain, would soon be known as Death Valley.

The Light Brigade was at one end of the valley, the Russian artillery and the bulk of the Russian cavalry at the other. Three-quarters of an hour passed before new orders arrived. Meanwhile the Heavy Brigade, after its victorious charge on one side of the hills, turned in full force to joint the Litht Brigade. But by the time Lucan received the order to advance both brigades, the Russians had been given sufficient time to regroup and replan and even to attempt to remove the English cannons from the redoubts captured from the Turks. To prevent the removal of these cannons, Raglan ordered the cavalry to advance. His orders were not understood, nor were they completely obeyed. Lucan ordered Cardigan to advance with the Light Brigade and himself prepared to follow with the Heavy Brigade. The tragedy had begun. Notwithstanding fire on its front and flanks from thirty cannons, the six hundred and seventy-three men of the Light Brigade advanced with incredible calm. Sapous, an old French officer, saw them from the hills and said: '*Je suis vieux et j'ai vu des batailles, mais ceci est trop.*' Like many others, he wept. It was too much for Lucan too. 'They have sacrificed the Light Brigade,' he said. 'They shall not have the Heavy.' He halted the dragoons, while the Hussars and the Lancers charged past firing at the enemy as they galloped through the dust.

Yard by yard, the six hundred increased their speed. They were four hundred when they started their lances lowered and their sabres flashing over the

A lancer of the famous 17th Regiment, (the so-called 'Death' or 'Glory Boys') in the uniform of 1914. He is wearing a Polish-style czapka with the white plume and is armed with a bamboo lance of Indian type that came into use in 1868.

CORPORAL. PRIVATES. OFFICERS.
93RD HIGHLANDERS. 14TH FOOT RIFLE BRIGADE. GRENADIER GUARDS. ROYAL ARTILLERY 26TH FOOT. ROYAL HORSE ARTILLERY.

TYPES OF THE BRITISH ARMY IN 1854. THE CRIMEAN EPOCH.

The Men of Balaclava. Mounted, from left to right: *ordinary soldiers of the 17th Lancers, 4th Light Dragoons, 2nd Dragoons, 1st Royal Dragoons, and an officer of the 11th Hussars.* On foot: *corporal of the 93rd Highland Infantry, soldiers of the 14th Infantry, of the Fusilier Brigade, officers of the Grenadier Guards, the Royal Artillery, the 26th Infantry, the Royal Mounted Artillery.*

Russian batteries, the burning cannons and the crushed gun crews. On and on they charged, forcing the Cossack cavalry contingents to withdraw.

But they had already achieved the impossible. Not knowing how or perhaps not wishing to surround and annihilate that handful of dust-covered youths, the Russians forced them to turn and withdraw at the gallop under the cannon fire that continued from the hills.

Thus it was that the day of Balaclava ended at four in the afternoon, and so, for the moment, did the Light Brigade. Nothing like that charge had ever been seen in cavalry history. Only a poet could do justice to the event. And that pacific poet laureate Tennyson wrote poems about Balaclava, one about the six hundred heroes of the Light Brigade, another on the three hundred of the Heavy Brigade.

Naturally the units did not perish. For some, Balaclava marked the beginning of a new period in regimental history. For the Hussars, for example, it marked

the simplification of the uniform. Before Balaclava, their uniform had been as elaborate and expensive as it could be. In 1892 there was an investigation of the cost of officers' uniforms. It cost forty pounds for an infantry officer, one hundred and fifty for a dragoon and three hundred for an Hussar. The highest cost was three hundred and ninety-nine pounds, seven shillings and six pence for an officer of the 10th Hussars.

This was the favourite regiment of George IV, who had become its colonel in 1793, when he was Prince of Wales. He ascended the throne in 1820 and continued to devote his attention to the Hussars, enriching the uniform beyond belief. The mounts were also richly caparisoned. Leopard skins on the saddles, saddle-cloths embroidered in gold and silver and even shell decorations were used. As if that were not enough, when William IV succeeded George IV in 1830, he authorised the Hussars and the Horse Guards to wear moustaches, forbidding them for the rest of the army.

Les terribles petits Grenadiers

In 1664 Charles II decided to equip the fleet with twelve hundred foot soldiers to be used as landing troops. This was the beginning of the Lord High Admiral of England, His Royal Highness the Duke of York and Albany's Maritime Regiment.

The marines were armed with flintlock muskets, weapons equipped with a mechanical firing device in place of the traditional slow-match which was so troublesome, inconvenient and often dangerous - safer and readier muskets in short. Many of the marines came from London units, and today the Royal Marines are one of the few regiments that are still entitled to march through the City, drums beating with their colours in the wind and with fixed bayonets.

In the beginning, during the reign of Charles II, the English Marines wore a yellow jacket with red facing, to distinguish them from land units which already wore the typical British red. Yellow was one of the colours of the Stuart House (the family of Charles II), and it was the favourite colour of the duke of York, the first commander of the marines.

But the real birth of the Royal Marines dates from 1755, the year in which they were given a permanent mandate. A great date in their history is 1761, the year of the siege of Belle Isle, when their French adversaries gave them the name of 'Les terribles petits grenadiers' In fact, the marines were wearing the tall bearskin caps that had already become distinctive of the grenadiers. As for the *petit*, it was a direct reference to their height, inferior to that of the real grenadiers.

English troops leaving the Transvaal in 1883. Notice the particular difficulties the men experienced in boarding and landing because of the structure of the vessels. The white helmet is now typical of the Royal Marines, who wear it on parade and at official ceremonies. In 1842 the Royal Marines were the first to occupy Hong Kong.

This was the time of the clandestine enlistment of Hannah Snell, the young woman who served with the marines at the siege of Pondicherry in India. She received twelve wounds and it is said that she herself extracted enemy lead from her wounds. Because of a leg wound, among others, she was given an annual pension of thirty pounds per year. She opened a restaurant and liked to circulate among the tables wearing her uniform from 'the good old days'

Today the marines are distinguished on ceremonial occasions by a white colonial-style sun-helmet. Like all important military units, the English marines have their legends. One of them has given rise to an expression that is still in use 'Tell it to the marines'. The story goes back to the foundation of the unit.

The anecdote - for it is this more than a legend - concerns Charles II, the captain of the *Defyance* (which had just returned from a voyage to the Indies), Sir William Killigrew, colonel of the Maritime Regiment, and Samuel Pepys, Admiralty secretary. One day the king was listening to the captain's account of the voyage of the *Defyance*. The king did not interrupt the captain's account, which was colourful to say the least, embellished as it was with digressions on the marvels, events and prodigies of which he had been a witness.

The king believed him, or pretended to believe him, but could not refrain from expressing his doubts when the captain spoke of certain flying fish which took off from the waves and dived into the sea again after spectacular flights and loops and nose dives and other aerobatics. Charles II silenced the captain and turned to Colonel Killigrew to ask him what he thought of a man who claimed to have seen fish fly like birds. To his surprise, the colonel replied that fish could fly. He, William Killigrew, had seen such flights during missions on which the king had sent him in tropical waters.

Then the King turned to Pepys. He commented that it was clear that no one could know more about the marvels of the earth and the sea than the men of the Maritime Regiment. Since then, whenever anyone is in doubt about the truth of an event, the standard reply has been to 'tell it to the marines'. If the marines confirmed the fact, then it was as good as true.

From left to right: *private, colour-sergeant and non-commissioned officer of the Royal Marines in uniforms of the mid-19th century. The regiment, founded in 1664, is one of the most famous in the British armed forces. With a few other units it shares the unique privilege of being allowed to cross the City of London with fixed bayonets, drum rolls, and colours flying. The Marines founded the first British colonies in Australia little more than 150 years ago. They took part in the Battle of Trafalgar. From 1804 to 1923 there was also a Royal Marines Artillery.*

The Honourable Artillery Company

Among the many singularities that distinguish the British armed forces is an artillery unit that is such in name only, or at least only in part. It is the Honourable Artillery Company.

The origins of this unit are lost in obscurity. The oldest record dates from 1537. This document sanctions the formation by the 'Guyld of St George' of a 'fraternity', whose members would be concerned with the 'science of Artillery', of bows, crossbows and 'hand gonnes'. Their purpose was to improve the defence of the realm. And, in fact, the Honourable Artillery made a significant contribution to defence from the very beginning. When the Spanish Armada was approaching the English coast, in 1588, the City of London mobilised about two thousand men. The officers and non-commissioned officers were for the most part members of the Honourable Artillery.

George I gave them red uniforms in 1722, and William IV gave them the uniform of the Grenadier Guards, which, except for different buttons, they still wear. There was a reason for the sovereigns' interest: the Honourable Artillery has always been the only armed unit that the sovereign could call out without the prior consent of Parliament. In 1801 the Honourable Artillery was given a light cavalry unit, and in 1860 it acquired a mounted battery.

Among the unit's duties is that of firing salvoes from the Tower of London during official ceremonies. In addition, the Honourable Artillery escorts the members of the royal family when they visit the City and accompanies the lord mayor on his official visits. The duty of serving as a bodyguard to the first citizen of London is assigned to one unit of the Company, that which incorporates the pikemen and musketeers.

During the Boer War and the two world wars, the Honourable Artillery served in the field alongside other British regiments.

As for the artillery, let us begin with the Royal Horse Artillery, whose units enjoy a place of honour, 'on the right of the line', in British Army parades.

The Royal Horse Artillery was created in 1793 under the direction of the duke of Richmond, then master-general of ordnance. Its origin is due to one of those events that often prove decisive in history, and not

only in military history. A mutiny broke out in Southampton aboard a ship loaded with French prisoners, and it was decided that modest-calibre guns would be required to restore order. But there were none at Southampton. A rider was sent to Winchester to find some. He found two, and he found a way of delivering them quickly. He had them hauled by postilion-ridden post horses. The gun crews crouched on the weapons in a manner not unlike that which was later to become regulation.

This incident is probably insufficient to account for the creation of a horse-drawn artillery, but it is illuminating enough to be repeated. The regiment that was created from it is certainly one of the finest in the world. The duke of Richmond gave it his special care. He equipped it with a movable smithy so that the smiths could work on the march, and he provided it with a laundry waggon, full of washerwomen constantly at work keeping the regimental linen clean.

The first barracks of the Royal Horse Artillery was Goodwood, the duke's private residence. The cannons were stationed in front of the house, and the men and horses were quartered in the duke's ample stables.

Today a single troop testifies to the past, with its blue uniform, its fur hat with red ornament and the thundering, large-wheeled cannon. The troop was preserved by the queen in memory of George VI, who was extremely attached to the Royal Horse Artillery. Consequently the troop is called the King's Troop.

Far larger is the basic corps of British artillery, the Royal Regiment of Artillery, which has recently celebrated its 250th anniversary. During the Second World War it numbered 750,000 men; one British soldier in four was a gunner. On 26 May 1716, the date of its formation, the Royal Regiment of Artillery consisted of two companies, with a total of ten officers, eighteen non-commissioned officers, sixty gunners and one hundred crew, the matrosses. One of those companies still exists, with the new name of Missile Battery Royal Artillery. But it preserves its old number of 19th Battery, which it had during the siege of Gibraltar (1779 to 1783). For three years and seven months the Royal Artillery fired continuously day and night on the French and Spanish besiegers - a total of two hundred thousand shots consuming eight thousand kegs of powder.

Left: *The Horse Battery of the Honourable Artillery Company, in a late-19th-century print.* Right: *a foot soldier of the Honourable Artillery Company, 17th-19th century. Between 1804 and 1854, the Company included a Chasseur Company.*

Next to two cannon lost at Mainwand and recaptured at Kandahar during the Afghanistan Campaign of 1880, stand nine brave men of Battery E, B Brigade, of the Royal Horse Artillery, who were decorated for their valour: from right to left, *the Trumpeter Jones, Gunner Collins (Victoria Cross), Sergeant-Major Paton, Sergeant Burridge, Corporal Thorogood, Cannoneer Tighe, the Driver Bishop, Bombardier Payne, and Sergeant Mullane (Victoria Cross). The regiment dates from 1793. A horse-drawn troop still survives and it wears the traditional uniform. It has been maintained at the wish of Queen Elizabeth II, in memory of her father, whose favourite regiment it was.*

The Heart in the Highlands

'My heart's in the highlands', begins that nostalgic verse by Robert Burns (1759-96). Not only the romantic heart of Robert Burns but those of all the Scots, particularly when they are under arms and far from home. Facile rhetoric? Perhaps. But there are few regions of the earth that evoke such a particular feeling, such devotion, such a sense of traditions worth keeping alive as Scotland. Gael or Anglo-Saxon that he may be, the Scot comes from a harsh, proud and discontented land. In uniform his character takes on new persistence and obstinacy, new responsibilities and additional immutable convictions. At the lost battle of Fontenoy, 11 May 1745, during the War of the Austrian Succession, the Scots of the famous Black Watch, a regiment about which more will be said later, threw down their muskets and advanced in the manner of their ancestors, a round shield on their right arm and the dirk and broadsword clutched in their hands.

For the Scot, to be a soldier is a gentleman's privilege. Three soldiers of one of the first Scottish companies (those that were later to form the Black Watch) once received a guinea each from King George I, for whom they had performed the sword dance. When they left the palace they tossed the coins to the porter.

For several decades one Scottish regiment abandoned the traditional kilt, the 71st Highland Light Infantry, which was formed in 1881 by the unification of the 73rd and the 74th. When these two regiments served in India, they abandoned the kilt for the more pratical trews. They resumed the kilt in 1948.

As for the 73rd, historians love to recount the story of Mrs Baird, the mother of Captain David Baird, a lively officer in that regiment. Baird was captured by the Indians and chained to another prisoner in a filthy cell for four years. When Mrs Baird heard the news, she exclaimed: 'Heaven help the poor lad who's chained to my Davy!'

The Highland Light Infantry was the only light infantry regiment to march 120 steps per minute with the rifle at shoulder-arms. Another characteristic of Scottish forces is the bagpipe. In 1781 the Highland Light Infantry Regiment received an entire band in silver from its commandant, Sir Eyre Coote, after a legendary and decisive encounter in India with Hyder Ali, the man who had put Captain Baird in chains. In eight hours, eight thousand Scotsmen destroyed Hyder Ali's army, which was reported to comprise one hundred thousand foot and fifty thousand horsemen.

Another famous bagpipe is that of Piper Mackay of the 79th Cameron Highlanders. He played the bagpipe as he marched around a grenadier company squared up to meet a French assault at Waterloo. He played it then with the same calm with which he had played it at dawn on the fatal 16 June 1815, when the regiment, at the head of the whole army, marched out of Brussels to Quatre Bras and the terrain of the great battle. This is the scene which Byron describes in *Childe Harold's Pilgrimage*, evoking the sound of the 'Camerons' gathering that 'thrills savage and shrill' 'in the noon of night': *And wild and high the 'Camerons' gathering rose...*

After Waterloo Piper Mackay received a gift of a silver trimmed set of bagpipes from the king. The Camerons were a fairly new regiment then. It had been organised by Sir Alan Cameron of Erracht in 1793. Stern trials awaited it in the Crimea, in Afghanistan and in Africa. It was called the Ciamar-tha Regiment, Gaelic for 'How do you do?' This was the greeting that the soldiers made to Alan Cameron every morning.

The origins of the 92nd, the 'Gay Gordons', are more romantic. They were founded by George, marquess of Huntely, in 1794, with the assistance of his mother, the beautiful duchess of Gordon, from whom each recruit received a kiss. They then formed a brigade, with the Royal Scots and the Black Watch. Waterloo was the great day for the Gordons as well. When the dragoons of the Scots Greys charged through their ranks, many Gordons grasped their stirrup straps and joined in that terrifying charge to the battle cry of 'Scotland Forever!' Napoleon was heard to exclaim: *Ces terribles chevaux gris! Comme ils travaillent!*

The Highlanders' and the Scots Greys' part at Balaclava has already been mentioned. The Scots Greys joined the Heavy Brigade in the Charge of the Three Hundred. The Highlanders (a battalion of the 93rd) known as 'the thin red line', assigned to defend Balaclava on the crest of some hills, repulsed the Russians with three musket salvoes. The 93rd Regiment, now the Argyll and Sutherland Highlanders, were recruited in 1800 by Colonel Wemyss of Wemyss. Each recruit was allowed to put his thumb and forefinger into the colonel's personal tobacco pouch. The temptation to join up was irresistible.

An 18th-century Milanese print, author unknown. The inscription reads: 'Uniform of the Scottish Highlanders who came to the Rhine to reinforce the English Army in aid of the Queen of Hungary and Bohemia against the French in 1745. There are ten free companies under the command of Lord Temple, their countryman.'

Beretone basso

di Color Celeste

Ritratto

Gibone
rosso

Mantello
Verde e Giallo
pendente dalle spalle
largo bra.ᵃ 12; e legato
in Centura serve in vece
de Calzoni.

Grembiale, Volgar-
mente scossale
d'avanti verde, e
giallo con borsa,
dove separatam
mente sta denari
e roba.

Senza Calzoni
alla Caccia, e
in Campagna

Calzette bian-
che

intreciate di rosso

Scarpe sotili

The Black Watch

Before concluding this survey of the most famous British units with a glance at the Black Watch, mention should be made of several other Scottish units that have played a part in the history of the British army. There are the Scots Guards, founded in 1642; the Lowland Brigade, or Royal Scots, who have already been mentioned; the Royal Scots Fusiliers ('Dinna fire till ye see the white o' their een' was the command they received from their commander, Sir Andrew Agnew of Lochnaw at the battle of Dettingen against the French); the King's Own Scottish Borderers (recruited in four hours' time in Edinburgh in 1689 by the Earl of Leven); and the Cameronians, or Scottish Rifles, not to be confused with the Camerons.

The Black Watch forms the Highland Brigade together with the regiments already mentioned: the Highland Light Infantry (Royal Highland Regiment); Seaforth Highlanders (the duke of Albany's Ross-Shire Buffs); the Gordon Highlanders; the Queen's Own Cameron Highlanders; the Argyll and Sutherland Highlanders (Princess Louise's).

The Black Watch originated from platoons that wore a blue, green and black tartan (from which their name) and in 1729 were assigned the task of maintaining order among the Scottish clans after the events of the preceding years, which had brought Scotland to the brink of secession and civil war. These platoons, provided by clans that had remained faithful to the king - the Campbells, the Grants and the Munroes - later became companies.

In 1743 the king transferred the regiment to England with the intention of sending them to Flanders, where the situation of his Dutch and Austrian allies was becoming dangerous (the War of the Austrian Succession was being waged). Subversive elements who wanted to overthrow the king in favour of the Stuart Pretender suborned the Highlanders and convinced them that they were to be sent to America. A mutiny resulted and the non-commissioned officers who had led the rebels were executed at the Tower of London.

The episode at Fontenoy two years later, when the Black Watch distinguished themselves with dirk and broadsword, restored the legendary name of the Black Watch. That was the regiment's first foreign action, and not even defeat could diminish the glory of their performance.

Men of the Black Watch took part in the Canadian campaign (1756) and in the attack on Fort Ticonderoga. They were present at the taking of Havana (1762) and, a few years later they took part in the American War of Independence, fighting those colonial troops alongside whom they had fought at Ticonderoga. They were in Egypt, at Waterloo, in the Crimea, Tel el Kebir, the Nile, India, the Boer War and the wars of the twentieth century. The motto of the 42nd Highlanders, *Nemo me impune lacessit*, has been verified on more than one occasion. One of the distinguishing marks of the regiment, earned at the beginning of the last century, has remained famous: the red plume of vulture feathers.

A soldier of the 1st Argyll and Sutherland Highlanders performing the sword dance (1882). Opposite: Uniforms of the Cameron Highlanders (79th Foot). Above, left: the first uniform (1796). The other uniforms are of 1807, 1815 (with the regimental colours, centre), 1828 (officer of the Light Company), 1850, and far right, a grenadier of 1832.

H. Payne

France

Beautiful Picardy

As an example of a kind of ideal continuity between the pre-revolutionary *Armée* and that which followed on the proclamation of the 'immortal principles' of 1789, one could cite Soult. He became a Marshal of the Empire in Napoleon's *Grande Armée* after having been a corporal in the Picardy Regiment of the king's army. And this continuity does nothing but honour to France.

The Picardy was the first French unit to be called a regiment. It was soon followed by those af Navarre, Piedmont, Lorraine, Champagne, Normandy and gradually by other regional troops. Picardy, Navarre and Piedmont provided a model of order, discipline and devotion to duty for all the others. Each regiment consisted of two battalions of seventeen companies each. One battalion was armed with pikes and the other with muskets. Each regiment had its own colours (vermilion for Picardy, black for Piedmont, *feuille morte* for Navarre, green for Champagne, etc.), but each flag bore the white cross of Charles VII, the first symbol of national unity. The men of these regiments were called *les vieux*.

The masterpiece of the Picardy vieux was the battle of Freiburg against the Bavarians in August 1644, when they were led by the Great Condé.

Twenty thousand men had to capture this city at the foot of the mountains of the Black Forest, an apparently impregnable site. The order to attack was given at sundown, about 6 o'clock. The count d'Espenan, colonel of the Picardy, sent his regiment out with the colours at the head of the regiment. The standard-bearer, a young officer, died in the first assault. The vermilion banner was passed to a twelve-year-old boy, and when he was killed, to a sergeant. Night fell and the battlefield was silent. Fighting was resumed the next day and the day after that. The third day of the battle began badly. The musketeers opened the action but were repulsed and almost encircled. Then there were seven infantry assaults, with the intrepid condé himself leading them in the final attack. Twenty officers were struck down around him, and he had to change his mount four times. Finally, the great gesture: in a fit of rage he threw his marshal's baton well beyond the enemy lines. And then the regiments hurled themselves one after another in a furious charge to recover that symbol. When Picardy's turn came, the vermilion banner finally reached the Bavarian trenches borne by a captain whose breast had been ripped open. And there he remained, supported and surrounded by the surviving soldiers of that beautiful regiment with its long pikes glittering in the August sunlight.

Above: *the Napoleonic eagle in the decoration of the diplomas of the Legion of Honour.* Opposite: *a 'Picardy' flag-bearer (1600) and musketeer (1680), one of the oldest regiments of the French army.*

The Musketeers: a Legion of Caesars

I speak of M. de Tréville, who was formerly my neighbour, and who had the honour to be, as a child, the playfellow of our king, Louis XIII, whom God preserve! Sometimes their play degenerated into battles, and in those battles the King was not always the stronger. The blows which he received increased greatly his esteem and friendship for M. de Tréville. Afterwards M. de Tréville fought with others: in his first journey to Paris, five times; from the death of the late king till the young one came of age, without reckoning wars and sieges, seven times; and from that date up to the present day, a hundred times, perhaps! So that in spite of edicts, ordinances and decrees, there he is, captain of the Musketeers; that is to say, chief of a legion of Caesars, whom the king holds in great esteem, and whom the cardinal dreads - he who dreads nothing, as it is said. Still further, M. de Tréville gains ten thousand crowns a year; he is therefore a great noble. He began as you begin. Go to him with this letter; and make him your model in order that you may do as he has done.

Thus D'Artagnan's father sketches ('in that pure Bearn dialect that Henry IV never totally managed to get rid of') the portrait of the ideal musketeer to his young son at the start of Dumas' most famous novel. The portrait is completed in the next chapter by Dumas himself, with his masterly novelist's skill in using history just enough to create genuine poetry.

A musketeer of the Restoration, in a drawing by Caran d'Ache. Opposite: The musketeers of King Louis XIII in a print by d'Epinal, who idealised the uniform. Richelieu also had a musketeer unit, which wore red cloaks. The King's Musketeers wore a blue cloak with a cross. They were armed with sword and pistol.

The picture we have today of the musketeers owes much to Dumas' novel. But the true history of the musketeers is not all that much different.

Their music, for example, at least what has survived, now seems closer to the gavotte than to barracks or parade music. For the most part, they were composed by Giambattista Lulli and had to satisfy Louis XIV and his court first of all. Nevertheless their sweet sixteenth century solemnity successfully evokes the world in which the musketeers came into being and the epoch in which they wrote some of the most glorious chapters in all of their history.

In the sixteenth century some men in the companies of pikemen were given a firearm called a *mousquet* and were therefore called *mousquetaires*. Between 1560 and 1600 the number of mousquetaires increased, eventually reaching the proportion of one musket for every three pikes. Finally, in 1600, Henry IV created a personal guard, a company of gentlemen armed with carbines and known as the *Carabiniers du Roi*. In 1622 Louis XII replaced the carbine with a musket, and so were born the *mousquetaires*.

The unit reached its apogee under Louis XIV, who was given Cardinal Mazarin's personal guard in 1660. The king reorganised the unit, modelling it after that of Louis XIII. Two companies were formed. the Grey Musketeers and the Black Musketeers, the colours corresponding to the saddle-cloths of their mounts. Their characteristic uniform was created at his time, with the blue cloak adorned with the large cross and fleurs-de-lys, the large boots and the plumed hat. This is the uniform one associates with the musketeers, much more than the equally beautiful uniform created for them in 1814 for the last year of their existence. After 1815 there were no more musketeers in the French army.

The most famous battle in which the musketeers took part was that of Steinkirk in 1692. The *Mousquetaires Gris* and the *Mousquetaires Noirs* then constituted part of the cavalry of the *Maison du Roi*. They charged the bodyguard of William III of England to the cry of *Vive le Roi!* Repulsed at their first attack, they reformed their ranks and charged again, urged on by the *Allez!* of the infantrymen of the Champagne regiment, who also joined the attack. With the loss of many lives, the Musketeers won the day for France.

But D'Artagnan (the real one, for he actually existed and his name was Charles de Batz) had already given his all. He fell, barely fifty years old, at the siege of Maastricht, 25 June 1673. He was struck down by a harquebus ball as he was trying to lead his musketeers into the city, to satisfy the king's pious and royal desire: to hear mass at any cost that very day in Maastricht or in its ruins.

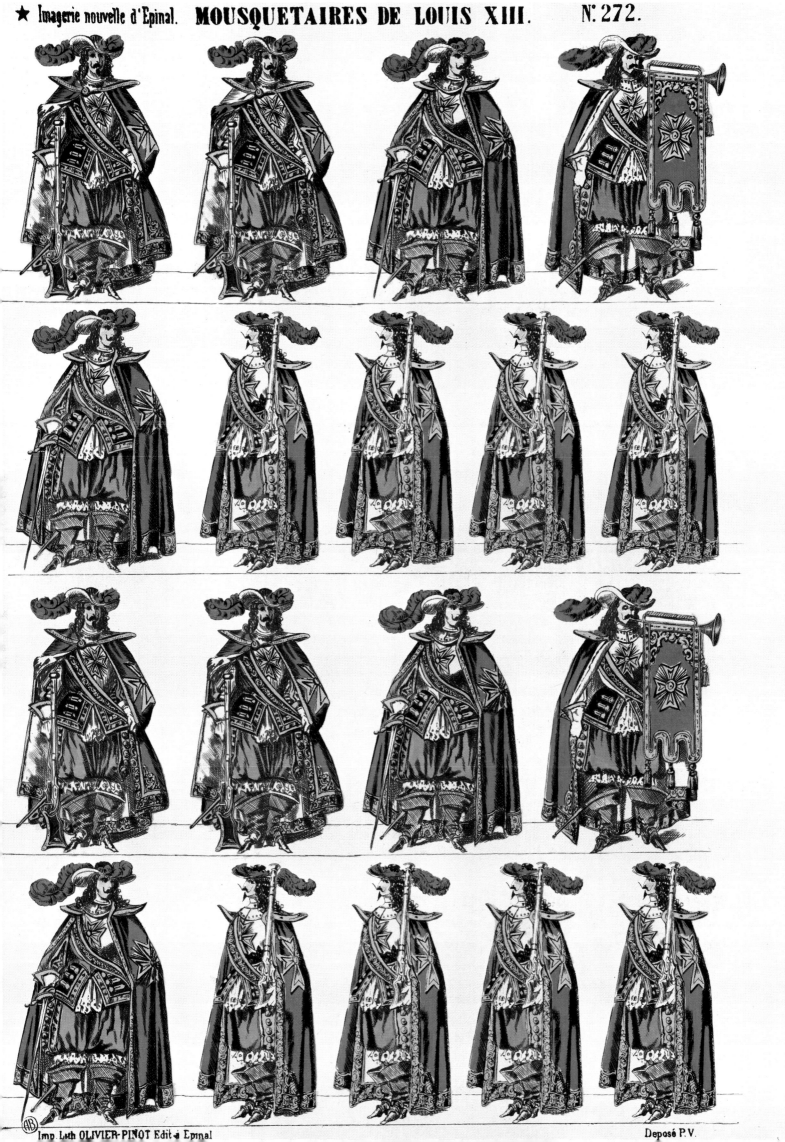

Imp. Lith. OLIVIER-PINOT Edit à Epinal

Deposé P. V.

The French Guards (Gardes Françaises) were founded by Charles IX and Catherine de' Medici. They came into being as King's Guards and were part of the Maison du Roi, that group of units which served as body guard to the kings of France.

The Sun King's Guards

Dix Enseignes de la Garde du Roy was the first name given to the regiment of *Gardes Françaises* at its foundation under Charles IX in 1558. Catherine de' Medici was present at their formation, which followed the capture of Le Havre. Like all royal guards, they enjoyed the king's special attentions and the consequent pomp and splendour. Under Louis XIII, the king who loved *les armes brillantes qui eblouissent les yeux et rendent l'appareil d'une armée plus terrible*, the parade of the Gardes Françaises was already a magnificent spectacle: officers with elaborately curled hair and bursting with lace and feathers and armed with a lance or *esponton*; colour-bearers in cuirass, sergeants with halberds, musketeers with their weapon braced against their padded right shoulders and holding their gunrests and tinder boxes in the left hand.

Under Louis XIV the Gardes Françaises received their first genuine uniform, one that made them the envy of the army. The Guards of the Maison du Roi were more beautiful than ever and could bear comparison with the English guards. The French guards had blue coats with scarlet lining, white or red stockings that reached above their knees, yellow belts and red trousers. Thus they marched against the enemy, the best foot soldiers of that great century, in the hundred battles of the Sun King. One of their greatest days was the battle of Fontenoy, 11 May 1745, during the War of the Austrian Succession. Louis XV, present at the battle, was certain of victory when the Marshal de Saxe threw the Guards into the fray to finish the enemy.

The first decisive encounter was preceded by a curious incident that, despite conflicting accounts, is worth recounting. At one point on the front a muddy trench separated the two forces, just in front of the Gardes Françaises. The Marshal de Saxe had fortified other points but not this one, for he was sure that no general would try to cross it. In fact, the main allied (English and Dutch) attack was launched exactly on to that spot. The fighting had been in progress for three hours at other points in the line (and a brand-new Franch regiment, the Legion of Grassin, had already distinguished itself), when at 8.30 in the morning the duke of Cumberland decided to send fifteen thousand English, Scottish and Hanoverians across the mud in an attempt to break through the centre of the French ranks. The nature of the terrain was such that the two forces, to their mutual amazement, found themselves within a few feet of each other. The English officers removed their hats in salutation, as did the French. Lord Hay, one of the senior English officers, called to the count d'Auteroche, lieutenant of the French Guards, and invited him to give the order to fire. 'After you' was his reply. 'The honour is yours.' This is Voltaire's version - it is certainly very chivalrous - but it is not supported by military historians. According to them, the guards could not have fired first, because they had been ordered since 1648 never to do so (it was considered that the tactical and moral advantage lay with the force which refused to fire first.) Nevertheless, on 20 August of the same year, at the battle of Lens (during the last phase of the Thirty Years War), in their excitement they were the first to fire, and in the time it took them to reload (twenty-four distinct actions were required to prepare a musket for refiring), the enemy managed to come dangerously close. (The imperial adversaries were finally defeated.)

Needless to say, the English have another, and much less poetic, version of the incident. According to them, after the famous greeting Lord Hay lifted his canteen as if to toast the enemy and then shouted: 'I trust you will stay where you are and give us the time to reach you, without swimming away down the river, as you did at Dettingen.' The River at Dettingen is the Main, and the battle of Dettingen, which took place on 27 June 1743, during the War of the Austrian Succession, was lost by the French. Their adversaries (an alliance of the English, Hanoverians and Austrians) did not take advantage of the victory, even though it was considered a great triumph. (Handel's Dettingen *Te Deum* was inspired by this battle.)

Non-commissioned officers and men of the French guards were among the first soldiers to pass from the royal army to that of the revolution. They joined the revolutionaries in taking the Bastille and abandoned their officers, all noblemen, to the fury of the populace. It was on that day that Sergeant Lazare Hoche, the son of a keeper in the royal kennels, began the brilliant career that was finally to see him as a general of the First Republic.

Red and blue were the basic colours of the uniform that Louis XIV provided for the French Guards. The print reproduced here shows a colour-bearer and an officer with an esponton *or pike, after the usage of the 17th and 18th centuries. The white cross on the flag was common to all the French regiments and was the symbol of national unity. The background colour varied however, from regiment to regiment. Among the many battles in which the Gardes Françaises took part was Fontenoy, the great battle of 11 May 1745, when they faced English, Scottish, and Hanoverian troops. The non-commissioned officers and troops of the Gardes Françaises were among the first military to embrace the cause of the French Revolution.*

The Republic and the Demi-Brigades

When the revolution broke out in 1789, the French army comprised, in addition to the Guards and the Swiss units of the Maison du Roi, one hundred and two infantry regiments, including twenty-three foreign regiments (Irish, Italian, Swiss and German), twelve battalions of foot chasseurs and seven colonial regiments for service overseas. The cavalry consisted of thirty-eight regiments - two of carabineers, eighteen of dragoons, and twelve of horse chasseurs, each comprising five squadrons, one of which was a depot unit. The artillery numbered seven regiments, each named for the school to which it was attached. Various specialist companies, sappers for example, were also part of the artillery.

Recruitment was voluntary and pay varied from branch to branch. The same uniform was worn by all. The coat, a kind of frock coat which the soldiers wore at the time, was light grey. The colour of lapels, cuffs and lining varied from regiment to regiment. The waistcoat worn under the coat was white, as were the trousers and the gaiters. Black gaiters, however, were worn in winter. The headgear was a black felt tricorn.

The infantry regiments had a grenadier company attached to the first battalion, and a chasseur company attached to the second. These were distinguished by details of uniform. The grenadier wore a bearskin busby, scarlet epaulets and a short sabre. The chasseurs had green epaulets and plume and carried a sabre. Each company had its drummers, who were dressed in royal blue.

32ND DEMI-BRIGADE 1796

The broad black felt hat, the dark blue tailcoat with red lapels and cuffs, and the tight-fitting trousers with leggings were typical of the infantry of the revolutionary and early Napoleonic periods. The infantry was organised in demibrigades.

In addition to this line, or royal army, there was also a territorial army: the militia, a common feature of all European states at the time. The militia consisted of forty-seven so-called 'provincial' regiments. The militia wore the uniform of the royal army, but the collar, lapels and cuffs were royal blue.

With the departure of many officers of aristocratic blood, six-thousand out of a total of nine thousand, after the revolution, the army had to be reorganised, and the militia was replaced by a National Guard, which became the real army of the revolution. In 1791 it totalled two million men, but very few of these had had the training necessary for troops about to enter the battlefield. And when France was attacked by the European monarchies, it was the old regiments that had to go to meet them in the name of Navarre and Touraine. They won their glory by repulsing the invader at Valmy and Jemappes.

In 1793 Lazare Carnot, the head of the 'war department', took on the task of reorganising the French army. There were now five hundred thousand men in the army; rank was abolished and the various units were given a structure quite different from that which they had had. The regiments were abolished and the infantry was organised in demi-brigades, consisting of one line battalion and two battalions of volunteers. A single uniform for all was adopted, the infantry donning the blue uniform that had hitherto been restricted to the National Guard and the volunteers. Regiments disappeared from the cavalry too and were replaced by demi-brigades of four squadrons each. In this way all the irregular and voluntary units were absorbed by the regular army units. It was Carnot who conceived and adopted the tactical unit known as a division, composed of two infantry brigades (i.e. four demi-brigades), two demi-brigades of cavalry and eight artillery pieces.

Thus reorganised, the French army won glory in all the wars of the revolution. When General Buonaparte took command of the army of Italy which he led victoriously as far as Leoben, he assigned to the demi-brigades banners with individual mottoes. The 25th demi-brigade had as its motto: 'The 25th has covered itself with glory'. The 57th: 'The terrible 57th that nothing can stop'. The 18th: 'Valorous 18th I know you; the enemy cannot withstand you!' These mottoes were embroidered in gold on the tricolour, the only colours of the demi-brigade.

In 1803 Napoleon, now first consul, suppressed the demi-brigade and restored the regiment. The term demi-brigade, associated with the period of the revolution, came back into use during the First World War, more than a century later, but then it was used to indicate battalion groups that did not belong to regiments like the

In the reform carried out by L. Carnot in 1793, the cavalry was also organised in demi-brigades, each of which consisted of four squadrons. Above: a drawing by Caran d'Ache of General François Severin Merceau-Desgraviers, known as Marceau, who died at Atlenkirchen on 19 September 1796. Below: The uniform of the Conflans Hussars. Note, below, the tall shako that was typical of hussars in all countries until the end of the 18th century.

chasseurs and the Alpine Chasseurs. Between the two wars, the term demi-brigade was applied to some formations of 'Fortress Alpineers', specially trained troops that were posted along the Franco-Italian frontier.

During the Second World War and later, during the campaigns in Indo-China and Algeria, the term demi-brigade was applied to battalion units of the famous Foreign Legion. It should be noted, however, that the traditional brigade disappeared in 1916, when in the French army, (as in other European armies), the structure of the division was altered - from two brigades each consisting of two regiments of three battalions to three regiments of three battalions.

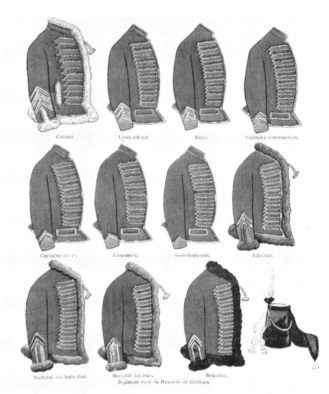

Foot and Horse Chasseurs

A CHASSEUR A CHEVAL 1806

The green-uniformed horse chasseurs of the Napoleonic army were employed on reconnaissance and harassing missions. The chasseur guards had the privilege of escorting the Emperor and, on the battlefield, of mounting the guard outside his tent.

The chasseurs were described as 'lightly armed soldiers, foot and horse, who are able to display in war the ability, skill and speed of wild-game hunters'. Although the chasseurs made their appearance some time after the invention of firearms, a comparison to the Roman Velites seems justified.

Beginning in the seventeenth century men were selected from the harquebusiers who were particularly expert shots and good runners, particularly suitable for ambushes and harassing actions.

William, landgrave of Hesse, formed a unit of marksmen with such qualifications in 1631. But it was really Frederick II of Prussia who should be considered the originator of this speciality. In select companies of his infantry he enrolled the sons of his Pomeranian gamekeepers - tall strong youths who were extremely good marksmen. Soon after, France formed chasseur units, and they were subsequently incorporated into all armies. In 1779, at the time of the War of Independence, the United States had six such regiments in its army.

In France in 1760, the prince De Broglie assigned a chasseur company to every infantry battalion. (A century earlier some regiments had included units of special marksmen who also fought singly.) Between 1766

and 1771 the chasseur companies were organised into six regiments armed with short-barrelled rifles. But the regiments were subsequently disbanded and twelve independent battalions were formed.

During the French Revolution they were organised into light demi-brigades, but Napoleon was against specialist units in the infantry and disbanded them altogether, later replacing them with skirmishers, or *voltiguers*. Chasseur battalions only reappeared in France in 1840 with the name of Chasseurs de Vincennes, later changed to Chasseurs d'Orléans, in memory of the duke d'Orléans, who had been responsible for their resumption. After 1848 they were called *Chasseurs à pied*, the number of battalions increased first to twenty-one and then to thirty-one, of which twelve were alpine specialists. From the beginning they assumed a darkblue uniform, called *bleu chasseur*, with green epaulets.

During the First World War the chasseurs, reorganised into demi-brigades, distinguished themselves in several actions, particularly in the Vosges and at Verdun. It was at Bois des Coures that the demi-brigade of Colonel Driant, a member of the Assembly, won great distinction. In 1940 they were again reorganised into light divisions and fought in Norway under General Bethouard. Some motorised units served as infantry in armoured units.

The *Chasseurs à cheval* were created by Fischer in 1743. They fought on foot and horseback and wore a green uniform with a plumed hat. The first unit, under the command of the Marshal de Saxe, also included a certain number of foot soldiers. In 1776 each dragoon regiment was assigned a chasseur squadron, and subsequently these squadrons were joined into regiments, as the chasseurs à pied had been. The tactical reason for the creation of these regiments was to have been the training of the men in single and platoon action. To all effects and purposes, the chasseurs à cheval were no different, from a tactical point of view, than other cavalry units. The only difference was the uniform.

The chasseur à cheval regiments in France numbered twelve in 1789, but by 1813 there were thirty. One was part of the Imperial Guard. There were twenty-three on the eve of the First World War. In their first military actions in that war they wore their characteristic uniform: a red kepi, a small yellow and green plume, a blue tunic with black frogging and red trousers.

In the Army of Napoleon the cavalry regiments were joined in homogeneous divisions according to type. The dragoons (an officer and a soldier are depicted opposite) wore this green uniform and crested helmet until 1870. Today they form armoured reconnaissance regiments.

Generale di Brigata

Ajutante Commandante

Officiale dei Dragoni

Officiale dei Cacciatori

Dragone

Cacciatore a Cavallo

The caption of this period print reads 'Review of Italian and Polish military units by Emperor and King Napoleon on the field of Montechiari, 10 June 1805'. Among the units on review one can distinguish the Polish lancers in the background by their typical czapkas. A similar light cavalry regiment was founded the next year by Napoleon after his entry into Warsaw. The grenadiers, above left, may also be easily recognised.

La Vieille Garde

Napoleon's Imperial Guard was born with the proclamation of the empire in 1804. Before then there had been special units assigned to the higher organs of the state: the Guard of the Executive Directory, composed of 287 foot and horsemen, and the Guard of the Legislative Body, composed of 1,256 men. Both units, created by the Directory in 1799, were responsible for public order as well as being Honour Guards.

When Napoleon became First Consul he joined the two units into the Consular Guard, which in 1803 consisted of 5,376 men, divided into a regiment of foot grenadiers, a regiment of foot chasseurs, a regiment of horse grenadiers, a company of horse artillery, and

Le vieux grognard.

other specialist companies. When the Guard was transferred to Boulogne, in preparation for the invasion of England, these forces were joined by a marine battalion. The proclamation of the empire changed only the name of these élite troops, the adjective 'consular' being replaced by 'imperial'. And the Guard was no longer responsible for the maintenance of public order. It became an élite reserve force to be used at decisive moments.

The Imperial Guard underwent notable inner transformations, and the specialities it included varied in number and composition. At first the infantry forces were composed of foot grenadiers and chasseurs. The Grenadiers Guards had to be at least five feet ten inches tall and have served for at least ten years. They wore a bearskin hat (nicknamed a 'beehive') more than a foot high, on the front of which was a copper badge with a crowned eagle, placed between two grenades, and a white braid. Their coat, a kind of tailed riding coat, was blue with red cuffs and white lapels, red epaulets, copper buttons, white trousers and gaiters. The white leather accoutrements were crossed on the chest, and the large cartridge belt was adorned with an imperial eagle. The officer's uniform was the same, but the buttons, epaulets and ornaments were gilt. The pioneers, with their white leather aprons, were assigned to the grenadiers, and there was a battery of twenty-four drums. The drum-major wore a uniform covered with gilt ornaments and a large scarlet sash embroidered in gold; his hat was topped with a tricoloured plume. The forty-six members of the band wore blue uniforms also covered in gilt ornaments. When Holland was incorporated into the empire (1810) a regiment of grenadiers of the Royal Dutch Guard was admitted into the Guard. They continued to wear their white uniforms with crimson lapels, cuffs and collar and a fur hat without the eagle badge.

In 1806 regiments were established of grenadiers fusiliers. Their uniform was like that of the grenadiers, except that the epaulets were white. Three years later regiments were created of grenadier marksmen and after the Russian campaign, flanker-grenadier regiments were instituted. In all there were nineteen regiments. These constituted the so-called Middle and Young Guard.

Originally the Imperial Guards consisted of three regiments of infantry, cavalry and artillery and engineer units. It later became a veritable army, divided into 'Old' and 'Young' Guards. These two pages show a detail of a print published in honour of the veterans of the Armée and a fine sheet of soldiers depicting the tall-bearskinned grenadiers, the faithful followers of the Emperor. The sheet of soldiers also depicts the charming vivandières, the women who followed the units and furnished the soldiers with food and supplies that were not part of normal rations. In battle they often spontaneously became nurses. Their characteristic costume was distinguished by their trousers and skirt.

GRENADIERS DE LA VIEILLE GARDE IMPÉRIALE.

The Horse Grenadiers and the Cavalry of the Imperial Guard

The regiment of horse grenadiers of Napoleon's imperial Guard was formed of those units which had participated with the foot grenadiers at Marengo in winning that difficult victory over the Austrians. The requirements - height, length of service, etc. - for admission to the horse grenadiers were the same as those governing admission to the foot grenadiers, and the uniforms, except for minor details, were alike. The horse grenadiers wore epaulets without a fringe, and they wore sheepskin trousers with their dress uniform. Their powdered

A horse grenadier escorts a captured Austrian officer from the battlefield. The horse grenadiers were an élite corps of the Imperial Guard. They rode black horses, except for the trumpeters, who rode white or grey horses.

hair was worn tied back in a knot. The busby had a small scarlet plume, and the chin strap was formed of copper scales. The curved sabre had a copper sheath, and the grenadiers used short-barrelled carbines. The horses were black and wore blue saddle-cloths with large 'dawn-coloured' galloons.

The regiment included thirty trumpeters mounted on light grey horses, which stood out boldly against the black mounts of the squadrons. The trumpeters wore a blue uniform with crimson lapels, cuffs and ribbons. Stripes were gold. In place of the bearskin hat, they wore a bicorn hat with gold braiding. The saddles were

of white leather. The kettledrummer rode ahead of the rest, dressed like a hussar with a blue dolman, and crimson trousers. He wore a brimless shako with a scarlet plume.

During the empire the horse grenadiers took part in every battle, from Marengo to Waterloo. Three hundred of them won the Legion of Honour, and all the officers were decorated with the rank of Officers of the Legion of Honour.

At the battle of Eylau the horse grenadiers were the centre of a curious episode. Colonel Lepic led the grenadiers in a furious charge at the head of Murat's massed cavalry that not only overran the Russian infantry and artillery batteries but carried them so far behind the enemy lines that they had to mount a veritable charge back to reach their companions again. That evening, Napoleon sent Colonel Lepic a commission making him a general and fifty thousand gold francs. Lepic accepted the promotion and divided the money among his grenadiers.

After 1812, the four horse regiments of the Guards of Honour formed part of the Imperial Guard. The members of this unit were sons of the prosperous who, upon being called to arms and being offered the possibility of promotion to the rank of second lieutenant after one year's service, provided their own uniforms and mounts. The uniform was particularly distinctive, consisting of scarlet Hungarian-style trousers, a green dolman and fur with white braid and frogs, and a scarlet shako with white braiding and plume.

A regiment of horse chasseurs was also part of the Imperial Guard. The regiment evolved from the 'guides' that had accompanied Napoleon during the Egyptian campaign. It was these 'guides' who became chasseurs in 1804. They then adopted the hussar uniform, consisting of a dark green dolman with five rows of copper buttons and yellow frogs. In ordinary dress they wore green trousers with a yellow stripe; in dress uniform they wore doeskin trousers. The bearskin hat had a copper chinstrap, a scarlet badge and a green and red plume. The ornaments and frogging of officers' uniforms were gilt. The trumpeters wore a blue dolman and a white fur hat.

The horse chasseurs of the Guard had the honour of escorting the emperor. In peace and war a squad of twenty-two chasseurs, with an officer and a trumpeter, escorted the sovereign, whether he was on horseback or riding in a carriage. During halts the chasseurs guarded the imperial tent.

The Guard Dragoons, also known as the Empress' Dragoons, were formed in 1806 - a regiment of six squadrons under the command of the Corsican Arrighi. They wore the traditional green dragoon uniform with a copper helmet *à la Minerve*, with its leopard-skin visor and a scarlet plume. The trumpeters, by contrast, wore a white uniform with scarlet lapels, cuffs and braiding.

In the same year Napoleon entered Warsaw escorted by an honour guard of Polish youths organised on the spot. Subsequently he organised a regiment of Polish light-cavalry lancers. These soldiers wore a particularly colourful uniform: the *kurtka* (a close-fitting jacket) was blue with crimson collar, lapels and cuffs, and a single epaulet of silver thread. The cloth trousers were crimson, with blue bands for the troops and silver bands for the officers. The traditional *czapka* was crim-

son and had a white plume hanging down one side. The trumpeters wore a white *kurtka*, and the kettle-drummer a curious Polish costume with large Turkish-style pantaloons and a fur trimmed surcoat. On his head he wore a toque with a long plume.

This regiment was joined in 1810 by a Dutch light-cavalry regiment known as the 'Red Lancers'. Together they fought with magnificent valour in Spain, Russia, Germany and finally at Waterloo, where the 'Red Lancers' were destroyed in an heroic charge.

The last unit that Napoleon created for his Guard was that of the scouts, a unit assigned to scouting and guerrilla actions.

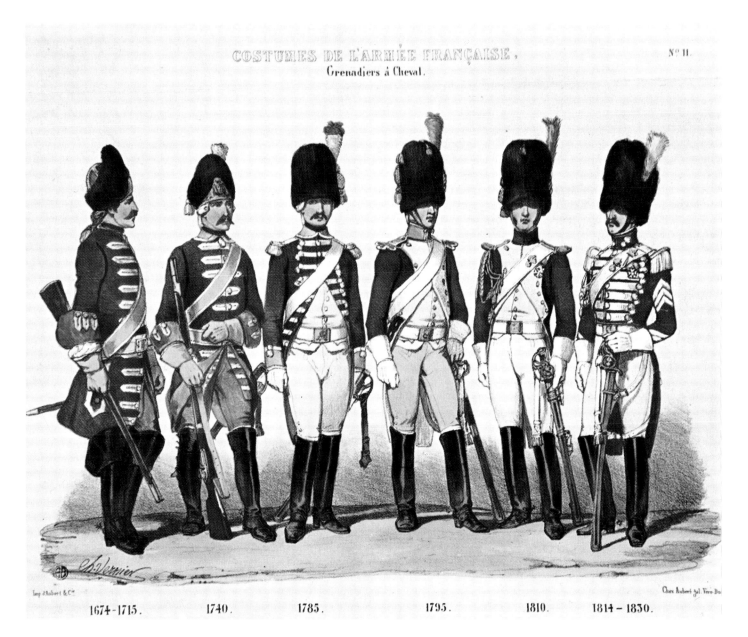

COSTUMES DE L'ARMÉE FRANÇAISE.
Nº 11.
Grenadiers à Cheval.

1674-1715.   1740.   1785.   1795.   1810.   1814-1830.

In the royal French army, the horse grenadiers did not comprise a special formation of their own. It was Napoleon who created the unit and took one squadron for his own guard when he became First Consul. The unit had its baptism of fire at Marengo. This French print shows the evolution of the horse grenadier uniform from the time of Louis XIV (1674-75) to Louis XV (1740), Louis XVI (Royal-Allemand Regiment, 1785), the Republic (Garde du Directoir, 1795), Napoleon I (Imperial Guard, 1810), and the Restoration (Garde Royale, 1814-30). It is said that at the Battle of Eylau the grenadiers awaited the order to charge in perfect immobility, while their commanding officer, Colonel Lepic, uttered imprecations at anyone who ducked his head under the snow.

The Emperor's Infantrymen

The Napoleonic infantry - which traversed the whole of Europe bearing the burden of war along a line of operations that extended from Moscow to Madrid - was always employed in Napoleon's tactics as the branch to receive the first shock of the encounter with the enemy, and consequently merited the greatest credit for his victories. There were few specialised units in the infantry. There were regiments of light infantry, but these were merely an inheritance from the demi-brigades of the republic. Within the battalions there were grenadier and voltigeur companies. But these were honourary distinctions rather than specialities with distinct functions.

The French infantry under Napoleon was a mighty and homogeneous power and was to retain this strength for a considerable time. In 1914, at the beginning of the First World War, the French infantry had a strength of 550 battalions of which only 31 were *cacciati*, including the alpines, whilst the Italian infantry was 362 battalions strong, of which 6 were grenadiers, 48 bersaglieri and 26 alpines.

In 1812, on the eve of the Russian campaign, Napoleon's infantry consisted of one hundred and eight line regiments and thirty-one light-infantry regiments, each comprising five battalions, of which one was a depot battalion and the other four were combat. Every regiment had its own company of gunners.

For a while the emperor's infantrymen kept their old republican uniform with the blue coat. Later a white coat was adopted, with collar, lapels and cuffs of different colours according to the regiment. The trousers and leggings were white. A black shako with a white braid, copper trim and chinstrap and a red plume completed the uniform.

But the white uniform did not last long. At Tilsit, Tsar Alexander of Russia saw the French infantrymen dressed in white alongside some units of recruits dressed in blue and commented that the latter colour seemed more practical. Napoleon was convinced by this remark and shortly thereafter adopted the blue uniform for his infantry. The light infantry had always worn a blue uniform. The short-skirted coat had red lapels, epaulets and cuffs. The trousers, leggings and shako, adorned with a hunting horn, were dark blue.

The Napoleonic infantry included several foreign regiments. It is estimated that in 1812 there were a million foreigners in the French army. There were Polish regiments, with uniforms modelled after their national costumes; there were red frockcoated Swiss regiments, green-coated Irish regiments, and Portuguese regiments that wore a blue and white uniform. In 1806 a regiment of former Prussian prisoners was created, and these troops fought loyally in Spain and in France and were only disbanded in 1815.

Left: A soldier protects himself as best he can from the African sun during the Egyptian Campaign. Overleaf: A sheet of Pellerin d'Epinal, late 19th century, with the song of the 106th Infantry and the illustrated history of the regiment. Note the detail that the words and music are the work of two abbés.

PELLERIN & Cie, imp.-édit.

UN CHANT DU 106me DE LIGNE

Paroles de l'abbé BOURGUIN

IMAGERIE D'ÉPINAL. N° 242

Musique de l'Abbé HENRY

Con-naissez vous l'his-toire De
ce bon Ré-gi-ment En voici de mé-
moire le ré-cit é-mou-vant.

Il débute en Bavière,
Où Biberach le voit
Sauver notre frontière
Par un brillant exploit.
Vive...

De Perrin, qui le mène,
Les braves Grenadiers
De l'armée autrichienne
Sabrent les canonniers.
Vive...

Des armes enlevées,
De nombreux prisonniers
Sont les nobles trophées
De nos rudes troupiers.
Vive...

Sous le ciel d'Italie,
Dans Gênes renfermé,
Pour sa rare énergie
Le Cent-six est cité.
Vive...

Sa belle résistance
A frappé les vainqueurs
Qui, pleins de déférence,
Lui rendent les honneurs
Vive...

A la grande bataille
Dont Wagram est le nom.
Il va, sous la mitraille,
Conquérir son renom.
Vive...

Témoin de sa vaillance
Napoléon passant
Dit à son ordonnance
« Ah! quel bon régiment! »
Vive...

Dans la froide Russie,
Malojaroslawetz
Couronne la série
De ses nombreux succès.
Vive...

Sept fois dans cette place
Les Russes sont entrés ;
Delzons, non moins tenace,
Sept fois les a chassés.
Vive...

Hélas! Par une bombe
Frappé mortellément,
Delzons, si brave, tombe
Devant son régiment.
Vive...

Sur ce champ de carnage
Nous demeurons vainqueurs
Par l'effet d'un courage
Plus grand que nos malheurs.
Vive...

REFRAIN
PAS REDOUBLE

Vi-ve le Cent sixième Ah Quel
bon Régi-ment Vi-ve le Cent sixième c'est mon
Cher Ré-gi-ment c'est mon Cher Ré-gi-ment.

O combats mémorables!
Que peut-on de plus beau ?
Vos noms impérissables
Sont inscrits au Drapeau !
Vive...

Devant-toi je m'incline,
Drapeau de nos aïeux !
Et jusqu'en ma chaumine
Je t'enverrai mes vœux.
Vive...

Gold and Silver Cuirasses

Although several French heavy cavalry regiments wore the cuirass, the name of cuirassiers was only adopted officially in 1804 for the eight regiments of so-called 'heavy' cavalry. The uniform of these regiments originally consisted of a grey coat over which was worn a cuirass of burnished iron with a leather breastplate.

In 1753 the regiments had coats of different colours - white, blue and red. In 1802 Napoleon replaced the 'republican' hat with a helmet decorated with a bearskin band and a black crest. The coat adopted then was blue, without lapels, and the epaulets were red. White trousers were worn and musketeer gloves.

After the restoration of the Empire in 1852, the number of cuirassier regiments was reduced. Under the Second Empire, the cuirassiers formed ten line regiments and two guard regiments. Their uniform was more colourful and included a white cape. During the war of 1870 the cuirassiers fought valiantly and sacrificed themselves at Reichshofen. After Sedan eleven regiments *à marche* were established, and in the reorganisation of the French army after the institution of the

Third Republic, there were first thirteen and then twelve cuirassier regiments. They were the only units to keep their epaulets when that ornament was abolished throughout the rest of the army.

During the First World War six regiments were employed on foot, and after the war they were partially and then fully motorised and incorporated into armoured units, with whom they fought in the operations of 1939-40, during the Second World War. Reformed in 1944, several cuirassier regiments were again incorporated in the most modern armoured divisions.

According to some military historians, the carabineers evolved from the *carabines*, light cavalry troops armed with a short harquebus. They first appeared in France during the reign of Henry II, about 1550, when Pietro Strozzi, created a marshal by Francis I, brought to France a company of mounted harquebusiers two hundred strong. The carabines had been organised in small units, and Henry IV assigned one of their units to his guards. Later a small nucleus of carabines was assigned to each musketeer mounted squadron. But it was Louis XIV who formed the first organic units of carabiniers. He gave them the sun as their badge. In 1809 Napoleon changed their uniform, and the carabiniers wore Roman-style helmets with a red horsehair plume and a copper crest. Their coats were white with blue lapels, and their white trousers were of doeskin. They also wore copper cuirasses. During the Second Empire the line carabiniers wore a blue tunic with a red collar and white trousers, while the carabinier guard regiment wore a sky-blue tunic and the typical Roman helmet.

Under the Second Empire a special cuirassier unit was formed to protect the sovereign and the palace. These were the 'Hundred Guards'. These splendid horsemen, who actually numbered 221, wore a steel helmet with a gilded crest, a white horsehair plume and a small red-feather plume; a sky-blue tunic with red collar, cuffs and lapels and golden epaulets; a steel cuirass, white skin trousers, black top-boots and white musketeer gloves. They used a short rifle with a very long bayonet. On horseback the 'Hundred Guards' carried the rifle with fixed bayonet against the right thigh.

The copper cuirass, polished bright as gold, and the crested helmet were characteristic distinctions of the uniform of the French carabiniers. Above, in a print dedicated to the veterans of the Grande Armée, *all the splendour of the carabinier uniform worn by the corps at Waterloo is illustrated.* Opposite: *In this evocation of the glories of the 1st Cuirassier Regiment one can observe that the cuirass was worn for the first time in 1803, together with the helmet with the long black plume. The Napoleonic helmet is still worn without major alteration by the Republican Guard.*

1ᵉʳ RÉGIMENT DE CUIRASSIERS

Le Régiment qui porte actuellement le nom de 1ᵉʳ Cuirassiers fut créé en 1631; il s'appela d'abord *Trefski Cavalerie*, et prit successivement le nom de ses Mestres de camp: *Flechstein* (1641); *Nimitz* (1649); *Turenne* (1651). — En 1657, Turenne ayant été nommé Colonel-Général de la Cavalerie, le Régiment prit lui-même le titre de *Colonel-Général* et le conserva jusqu'à la Révolution. — En 1791, il devint 1ᵉʳ *Régiment de Cavalerie*. Cuirassé à la fin de 1802, il s'appela, en 1803, 1ᵉʳ *Régiment de Cuirassiers*. — La première Restauration (1814-1815) lui donna le nom de *Cuirassiers du Roi*. — Il reprit son nom de 1ᵉʳ Cuirassiers pendant les Cent-Jours, et fut licencié à la fin de 1815. On forma alors un Régiment dit des *Cuirassiers de la Reine*, qui, en 1830, s'appela définitivement 1ᵉʳ *Régiment de Cuirassiers*.

BATAILLES & SIÈGES PRINCIPAUX
AUXQUELS LE CORPS A PRIS PART

1638 — Campagne de Flandre. Combat de Polinkove, où le régiment fait une charge superbe.

1643 — Victoire de Rocroi, remportée par le duc d'Enghien sur les Espagnols; le régiment enfonce à deux reprises l'infanterie ennemie.

1645 — Bataille de Nordlingen gagnée par le Grand Condé sur les Allemands; Turenne charge à la tête du régiment.

1652 — Guerre de la Fronde. Combat du faubourg Saint-Antoine, sous Turenne.

1658 — Bataille des Dunes, gagnée par Turenne sur les Espagnols.

1667-1668 — Conquête de la Flandre et de la Franche-Comté.

1672 — Conquête de la Hollande; prise de Maëstricht.

1674 — Victoire de Sintzheim, remportée par Turenne sur les Allemands.

1675 — Nouvelle campagne sur le Rhin; bataille de Turkheim gagnée par Turenne sur les Allemands; l'Alsace est conquise. — Victoire de Cassel (1677).

1688 — Prise de Philipsbourg, par Vauban.

1702 — Campagne d'Italie; bataille de Luzzara gagnée par le duc de Vendôme sur les Autrichiens. — 1705, victoire de Cassano, et 1706, victoire de Calcinato, remportées par le duc de Vendôme sur les Allemands. A Calcinato, le régiment prend 4 drapeaux, 12 étendards et 10 canons.

1707-1712 — Campagnes de Flandre. — Bataille de Malplaquet (1709). — Bataille de Denain (1712), gagnée par Villars sur le prince Eugène; elle sauve la France.

1713 — Prise de Landau et de Fribourg.

1733 — Guerre pour la succession de Pologne; campagne sur le Rhin.

1740 — Guerre pour la succession d'Autriche; prise de Prague (1741). Célèbre victoire de Fontenoy (1745), remportée par le maréchal de Saxe sur les Anglais. — Batailles de Rocoux (1746), de Lawfeld (1747), gagnées par le maréchal de Saxe.

1756-1763 — Guerre de Sept ans; bataille de Hastembeck (1757), gagnée par le maréchal d'Estrées sur les Anglais. — Conquête du Hanovre.

1792 — Commencement des guerres de la Révolution. Victoire de Jemmapes, remportée par Dumouriez sur les Autrichiens; le 1ᵉʳ Régiment de cavalerie enlève quatre redoutes autrichiennes et se couvre de gloire.

1794 — Victoire de Moucron; le sous-lieutenant Alix, à la tête de 10 cavaliers, s'empare de 5 canons et fait 700 prisonniers.

1796-1801 — Campagnes d'Italie. En 1796, le capitaine Lasalle, à la tête de 25 cavaliers du 1ᵉʳ Régiment, traverse l'armée autrichienne, entre dans Vicence occupée par l'ennemi, et rejoint son poste en sabrant tout ce qu'il rencontre; Bonaparte le nomme chef d'escadrons à vingt-deux ans.

Victoires d'Arcole, de Rivoli (1797), remportées sur les Autrichiens. — Au passage de la Piave et du Tagliamento, Kellermann se met à la tête du régiment et enfonce la cavalerie ennemie.

1800 — Célèbre victoire de Marengo, remportée par Bonaparte sur les Autrichiens. — Combat de Vérone (1801).

1805 — Napoléon fait l'armée autrichienne prisonnière devant Ulm. — Bataille d'Austerlitz, gagnée par l'Empereur; les Russes sont anéantis; le capitaine de Berckheim, à la tête de son escadron, enlève 5 pièces de canon.

1806 — Victoire d'Iéna. La Prusse tout entière est conquise en un mois par Napoléon. A Lubeck, les cuirassiers forcent le général Blücher à mettre bas les armes avec 16,000 hommes.

1807 — Campagne de Pologne. A la bataille d'Eylau, gagnée par Napoléon, les cuirassiers écrasent 20,000 hommes d'infanterie russe.

1809 — Campagne contre l'Autriche. Victoire d'Eckmühl; le 1ᵉʳ Cuirassiers enfonce un carré, taille en pièces les cuirassiers autrichiens et se couvre de gloire. — Célèbre bataille de Wagram gagnée par Napoléon. — Combat de Znaim, où le 1ᵉʳ Cuirassiers sabre les grenadiers autrichiens.

1812 — Campagne de Russie. Bataille de la Moskowa, où nos cuirassiers s'emparent de la grande redoute russe, après des charges admirables.

1813 — Campagne d'Allemagne. Bataille de Leipzig — Bataille de Hanau, gagnée par Napoléon sur les Bavarois.

1814 — Campagne de France; batailles de Montmirail, de Vauxchamps, où Napoléon écrase Blücher.

1815 — Victoire de Ligny, remportée par Napoléon sur les Prussiens. — A Waterloo, le régiment prend part aux charges fameuses sur les carrés anglais; dans ce sublime fait d'armes, le 1ᵉʳ Cuirassiers termine sa 95ᵉ campagne.

1831 — Expédition de Belgique. — 1832. Siège d'Anvers.

1870 — A la bataille de Reichshoffen, le 1ᵉʳ Cuirassiers participe aux charges de la division Bonnemains, qui arrêtent le mouvement des Prussiens et assurent la retraite de l'armée.

A la bataille de Sedan, le commandant d'Alincourt, à la tête du 4ᵉ escadron, fait une tentative héroïque pour percer les lignes de l'ennemi.

Le 1ᵉʳ Régiment de Cuirassiers de marche, formé au mois de septembre, assiste aux affaires de Toury, de Coulmiers, de Chevilly, et à la retraite d'Orléans, où le 4ᵉ escadron est cité à l'ordre de la division; après la guerre, il est fondu dans le régiment actuel.

HONNEUR ET PATRIE

VALEUR ET DISCIPLINE

The Francs-Tireurs

The Franco-Prussian War of 1870 saw the emergence of small units comprising a few dozen men who, exempted from service in the regular army and national Guard, nevertheless wanted to share in the events that were involving their homeland. Thus were born those independent units known as *francs-tireurs*, a military speciality that was to become proverbial.

Needless to say there was no organisational uniformity, nor were the training and uniform of these troops homogeneous. In fact, there were some notable curiosities in dress. Some units had particularly spectacular uniforms, with a variety of headgear, from the fur hats of the Greek volunteers to the Louis XIV hat with immense plumes. And some even wore the red cape of the 'explorers of La Plata'. Some units did not serve with great honour, but many others conducted actions in which they distinguished themselves by their courage and spirit of self-sacrifice.

The ranks of the francs-tireurs included such men as the Garibaldino Stefano Cangio, Baron Charette, former commander of a battalion of papal Zouaves, and the sculptor Barholdi who later created the famous Statue of Liberty in New York Harbour. At that time Bartholdi represented Garibaldi at the National Defence government in Paris and alway wore the red shirt. The names of the units were distinctive: *Les Enfants Perdus, Les Ours Nantais, La Compagnie de la Revanche, Le Battaillon Egalité*, and others.

From a report by a committee set up by the National Assembly of Bordeaux for examining the possibilities of continuing the war in the spring of 1871, it appears that the number of francs-tireurs in service totalled forty thousand.

The Vosges chasseurs, commanded by Garibaldi, won the victory of Dijon in January 1871 and captured the only flag that the Prussians lost in the course of the entire war. Worthy of mention, too, is the franctireur unit of Parmain, a town near Isle Adam on the Oise, which gathered around a pharmacist named Capron and with two hundred hunting rifles resisted the attacks of an entire brigade supported by artillery. Among the units that rushed to the defence of Paris during the siege, which included American volunteers, were the Legion des Amis de la France, a unit of Algerian volunteers, the Francs-Tireurs de la Presse, and the Legion Gutenberg, a squadron of creoles and mounted scouts, who rode horses from the imperial stables.

A column of francs-tireurs *in action during the Franco-Prussian War of 1870-71.* Opposite: *a print by Pinot d'Epinal depicting the men who were at Garibaldi's disposal in the so-called 'Army of the Vosges.' It comprised a mixture of 'French, Spanish, Polish, Greek, Algerian troops, including mobile guards, garrison soldiers, volunteers, forcibly enlisted recruits, decked out in the strangest garbs some military, some brigandlike, some heroic, commanded by officers whose moral authority was that of the professional adventurer, the broken lance of all causes, and the pure paladin ready to die for the republic, all types from the coward who should have been shot to the hero worthy of apotheosis.' (Guerzoni)*

Compagnie des Vosges.

Garibaldiens & Francs-tireurs.   Officier garibaldien.

Imp. Lith. CH. PINOT édit. à Epinal.   Deposé.

The Foreign Legion

Captain Danjou had an artificial hand, the result of an injury sustained in the Crimea. He was the hero of the Cameron episode in Mexico (30 April 1863).

As we have seen, the French kings had used foreign units in their service since the Renaissance. In addition to the Swiss, traditional mercenaries, Francis I recruited Italian troops into his army, as did Henry III. And before the revolution there were soldiers from every country in Europe in the French army. The French Foreign Legion is something of a symbol of this tradition. It was founded by Louis Philippe by a decree of 9 March 1831, issued after the occupation of Algeria.

An entire body of legend has grown up around the Foreign Legion, but we should be more concerned with the true story of this unit whose men were always, and only, foreign volunteers driven by personal disappointment or misfortune to find escape in the adventure of war. The first element of the Foreign Legion consisted of a battalion of Polish exiles who were already enrolled in the 67th Infantry Regiment. The legionnaires were organised into various battalions by nationality. The first was Swiss, the second and third were German, the fourth was Spanish, the fifth was Italian, the sixth was Belgian and Dutch (which is to say, it was compo-sed of Frenchmen who were trying to pass as Belgians) and the seventh was Polish. The legion had its baptism of fire on 27 April 1832, and its valiant performance won it a flag and red grenadier epaulets.

The legionnaires became extremely proud of their uniform: the red kepi covered with a white cloth and the famous neck-guard, and the dark blue tunic with a white collar and red trousers. This uniform has been altered somewhat but the kepi and red epaulets have been preserved.

To recount all the adventures of the Foreign Legion would be, in one of their own phrases, like crossing the whole earth. From Algeria to Madagascar, to the far east, Mexico and the battlefields of Europe, it is no exaggeration to say that the Foreign Legion has fought on every continent. In 1859 the two regiments that then made up the legion were in Italy and took part in the battles at Magenta and Solferino. On 30 April 1863, at Cameron in Mexico, some sixty legionnaires fought to the last man under the assault of thousands of Juarez's soldiers.

In 1870 the legion fought in France. Subsequently they were engaged in Dahomey, Madagascar and Tonkin. In 1885, two companies of legionnaires, a company of Tonkin marksmen and a naval artillery unit - some six hundred men in all - were stationed at Tuyn Quang on the River Claire, under the command of Major Domine. For two months they repulsed the attacks of twenty thousand Pavillons Noirs.

The legion was in Europe during the First World War. The 4th regiment, composed of Italians under the command of Ezio Garibaldi, fought valiantly in the Ardennes, where, at Bois de Bollante, Bruno Garibaldi died. The legion took part in the Second World War, first in France and then in the Free French territories. It also had its paratroopers at Dien Bien Phu and then in Algeria.

'A nous, la Légion!' This was the cry that united the legionnaires in all their battles. It was almost as if they wanted to brandish the fact that they were mercenaries. This seems to be confirmed by one of their songs:

> Jamais Garde de Roi, d'Empereur, d'Autocrate,
> de Pape ou de Sultan, jamais nul régiment
> chamarre d'or, drape d'azur ou d'escarlate
> n'alla d'un air plus mal et plus superbement.

Danjou's artificial hand is one of the relics of the Legion and is as famous as the classic white kepi of the Legion, which is not, however, shown in this print by Pellerin d'Epinal. Notice the red grenadier epaulets which the légionnaires were granted from the time of their baptism of fire.

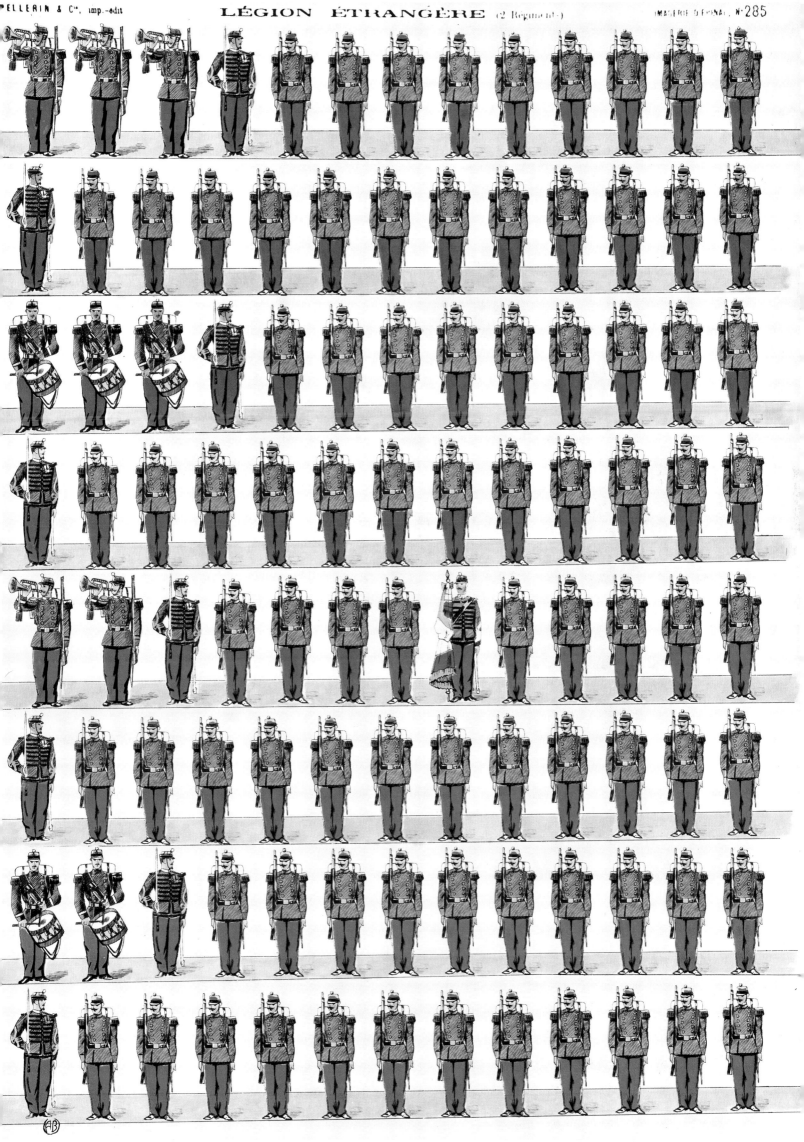

The Blue Devils

The *Chasseurs Alpins,* known as the Blue Devils because of their dark blue uniforms and their bravery, were constituted after the example of the first Italian Alpine companies. The Italian units were formed in 1872, and the French unit was created sixteen years later, in 1888. In that year the Triple Alliance of Italy, Germany and Austria was renewed, and the French general staff decided that special mountain units would be necessary to face the Italian units on the frontier. Thus twelve of the thirty chasseur battalions were transformed into Alpine Chasseurs and transferred to the Franco-Italian borde. At the same time twelve mountain pack-batteries were created so that each battalion could have its own mountain battery support. There were six Italian Alpine regiments at the time, so the forces rather well matched.

The Chasseurs Alpins kept the dark-blue uniform of the regular chasseurs. The kepi was replaced by a beret, and the dark blue coat with tails that buttoned on the back was replaced by a jacket and cape of the same colour. The white buttons and braid were kept, as were the jacket frogging, the trouser facing and the yellow braiding, characteristic elements of the chasseur uniform.

The new battalions were never organised into regiments but remained corps battalions, a typical system in the French army. They formed 'Alpine groups' supported by mountain batteries and units of customs men and forest guards. Finally they were incorporated into the two army corps garrisoning the Italian frontier: the XIVth of Lyons and the XVth of Marseilles. In the strategic plan of General Joffre, the Alpine Chasseurs were to form the backbone of defence against any attack from Italy. When Italy declared its neutrality, the French general staff transferred the units to the Vosges.

At this time additional battalions were formed, and they were all organised in demi-brigades, thus reviving the kind of unit which had replaced the regiment at the time of the revolution. After the war, the alpine battalions returned to their garrisons, and their number was reduced to nine. It is worth noting that although France had mountain borders with Switzerland, Spain and Germany, it only established mountain troops on the border of Italy. Thus recruits from Savoy, the Briançonnais and the Maritime Alps, who were normally assigned to mountain units, were joined by contigents from the Pyrenees, the Auvergne, Cevennes, the Vosges and Corsica.

When the political situation of Europe deteriorated again in the years before the Second World War, the alpine chasseur battalions were increased to eleven, and another speciality was created - *fortress chasseurs.* There were seven battalions, entrusted with garrisoning the fortifications on the Italian frontier. In 1939, eighteen of the thirty French chasseur battalions were Alpine Chasseurs.

These battalions have always been remarkable for their continuity and homogeneity. In 1914 the thirty-one battalions numbered more than twenty thousand men. They were easily mobilised, for they were recruited exclusively among the mountain districts and the garrison headquarters were all but at their front doors.

At the beginning of the Second World War, the Alpine Chasseurs were marshalled along the Italian border, but when the offensive was launched in the northeast of France, almost all the units were transferred to that sector. After the Armistice, the surviving battalions returned to their garrisons in Savoy and the Maritime Alps, where they remained until November 1942, when the Germans occupied continental France and the French army was forcibly disbanded.

Most of the Alpine Chasseurs turned to guerilla warfare and their activities in the mountains made a notable contribution to the Resistance. In February-March 1944 some five hundred *maquisards,* former Alpine Chasseurs for the most part, under the command of Lieutenant Morel, resisted on the Plateau des Glières for almost sixty days under the attacks of the joint forces of the Darlan militia and German troops. About two hundred and fifty fell, but the enemy's losses were much greater, more than a thousand men. After the disbanding of the alpine chasseur battalions, a tough band of resistance fighters was formed in the Vercors zone; by the spring of 1944 they numbered four thousand men. These men fought bravely for a month and a half before they laid down their arms.

After the Franco-American landing on the Mediterranean coast the Alpine frontier was abandoned after the retreat of the XIXth German army. Former chasseurs who had been serving in the Resistance reconstructed their battalions and remained on the frontier until the end of the war. The old dark-blue uniform with its yellow frogging and braids was still a symbol of endurance and valour.

The Chasseurs des Alpes *are called 'Les diables bleus' because of their dark blue uniforms. They serve in the mountain regions where they are recruited. They are depicted* (opposite) *in a water colour by Georges Scott entitled* 'Nos chasseurs en Haute-Alsace (Saint-Amarin)'.

From Poilu to Para

In 1914 the French army was the only one that still did not have a field uniform. The infantry entered the war with its beautiful gold-buttoned uniforms, the red kepi, the blue coat and red trousers. The chasseurs still had their dark blue and yellow uniforms, the cavalry its helmets with horsehair plumes, dark and light blue jackets, red trousers and frogged dolmans, and the cuirassiers covered their shining cuirasses with a kind of yellow waistcoat. Artillery and corps of engineers had black uniforms, the Zouaves white; tirailleurs and colonials still put on their typical nineteenth-century uniforms. France won the battle of the Marne in these uniforms. Trench warfare, barbed wire obstacles and new deadly weapons, however, made uniforms of neutral colour essential. The French chose horizon blue, and it was in this uniform that the foot soldier - called a *poilu* because of his ragged beard - won his war. Almost all the infantry regiments were decorated, or *cravatés* in French military jargon. At Verdun the chasseur demi-brigade (56th and 59th battalion) and the 165th and 137th infantry won particular distinction.

In the Second World War the French army mobilised five and a half million men. There were eighty-one infantry divisions (of which only about forty were regular army), two light mechanised divisions (comprising armoured cavalry and transport), three armoured divisions and two brigades. Later, between the winter and spring of 1940, four armoured divisions were added, the last of which (commanded by General De Gaulle) was only ready on 15 May, five days after the German offensive had begun. It is worth describing the composition of the division, because it achieved one of the few French successes in the campaign. It included the following units: the 6th and 8th demi-brigades of tanks, the 4th chasseur battalion, the 10th motorised cuirassier regiment, the 322nd artillery regiment, and the 7th motorised dragoon regiment.

Many French units in that tragic campaign fought with magnificient valour. Mention should be made of the 22nd Regiment of Colonial Infantry and the 3rd Cuirassier Regiment with its Samoa tanks. Notable units were the 136th and 147th Fortress Regiments, which were attacked by the armoured corps of General Guderian at Sedan. The 14th Motorised Dragoons fought so furiously at Sedan that Rommel testified to their strength. Finally one should mention the units that formed the 2nd and 3rd Armoured Divisions and the Red Devils of the 152nd infantry who bravely withstood the attacks of the German tanks.

After the Armistice the few units that remained to conquer France tried to reorganise, but when France was occupied by the Axis forces in November 1942, some units went into the Maquis. The officers and men of the 2nd Dragoons stationed at Auch, for example, dispersed into the countryside posing as forest guards or office workers. Before dissolving the regiment, Colonel Schlesser had all his men parade before the flag. The flag was then taken to Africa, where the regiment was reformed. In 1944 it landed with the army of General de Tasigny in Provence and fought in Alsace, on the Rhine, in Baden, and on the Danube. Among the metropolitan troups that were part of this army one should mention the 2nd Cuirassiers (a regiment quartered in Paris in peacetime), the 141st Infantry (which fought in the Alps), the armoured regiment of naval fusiliers, and the 64th Artillery Regiment.

Probably the most famous French forces today are the paratroopers. The Paras were founded in 1936, with the formation of two paratrooper companies, the 601st and 602nd Air Infantry Companies. In the 1939-40 campaign, the two units were not employed in the type of combat for which they had been trained. Instead,

In his sky-blue uniform, his round hat, loose puttees, a pipe in his mouth and his full beard, the poilu *became the symbol of French resistance and will to victory. His nickname (lit. 'the shown one') assured that he would be distinguished from the rear-guard soldiers who are credited with the foolish question: 'How do you get your beard into a gas mask?'*

they were used as assault units on the Sarre front. They avoided capture and were sent to Algeria after the armistice.

The Free French organised in Great Britain also included paratrooper units. The parachute company of the Free French army performed several missions in French territory from 1941 onward. They later fought with British troops in the middle east, Egypt and Libya. Three parachute regiments were created in 1943, after the Allied landing in North Africa: the 1st at Fez, in Morocco, and the 2nd and 3rd on British territory. The regiments were officially called Parachute Chasseurs.

The 2nd can boast the honour of being the first Allied unit to have set foot on French soil on the night of 6 June 1945. Their action was decisive for the success of the landings. The 3rd regiment was hurled into the heart of France and worked in small groups, with the task of cutting the communications of the enemy columns and effecting raids on warehouses, camps and command posts. When the war ended, the paratroopers were transferred from the air force to the army. Thus the 25th Infantry Division, an air transport division, was created. The Indo-Chinese situation saw the 2nd and 3rd regiments sent to the far east. These regiments fought to reoccupy the main cities of Cochin-China and Laos. The following year a marching demi-brigade of paratroopers was created in France and sent to Indo-China, and they were followed by two parachute battalions of the Foreign Legion.

In 1956, when France and Great Britain sent a force to Egypt, during the war between Egypt and Israel, the Paras were dropped in the zone adjacent to the Suez Canal and quickly subdued the Egyptian troops. Two years later, the Paras, ordered in eleven regiments stationed in south-western France and in Algeria, assumed a position that spelled the end of the Fourth Republic.

A picturesque illustration painted by Georges Scott captures all the touching and heroic flavour of the homage rendered to the flag by an infantry regiment at the beginning of the First World War. The year is 1915, and the sky-blue uniform has only recently replaced the red and dark blue of the 19th-century uniform.

Germany

The Giant Grenadiers

The term 'grenadier' came into usage in the middle of the seventeenth century in France and was applied to those men in the infantry regiments whose task it was to precede the attack columns and hurl grenades at the enemy. Obviously these men had to be tall and particularly robust. The name 'grenadier' was later given to those soldiers recruited into the bodyguard of the sovereign.

Frederick William of Prussia, father of Frederick the Great, loved drink and money, but he made no economies when it came to acquiring tall, well-built men for his favourite grenadier units, the 'Blue Prussians' or 'Giants of Potsdam'. Some of the strongest grenadiers of the first battalion, the 'red unit' of the guards, were seven feet tall, and none of them was shorter than six feet, not even the bassoon players or the turbaned Moors in the pipe band. The first units of these giants were formed in the royal hunting preserve of Wysterhausen, two battalions of six hundred men each. (The number of battalions was increased to three in 1740 by Frederick II.)

Frederick William I spent the equivalent of sixteen million pounds to recruit and equip his favourite units. A colossal Irishman was bought for six thousand pounds by the king's recruiting agents. Foreign ambassadors at Frederick's court knew that the way to win his favour was to offer him wine, tobacco and grenadiers. Thus the ambassador of the tsar offered him fifty Russian giants every year, and the Saxon ambassador accompanied his birthday greetings to the king with the gift of

several 'seven-feet-tall Adonises'. The English plenipotentiary, knowing that King George I wished to strengthen his relations with Prussia, sent in his dispatches the requirements for Frederick's giant grenadiers so that George I could make him a gift.

The grant to each new recruit was made personally by the king. The pay was high, gifts were frequent and even the messing of the grenadiers was far superior to that of the rest of the army. The grenadiers wore a typical hat with a brass plate and red trim. Their jacket was blue with gold frogging and scarlet lapels. The trousers were scarlet, the long stockings white, and the garters and shoes black. They carried a large leather bag with a white bandoleer, and they were armed with a short dagger and a musket.

The king was the colonel of these battalions, two of which were garrisoned at Potsdam and one at Brandenburg. He never exposed his grenadiers to enemy fire, but he still required them to undergo thorough training. Their exercises lasted all day. There were frequent night alarms, as many as three in a single night, and the officers had to be mounted and in marching order within eight minutes. Even the battalion mascot, an enormus bear, could execute all the commands. At his death Frederick William I asked to be buried in the uniform of his grenadiers and ordered that his coffin be carried on the shoulders of his giant soldiers.

Opposite: *Mit Gott für Koenig und Vaterland (With God for King and Country), the Prussian motto on a badge for 19th-century military headgear.* Above: *Next to the officer in a tricorn hat is a giant grenadier of the* Potsdamschen Rothen Leib-Bataillon Grenadiere No. 6, 1730. *On his hat is a badge with the motto 'Suum cuique', similar to that reproduced on p.3. Frederick William I, the founder of the corps, received from rulers of various countries gifts of gigantic men to be enrolled in his grenadiers. The Tsar of Russia sent him one hundred and fifty every year. The giant grenadiers earned glory on many occasions under Frederick II. An Austrian ambassador, who had the physical requirements of the grenadiers, was almost forcibly recruited.*

The Von Seydlitz Cuirassiers

A VON SEYDLITZ CUIRASSIER 1757

The Von Seydlitz Cuirassiers wore a white uniform with blue cuffs. They had skin trousers and a burnished cuirass. They were the typical representatives of the heavy cavalry of Frederick the Great, for whom they fought bravely.

The Prussian army, which in the eighteenth century was admired throughout Europe, was organised by Frederick William, the Great Elector, and turned into a perfect instrument of war by Frederick I, the first king of Prussia, and by Frederick William, who was called the 'Sergeant-King'.

The officers were trained in the schools at Kolberg and Berlin, and the general staff cadres were instructed at the famous Berlin War Academy. The cavalry was the backbone of the army, and it included the famous cuirassiers of Wilhelm von Seydlitz. One could almost say that Von Seydlitz was born in the saddle, and he was a major at the age of twenty-three. It was a common saying that a cavalry officer had no need to surrender as long as his horse was alive. The king wanted to see if this cliché was true, so he had his escort surround Von Seydlitz when he was half-way across a bridge, and asked the young officer to show what he would do if those surrounding him were enemies instead of friends. Von Seydlitz spurred his horse and with a single spectacular jump, leaped into the river. Von Seydlitz exlaimed: 'That is my answer, Sire!'

Trained, inspired and spurred on by Von Seydlitz, the Prussian cuirassiers performed with incomparable valour at Kolin, Rossbach, Leuthen and Hochkirch. At Leignitz they captured six enemy colours, and at Torgau they competed with the hussars for the victory. It would be no exaggeration to say that the decisive action of the Seven Years War was the last charge of Von Seydlitz's cuirassiers at the battle of Freiburg.

At the battle of Rossbach Von Seydlitz's cuirassiers surprised the French army on the march. With a terrific charge the cuirassiers overwhelmed the enemy cavalry and prevented the infantry from getting into battle formation. (Von Seydlitz's gesture when giving the signal to attack has become famous: he threw his pipe in the air.) The French fled back across the Rhine leaving their waggons and rich booty behind. Following this charge, Von Seydlitz was promoted to the rank of lieutenant-general and given the Order of the Black Eagle.

At Zorndorf it was Von Seydlitz's cuirassiers who decided the outcome of a battle that was uncertain till the very end. This time the cuirassiers faced the Russians, who adopted the traditional tactics of squaring up their forces with the cavalry and waggons in the middle. The Prussian infantry broke the square but soon faltered and would have been crushed by the Russians if Von Seydlitz's cuirassiers had not driven them back with a furious charge. It was a terrible battle. The smoke of fires was so dense that the soldiers could hear the king's voice but could not see him. All the men in Frederick's personal guard fell around him, and at a certain point the king dismounted and led the infantry to the attack, shouting: 'Follow me, boys, not because you love me but for God and Country!' The Russians fought to the last cartridge, but Prussian discipline won the day. Von Seydlitz died in 1772 and was buried in Namslau in a bare stone tomb.

The Prussian army under Frederick had thirteen cuirassier regiments; the army that faced Napoleon had twelve. After the Napoleonic wars the Prussian cuirassiers were reorganised into ten regiments, two of which became part of the Guards.

After the war of 1870, during which the Prussian cuirassiers won distinction at Gravelotte and Saint Privat, the army of the new German empire was reorganised, and two regiments of Saxon cuirassiers and two Bavarian heavy cavalry regiments joined the old regiments of Prussian cuirassiers. But differences in uniform were kept. And the Prussians continued to wear their helmets with the white spike on top.

Opposite: *Details of the uniform of the Prussian cuirassier regiments in the period 1756-1763. In the War of 1870-71 the Prussian cuirassiers wore a helmet topped by a white spike (or, in the case of the two Guard Regiments, a yellow spike). The 1st Cuirassier Regiment was founded in 1672.*

Die Preußischen Kürassier-Regimenter 1756-63 (II. Teil.)

1) 1688	1691	1691	1691	1691	1704
Nr. 7	**Nr. 8**	**Nr. 9**	**Nr. 10**	**Nr. 11**	**Nr. 12**
1755 Driesen	**1742 Rochow**	**1751 Prinz von**	1691—1807 Regt.-	**1738—1807 Leib-**	**1743 Kyau**
1758 Horn	**1757—74 Seydlitz**	**Schönaich - Carolath**	Gensdarmes 6)	**Karabiniers-Regt.**	**1759 Spaen**
1762—77 Manstein	16. 10. 1807 Reste des	**1758/69 Bredow**			**1763—96 Dalwig**
2) Kür. Regt. v. Seydlitz	Kürass. Regt. Heising	1807 als Kür. Regt.	Verbleib wie beim	wie beim Regt. Nr. 2	1807 als Kür. Regt.
(Magdeburg)Nr.7,3.Esk.	(Nr. 8). Zum Kür.Regt.	Holzendorff (Nr. 9)	Rgt. Nr. 2		Bünting (Nr. 12)
3) 1.Esk.Reit.Regt.Nr.10	Wagenfeld (Nr. 4)	aufgelöst			aufgelöst

Hutquaste

Mannschafts-Kollett

Kollettborten

Säbeltaschenbesatz

Unteroffizier-Tressen,

Schabrackenbesatz

Westenborten

Trompeterborten

Offizier Kollett

Salzwedel, Osterburg,4) Tangermünde, Arendsee,Seehausen, Lenzen, 5) Werben.

Lowositz, Prag, Kolin, Roßbach, Leuthen, vor Schweidnitz und Olmütz,Kay,Kunersdorf,Maxen vor Schweidnitz.

Ohlau, Grottkau, Münsterberg, Strehlen.

Lowositz, Prag, Kolin, Roßbach, Leuthen, vor Breslau, Schweidnitz und Olmütz, Zorndorf,Hochkirch, Hoyerswerda, vor Dresden, Liegnitz, Torgau, Langensalza, Kloster Wallstadt, Leutmannsdorf, Reichenbach, v. Schweidnitz.

Oppeln, Löwen, Groß-Strehlitz, Falkenberg.

Prag, Moys, Breslau, Leuthen, vor Schweidnitz und Olmütz, Hochkirch, Maxen vor Schweidnitz.

Berlin.

Lobositz, vor Prag, Roßbach, Leuthen, v. Olmütz, Zorndorf, Hochkirch,Hoyerswerda, vor Dresden, Hohen-Giersdorf, Liegnitz, Torgau, Adelsbach, Reichenbach.

Rathenow,Wolmirstedt Neuhaldensleben, Sandau, Havelberg,Coburg.

Lowositz,Prag.Kolin,Breslau, Leuthen,Wischaur, Zorndorf, Hochkirch, Liegnitz, Torgau, Langensalza, Freiberg.

Ratibor, Leoschütz, Gleiwitz.

Prag. Kolin, Breslau,Leuthen, Torgau, Burkersdorf, Leutmannsdorf, Reichenbach.

Von Ziethen's Hussars

The first hussar regiments appeared in the Prussian army during the Seven Years War. Assigned to command them was Hans Joachim von Ziethen, a curious figure who had shown such lack of discipline at the beginning of his military career that he had been obliged to resign from the army. But Frederick sensed that the man had remarkable qualities and readmitted him to the army. Von Ziethen was sent to Hungary to study the battle tactics of the hussars, where he became the student of Baranyai, one of the creators of that light cavalry known as the hussars. And when Von Ziethen later faced Baranyai at the battle of Rothschloss, in 1741, he beat his old master.

Von Ziethen won distinction in the Silesian campaign and was repeatedly promoted. Finally he was given the command of a regiment of hussars, the 3rd, which was later named after him. He turned his light horse into a highly skilled unit, disciplined and well trained. Von Ziethen's enterprise and his hussars' valour were determining factors in many battles. At Torgau in 1760 Frederick found himself in a perilous situation, when his army of only forty thousand men had to face the Austrian and Russian armies. Had the two enemy armies managed to join forces, their superior numbers would have been fatal to Frederick. The battle swung back and forth. Frederick's horse was shot from under him twice and he himself was wounded.

'Courage, boys,' he urged his soldiers, who were fighting desperately, 'Von Ziethen is to the rear of the enemy. He will surprise them and the battle will be won.' In fact, during the night, Von Ziethen succeeded in opening a passage through the Austrian ranks and forced them to retreat.

'Papa' Ziethen became so famous that everyone wanted to serve under his command. The king was devoted to him. Once, after the Seven Years War, the general, old and infirm by now, was received at court. The king made Von Ziethen sit while he remained standing in front of his faithful officer. And it was certainly Von Ziethen's valour and merit that made the hussars Frederick's favourites. In the battle of Leuthen at which twenty-six thousand prisoners were taken and one hundred and sixteen cannons and fifty-one flags were captured - Frederick had his own escort manned by hussars.

At the end of the Seven Years War Prussia had eight regiments of Hussars, comprising 9,288 men. Each regiment had a name; the one that bore Von Ziethen's name was also known as the 'bodyguard hussars'. One of the victors at Waterloo served in this regiment, Field Marshal Von Blücher. Von Ziethen's hussars wore a tall black fur hat with a plume and a scarlet badge. The hussar dolman was scarlet, the pelisse light blue, the trousers dark blue and the tall boots were black.

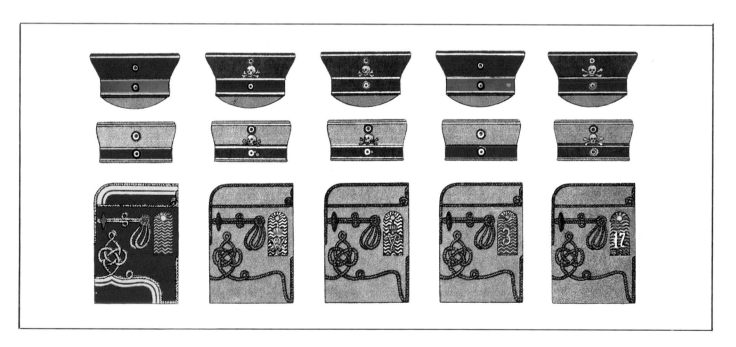

Opposite: *A member of the 5th Regiment, the so-called Black or Death Hussars* (Regiment Schwarzen Husaren), *created by Frederick the Great on 9 August 1741. After the defeat at Jena (1806), the regiment was reformed and became part of the regiments of* Leib-Husaren, *the 1st and 2nd, which maintained the skull badge on their headgear. During the First World War this emblem was extended to another regiment, which was part of the Danzig garrison, the 17th. The uniforms that these three regiments, the Guard Hussars and the 3rd, wore on the eve of the First World War, are schematically illustrated above. The details of the uniform depicted here are the rigid hat* (Schirmmütze), *the field hat* (Feldmütze), *and the dolman* (Attila).

The Uhlans

The uhlans were a particular kind of light cavalry which had Tartar origins. It comprised excellent riders who were experts in handling the lance; they were also armed with a long scimitar for hand-to-hand combat. They appeared in Europe at the end of the seventeenth century and were first organised in 'bands'. The name, which is derived from the Turkish oghlan, means 'comrade'.

Poland, which had a fine cavalry since the fourteenth century, made the uhlan its own, keeping the Asian uniform, but adding the typically Polish hat called the *czapka*. When the use of firearms diminished the efficacy of the lance, the uhlans were given a carbine.

A Prussian uhlan in the uniform worn at Sadowa. The final episode of Sadowa, the beginning of the pursuit, is illustrated in the print reproduced above. The uhlans were intrepid horsemen and represented the German equivalent of the Russian Cossacks. The uhlans were armed with a lance and a straight sword. This illustration is by Christian Sell.

The use of uhlans soon became common in the armies of eastern and central Europe, Thus, in addition to Poland, there were uhlans in the armies of Russia, Austria and Prussia and, for a while, in that of France, where Marshal Maurice de Saxe armed them with a lance twelve feet long which could also be used as a tent pole. Uhlans appeared in Prussia after the Seven Years War, but by 1745 there was already a Bosnian corps which had all the characteristics of uhlans. In 1788 this corps became the Regiment of Bosnian Uhlans. When the Polish provinces were annexed, fifteen uhlan squadrons were formed: they were called *Towarzyszy* ('comrades'). After the Peace of Tilsit (1807) the uhlans became even more popular.

The 8th Regiment, organised in Russia in 1812 by the exiled duke of Holstein-Oldenburg from German deserters (originally part of the Russo-German Legion), passed into the service of Prussia in 1814.

After the Napoleonic wars the Prussian army had two uhlan guard regiments. Their typical costume, called a *ulanka*, had lapels, plastron and cuffs of different

colours according to regiment. After 1870, it was dark blue for the Prussian regiments, light blue for the Saxons, green for the Bavarians. The trousers were blue-grey and the boots reached to above the knee. The traditional *czapka* was adorned with long braided cords.

The Bosnians won distinction at Gross-Soegendorf, Kant, Adelsbach and Barkensdorf. The *Towarzyszy* were engaged in the Polish campaign at Piontnitza, Kölln Magniszewo and at other places, where they demonstrated their reputation for invincibility.

In the Franco-Prussian War of 1870-1, the German uhlans counted twenty-one regiments. Their tactic was the rapid long-distance raid, which had been the tactic of the Confederate cavalry in the American Civil War. A particularly memorable action was that of Count Zeppelin, who managed to pass the French outposts with only eight men. When they had already covered a great distance they were surprised by a French platoon, but Count Zeppelin managed to pass the outposts again and deliver important information to Crown Prince Frederick.

During this war, Nancy surrendered to a platoon of six uhlans. The uhlans guarded the advance of the German armies across France and played an important role in the siege of Paris, but they met deadly adversaries in the *francs-tireurs*. The imperial German army had some thirty uhlan regiments. Three of them were Guard Regiments garrisoned at Berlin and Potsdam, two were from Württemberg, two from Saxony and two from Bavaria. Austria-Hungary and Russia also had uhlan regiments. One of the Russian regiments was assigned to the Guard. During the First World War, when troops were on the march the uhlans preceded the advance columns at a great distance. Their duty was scouting and security. So famous did they become that all cavalry units came to be referred to as uhlans and they struck real terror into the hearts of the populace.

In the period between the two world wars, Poland, in homage to its military traditions, created twenty-seven uhlan regiments. They lost their lives in their heroic cavalry charges against the German tanks in 1939.

Black Cuirassiers and White Guards

Theodor Korner, the poet who was a supporter of German resurgence, is depicted here in the uniform of the Black Chasseurs of Luetzow. He lost his life fighting against the Napoleonic French army at Gadebusch.

During the Seven Years War, Frederick II employed several free corps of infantry and cavalry. One of them was Schony's corps, which consisted of about six hundred grenadiers and three hundred hussars, all dressed in Hungarian style. Another unit was formed by Von Kleist, of infantry, chasseurs, dragoons and hussars, and there were two battalions of 'Green Croats'. There were seventeen hundred men in all, including the musicians, all dressed in dark green with red lapels and cuffs, a tall round hat with silver braid and a leopard-skin sash at the waist.

There was another free corps which appeared during the Napoleonic wars, the Black Chasseurs of Luetzow. Count Von Luetzow had been an officer in the Prussian army, which he left after the Peace of Tilsit. When he rejoined the ranks, he was authorised to form a *Frei-Korps*, comprising infantry, cavalry and Tyrolean marksmen. In 1813 General York, who had commanded the Prussian troops in the Grand Army, went over to the Russians, and it was not long before the king himself turned on Napoleon and declared war. Germany was caught in a great fever of patriotism and volunteers arrived from everywhere (ten thousand from Berlin alone). Von Luetzow's chasseurs tended to recruit students, artists, poets and adventurous young men for the most part.

This unit maintained a rigid discipline on the march and in battle, but during halts it became a regular band of bohemians, who got themselves up in outlandish costumes and organised dances and games. Because of the audacity of its men, it was often employed in gathering information, frequently behind the French lines. The men communicated by writing messages on walls using conventional phrases as a code.

Von Luetzow's chasseurs wore a black uniform with a red and gold sash. These three colours were later adopted for the German flag by the Federal Assembly of Frankfurt in 1848, by the Weimar Republic in 1918 and by the two republics that today divide the land of Germany. The Black Chasseurs were attacked by the French at Kitzen in 1813 and almost annihilated. Von Leutzow himself was wounded and surrounded but just managed to reach the Prussian forces. He reorganised his formation at once, and they had their baptism of fire at Gadebusch, where the poet of German recovery, Theodor Korner, the celebrated author of the *Song of the Sword*, was killed. Later Von Luetzow's chasseurs were sent to Denmark and took part in the siege of Julich. They were later dissolved and incorporated into the 25th Infantry and the 10th Uhlans.

In marked contrast to the Black Chasseurs were the Prussian army's White Guards, so-called after the French *garde du corps*. They originated from a squadron created by Frederick William I in Potsdam essentially as a parade unit. Frederick II turned them into an excellent cavalry regiment, of which he was the colonel. At Zorndorf on 25 August 1758, during the Seven Years War, the regiment, under the command of Colonel Von Wackenitz, was drawn up in reserve until the battle took a turn for the worse. Frederick II said to Von Wackenitz: 'Things are going badly. We shall lose'. The colonel replied: 'Majesty, I do not consider the battle lost until the *garde du corps* has charged.' 'If that is what you think', the king answered, 'then charge'. The White Guards did charge and they tipped the balance of the battle. The Prussian White Guards did, in fact, have a completely white uniform, with tall topboots, a bronze cuirass and a helmet crested with the imperial eagle.

A German cuirassier of the Garde du Corps *in a picture by De Neuville. At Zorndorf the Prussian* Garde du Corps *earned the praise of the greatest cuirassier of all time, Von Seydlitz. The Guard was commanded by General Wackenitz, who asked to lead the charge when the battle seemed lost.*

From the Pickelhaub to the Afrika Korps

The modern German army which fought in two world wars was born with the proclamation of the empire at Versailles in 1871. On the eve of the First World War the German army consisted of four blocks, representing the national armies of Prussia, Saxony, Württemberg and Bavaria. The Prussian army was very much larger than the other three in number of regiments, but there was, of course, a single general staff. To give an idea of the division of forces among these armies, it should be noted that out of two hundred and seventeen infantry regiments, one hundred and sixty-six were Prussian, ten were from Württemberg, seventeen from Saxony and twenty-four from Bavaria. Almost all the infantry regiments, except the Bavarians, had two numbers, one representing their order in the imperial army and the other their order in the national amy. Thus, for example, the 74th Imperial Regiment was also the 1st Hanoverian Regiment; the 99th was also the 2nd Upper Rhine Regiment, and so on. And several regiments also bore the names of famous men or of members of foreign royal houses. The 145th regiment, from Lorraine, was named after Victor Emmanuel III, king of Italy.

The cavalry was organised in one hundred and ten regiments, of which eighty-six were Prussian, eight Saxon, twelve Bavarian and four from Württemberg. The cavalry included several special branches: eight regiments of cuirassiers, twenty-five of dragoons, twenty of hussars, twenty-three of uhlans, thirteen of horse chasseurs, four of heavy cavalry and one of horse grenadiers. The 13th Hussar Regiment, recruited in Hesse, was named after Humbert I, king of Italy.

The artillery included two special branches: one called field (one hundred regiments) and one called foot (twenty-seven regiments). Likewise the corps of engineers included two specialities: the engineers and sappers, on the one hand, and on the other, the so-called communications units: railwaymen, telegraph operators, air supply, pilots and drivers.

As for the infantry uniform, it consisted of a dark-blue tunic with red collar and cuffs, iron-grey trousers with red braid and the classic leather helmet with spike. The chasseurs wore a green uniform and a shako.

The cavalry had various opulent uniforms. The Bavarian cuirassiers wore a white jacket, the Saxon heavy cavalry wore sky blue, the uhlans wore the short tunic called the *ulanka*, the colour varying according to regiment (dark blue for the Prussians, light blue for the Saxons and green for the Bavarians), and the hussars wore their own dolman, which was called an *attila*. The artillery and engineer uniform was dark blue with black trim, but the artillery helmet was distinctive, the spike being surmounted by a yellow metal sphere.

During the course of the First World War Germany mobilised an immense force consisting of some fifteen million men. At the beginning of the war there were 2,143 battalions, 406 machine-gun units, 806 squadrons, 1,070 field batteries, 778 foot artillery batteries, 394 sapper companies and 46 air squadrons, in a total of 94 divisions. The employment of reserves side by side with regular army troops was a genuine surprise. At the end of the war, the German army counted 73 army corps, with a total of 692 infantry regiments, 102 cavalry, 297 artillery, in addition to several special corps, such as the *Alpenkorps*, and the *Deutsche Jager Division*, which fought on the Italian front.

At the end of the war, the German army was reduced to seven infantry divisions and three of cavalry. Altogether there were twenty-one infantry regiments, each with a training battalion, eighteen cavalry regiments, and seven field artillery regiments. The collapse of the empire and the difficulties of reconstructing an army through the formation of many volunteer corps, (later disbanded), made it difficult to maintain the traditions of the old corps of the imperial army. And some units, like the Guards of the imperial army and of the federated states, disappeared entirely. The division into contingents was also abandoned, although the troops of the 7th Division, stationed in Bavaria, maintained a certain autonomy. The *Reichswehr*, the name assumed by the army of the Weimar Republic, was a new organism. Only a few regiments, like that of the Bamberg Cavalry, survived the old traditions. Thus the 67th Infantry Regiment inherited the traditions of the 'Alexander' Regiment of the Imperial Guard.

The German army was officially reconstructed after the Nazis came to power, in 1934, when each infantry battalion and each infantry group was transformed into a regiment. Thus there were twenty-one infantry divisions and three of cavalry. The latter were soon transformed into two armoured divisions. On the eve of the Second World War, the forces o fthe German army included thirty-five infantry divisions.

German officer uniforms during the First World War as worn by infantry and grenadier regiments and by the line guard. The spiked helmet with a nail originated in Denmark about 1850. It was adopted by the Prussians and all but became their symbol, despite the fact that it was used by all the more important armies in the world.

HEER UND TRADITION

Die historische Uniformierung, Ausrüstung und Bewaffnung, sowie geschichtliche Entwicklung von Heer, Kriegsmarine und Luftwaffe der Welt.

Gegründet von H. Knötel d. J. und Hans M. Brauer

Herausgeber: Dr. K.-G. Klietmann, Berlin.

© Alle Rechte beim Verlag „Die Ordenssammlung - Historia Antiquariat", Berlin 12

Offizier des 4. Garde-Regiments z. F.
Garde-Grenadier-Rgt. 4

Offizier vom 5. Garde-Regiment zu Fuß,
Garde-Grenadier-Rgt. 5

Leutnant vom Grenadier-Regiment Nr. 5.
weiße Patte: Gren. Rgt. 1–4
gelbe „ „ „ 5, 6, 7, u. 11
rote „ „ „ 8

Feldmütze der Offiziere

Helm der Offiziere

Offizier vom Füsilier-Regiment Nr. 80

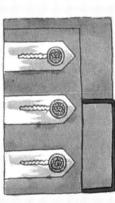

Ärmel für Grenadiere der Garde
und Linie

Ärmel für 5. Garde-Grenadier-
Regiment (5. Garde-Regiment
zu Fuß — weiße Knöpfe)

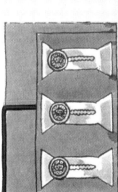

Ärmel für Regimenter der Garde
(hier 1. Garde-Regiment z. F.,
Garde-Füsilier-Regiment
und Lehr-Infanterie-Regiment)

The Panzerdivisionen

The first Panzer divisions were formed by the transformation of several cavalry regiments into armoured divisions. On the eve of the Second World War, the German army had nine Panzer divisions, each comprising a *Schützenbrigade* (a fusilier regiment and a battalion of motorcycle fusiliers), a *Panzerbrigade* (two regiments of tanks), a motorised reconnaissance group with armoured cars, motorcyclists, sappers, a battalion of motorised sappers and a regiment of self-propelled artillery.

These divisions were boldly employed in Poland

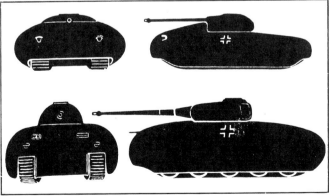

with drives against long-distance objectives without any concern for protecting their flanks. The results of this technique were spectacular. It was the 3rd Panzer Division, under the command of General Guderian (the founder of the armoured units), that cut the Polish 'corridor' to Danzig.

Ten *Panzerdivisionen* were arrayed against France and organised in armoured army corps. The use of these divisions was decisive in crushing French resistance. It was in this campaign that General Rommel, in command of the 7th Armoured Division, performed his first brilliant actions.

After the victory over France, Hitler decided to double the number of his armoured divisions, but reduced their size. From then on each division had only one tank regiment. When General Rommel was sent to Libya, his division comprised the 8th Armoured Regiment, the 15th armoured brigade, the 115th Motorised Infantry Regiment, the 200th Regiment of motorcycle and motorised machine-gunners, the 33rd Artillery Regiment and the 33rd Reconnaissance Group. Later a second armoured division joined this one under the command of Rommel. In June 1941, when the German army attacked the Soviet Union, three tank groups and four armoured groups were formed to effect a rapid and deep advance. (In the same year the regiments of *Panzergrenadieren*, or armoured grenadiers, with light tanks, and the famous Tiger and Panther tanks, were created.)

The results of the Russian campaign are common knowledge. After the first crushing advantage which they won over the Russians, the German forces were horribly decimated and ended in a decidedly inferior position. Suffice it to point out that, towards the end of 1944, the ratio of German armoured units to Russian ones was one to seven. When, at the beginning of February 1945, the Russians attacked and reached the Oder, there were twenty-three German armoured divisions in service, as well as the nine of the southern tank group (between the Carpathians and the Drava) and two more blockaded in Courland.

The last major unit to participate in the defence of Berlin was the 52nd Armoured Corps, whose commandant, General Widling, signed the surrender of the capital's garrison to the Russians.

German designs for tanks published by the review Signal *during the Second World War; they were never executed. The caption reads: 'Soldiers and builders dream of a kind of tank that while maintaining its normal outer dimensions can achieve the greatest technical capabilities and satisfy all military needs'. This dream must have been shared by those who had to do with the first tanks. An example is illustrated opposite in a page of an Italian series, the* Marca Aquila. *It was well known to collectors of paper soldiers and students of military iconography.*

Russia

The Streltsi

The exact meaning of 'streltsi' is 'sharpshooters' or 'chasseurs', and the name was given to the free bowmen and communal militias organised in the Grand-Duchy of Moscow at the time of Ivan the Terrible, about 1545, They were a caste of free men, the career of soldiering being handed down from father to son and they were lodged, equipped and paid by the state. In peacetime they were the backbone of the army. Their numbers were about forty thousand, and some twelve thousand of them were garrisoned in Moscow, at least until the time of Peter the Great, who in 1697 decided to remove them from the capital on the pretext of assigning them to the defence of the frontiers.

As a boy, Peter had more than once risked death at the hands of the streltsi. On 15 May 1682 they were urged on by Sophia, the tsar's step-sister, to enter the Kremlin and exterminate the family of Peter's mother. Peter was ten at the time, and the fright of that incident left him with a permanent facial tic. The second time was in 1689, but he was saved by some of his soldiers, of whom more will be said later, and by a soliaary flight of some forty miles on horseback.

The decision to send the streltsi away was a source of disappointment to the soldiers, long accustomed to the comfortable life of Moscow, many of whom had set up businesses in the capital and would now be obliged to leave their families. When Peter the Great went abroad for a while, the streltsi organised a revolt, which increased in violence when the rumour was started that the tsar was dead. Four streltsi regiments, stationed along the southern frontier, conferred with the tsar's sister Sophia (who opposed Peter the Great's European policies), and marched on Moscow, determined not to let the tsar return. It was decided to put the Tsarevitch Alexis on the throne, under the regency of Sophia, and to massacre all the boyars, or feudal lords of Moscuvy as well as all the foreigners living in the capital. But on 18 June 1698, near the monastery of Vokresenskij, the regiments of Peter the Great, under the command of General Gordon, met the rebel streltsi and dispersed them with cannonades. Fifty-six streltsi were captured and hanged on the spot, but the tsar was not content with this easy victory. He returned to Moscow in August and gave orders that Prince Rodomanavski (chief of the secret police at the time) was to be brought to trial on charges of conspiring with the streltsi. This trial was the signal for a terrible series of executions.

In 1705 the streltsi were abolished as a special corps and incorporated into the army, which, thanks to the efforts of Peter the Great in reorganising it, now had a strength of forty-eight infantry regiments and twenty-eight cavalry, as against the twenty-one infantry and two of cavalry that had constituted the army at the time of the streltsi revolt.

Above: *The helmet of the Tsar's mounted Life Guards. It is surmounted by the silver double-headed eagle.* Opposite: *The commanding officer of the Streltsi, a kind of Praetorian Guard of the 16th-17th centuries. In peacetime they were the Tsar's guards and in wartime they were the backbone of the army.*

The Cavalry of Peter the Great

As we have seen, the backbone of the Russian army when Peter the Great ascended the throne was represented by the streltsi. Peter devoted himself at once to the creation of a modern army, modelled on those of the countries of western Europe. The first thing he did was to transform into an efficient military force the two regiments which had served him as a child in his war games. He then established a brigade of regular troops named after their commandant, the Scotsman Lefort. These units were trained in spectacular and not always bloodless manoeuvres.

When in 1699 Peter formed an alliance with Poland and Denmark against Sweden, he actually had only four regiments, and to meet the requirements of the war he ordered each community to furnish the army with one hundred men. In this way he managed to organise sixteen infantry regiments and two dragoon regiments. The infantry immediately adopted a dark green uniform, which it kept until the First World War. The dragoons had a blue coat with red or white lapels, skin trousers and a metal helmet. They were the first great cavalry of modern Russia, even though, as is always the case with dragoons, they ought more properly to be considered 'mounted infantry' rather than actual cavalry. In fact, they had to fight to foot as well as on horseback, and were extremely formidable with their long straight swords. The new army's trial by fire was, however, a disaster. The Swedes, nine thousand strong

Great's army included - in addition to forty-eight infantry regiments, five grenadier regiments and three guard regiments - twenty-three cavalry regiments, five regiments of horse grenadiers, seven of hussars and nine of dragoons - not to mention the Cossacks, seventy-two thousand strong (of whom more will be said later) - and the garrisons stationed along the borders of this vast empire. General Potemkin as responsible for the excellent training of the Russian cavalry and it is to his credit that the cavalry was strategically employed as an autonomous branch in the occupation of the vast territories of southern Russia.

Peter the Great's army did not have uhlans, which were only formed in 1803, when the Russian empire incorporated the eastern regions of Poland. But in 1882 all the cavalry specialities were abolished, and all the regiments of hussars, uhlans cuirassiers and horse grenadiers became simple dragoons, an event which created much distress among the various units compelled to abandon their traditions. Some units even organised processions to carry their old uniforms to the depots in open protest against the authorities who had ordered their suppression.

under the command of their king, Charles XII, defeated sixty thousand Russians at Narva and captured a vast amount of botty: one hundred and forty-five cannon, one hundred and fifty-three flags and large quantities of valuable material. Eighteen thousand Russians died on the battlefield. But the Russians had their revenge, at Narva again four years later, and at Poltava on 8 July 1709. At Poltava, Peter attempted to deceive the enemy with the stratagem of having one of his best regiments put on the uniforms of recruits. But what decided the Swedish defeat was the fact that Charles XII's leg was gangrenous from an old wound and he was forced to hand over the command of the army to General Renskold, who was not only beaten but was actually captured by the Russians.

Now organised on the model of western European armies (and the Prussian army in particular), Peter the

Left above: *an encounter between Russian and Turkish light cavalry towards the end of the 18th century. Peter the Great had about thirty cavalry regiments. General Potemkin was responsible for the training of the cavalry.* Above: *A Circassian horseman with a medieval style uniform.*

The Tsar's Playthings

Two of the most famous Russian regiments were the Pre-obzhenski (above) and the Semenovski (below), shown here fraternising with the local civilian populace. Both regiments wore the spiked helmet. But the spike of the soldier of the Preobzhenski Regiment is hidden by the hanging plume.

Peter the Great, who became tsar at the age of ten, had a great passion for playing at soldiers and lost no time in substituting flesh-and-blood soldiers for his tin and lead toys. In exile at Preobrazhenskoye, where he had been sent by Sophia, he organised a regular little army, which he engaged in mock battles (at which quite a few of his 'toys' lost their lives). He recruited these soldiers from among the stable boys and falconers such as Menshikov, who became his adviser for life, and that robust groom Serghey Bochvotoff, who, as he had been the first recruit, always had the honour of being the first man registered in the regimental rolls, even when in 1720 it became a genuine regiment, the lst Preobzhenski Guards.

There are those who maintain that this casual use of men as toys was, from the very beginning, a plan thought up by the precocious Peter to develop a size-able group of devoted followers, to be used at the right moment. Whatever the truth of this, the *potechni* ('playthings') were certainly faithful to Peter. The young boy summoned German officers for their training and insisted on them going on long marches (on which he joined them), when he lived as they did, sleeping on the ground and sharing their mess. Later he created a second regiment of *potechni* in another village near Moscow, Semeniov, a regiment which was named after that village, the Semenovski Regiment.

The two regiments, soon joined by a third, the Ismailovski, were so well trained and so perfectly orga-nised that young Russians soon aspired to join their ranks. The tsar did not hesitate to spend his leisure hours with these troops, aften getting drunk and com-peting with them in intemperate and wild behaviour.

The Preobzhenski regiment had an artillery comp-any commanded by the tsar himself under the pseudo-nym of Peter Alexeyeff, in which he held the rank of sergeant. (The assumed name consisted of his first name and patronymic, i.e. Peter, son of Alexis. Since the tsar had ordered that all the officers must be foreign, he could not give himself a higher rank.) From this nuc-leus of *potechni* was born the Imperial Guard, the subject of the next section.

A curious detail, mentioned by Ogden, is worth citing here. Only fair-haired men were admitted to the Preobzhenski regiment. Dark hair and blue eyes were required for entry into the Semenovski regiment.

Opposite: *Russian infantry between 1742 and 1763. In the foreground is an officer of the Grenadier Guards. Seen from the rear are a musketeer and a grenadier of the Panduri Regiment. On the far right is a Novgorod Grenadier. In the background is a sergeant of the Preobzhenski Regiment and two musketeers.*

Russland.

Sergeant und Musketiere
der Regimenter Preobraschenski, Semenowski und Ismailowski
1742—1762.

Musketier und Grenadier
vom Panduren-Regiment 1752—1763.

Grenadier
der Garnison von Nowomirgorod
1760—1763.

Garde-Grenadier-Offizier
1742—1762.

The Imperial Guard

1877 in the Winter Palace, St. Petersburg, Alexander II receives the recruits assigned to the units fighting against Turkey. The Tsar personally assigned the recruits to the various regiments by marking the number in chalk on the chest of the recruit. In 1861 the Tsar had abolished serfdom, thereby freeing 47 million peasants.

The Russian Imperial Guard was formed in the reign of Peter the Great. It was this 'modern' tsar, who, during his travels in Europe, had observed that many sovereigns had a kind of army within the army, known as the Guard, and decided to organise one for himself, modelling it after the Prussian Guard, i.e. a guard organised as a proper fighting unit. In an army with an infantry of less than fifty regiments, there could hardly be more than three of four Guard Regiments. There were three regiments of Foot Guards in 1720, the Preobzhenski, the Semenovski and the Grenadiers. They had a simple dark green uniform with red frog-

ging and lining. The Preobzhenski collar was red, and the Semenovski was blue. The grenadiers had a large plume of ostrich feathers on their cocked hat, the front of which was turned back.

The Guard took part in several campaigns, especially those against Napoleon in Austria and Poland. They were in the 'National War' of 1812 and in the later campaigns in Germany and France. In addition to the infantry regiments there was from the beginning a regiment of Cavalry Guards, with a silver helmet and black feathers, red coat and trousers, and dark-blue lapels and waistcoat. When the cuirassier regiments changed their uniform, the officers kept the red tailcoat for court wear, as a memento of their original red coat.

Following the Napoleonic example, this chosen corps was carefully developed. As in other armies, the three Guard Regiments included chasseur units, similar to those in other forces. They had a very simple dark-green uniform with a single epaulet on the left shoulder. The chasseurs of the Ismailovski regiment, the fourth regiment to be formed, wore a green casque. By the end of the Napoleonic wars, the Tsar's Guard counted twelve regiments, all of which survived until 1917. These regiments did not have numbers, but bore the name of a place, an area or a famous person. Preobzhenski, Semenovski, Ismailovski, Iegerski, Moscovski, Guard Grenadiers, Pavlovski, Finland, Lithuania, Petersburg, Kegsholm, Volinski.

The Foot Guard Regiments were distinguished from the line regiments by their double braiding. The headgear consisted of a low sheepskin kolback with a badge bearing the St Andrew's Cross. This was replaced by a shako in the form of a truncated cone when the old uniforms were revived in 1910. The Pavlovski dress uniform was completed by a scarlet cloth mitre with white decorations, a metal badge and a pompom.

In addition to the twelve regiments divided between three infantry divisions, there was also a 'Regiment of the Emperor', which, unlike the twelve other regiments, comprised two instead of four battalions. The soldiers of this regiment were hand-picked from the Guard Corps and were charged with assuring the safety of the imperial palaces at St Petersburg and Krasnoye Selo. In addition to manning the guard posts at the gates and the look-outs in the park, they provided some thirty sentinels scattered in the halls and corridors, staircases, kitchens, pantries and cellars of the palaces.

With the reforms of General Miliutine, who reorganised the tsarist army in about 1850, the chasseur battalions of the imperial family were created. There were four battalions to a brigade; they too had their own names. The fourth battalion wore the long national tunic known as a *kaftan*, with thousands of pleats from

the waist to the knee, and a Polish-style hat.

The cavalry was also enlarged in the Imperial Guard. The cuirassiers, who first appeared in Russia in 1731, were organised in three regiments, which together with other units composed the First Cavalry Guard Division. On the eve of the First World War, there were the Cavalry Guard Regiments, Horse Guards, the Cuirassier Guards of His Majesty the Emperor, and the Cuirassier Guards of Her Majesty the Empress. They all wore the white tail-coat, a yellow metal cuirass and a brass helmet. In dress uniform the helmet was topped by the imperial eagle; in ordinary uniform by a stiff plume which stood erect like a slender spike. The trousers were blue-grey, the gloves, epaulets and stripes were of various colours. The cuirassiers constituted the heavy cavalry, but the First Division included two regiments of Cossacks, one called that 'of His Majesty the Emperor'; the other called that 'of the Hetman Hereditary Prince'. There was also a *sotnia* (squadron) of Ural cossacks, also known as 'His Majesty's'.

The light cavalry constituted the Second Division and included a dragoon regiment, two regiments of uhlans, and two regiments of hussars (one of which was 'His Majesty's' and the other the 'Grodno Guards'). The grenadiers had a coat of green cloth with narrow tails and metal buttons, and blue-grey trousers. The typical distinguishing mark of the grenadier was the helmet with a transverse crest running over the top of the head-piece. In dress uniform a scarlet cloth with three yellow stripes reaching to the shoulders was attached to this crest. The dragoons had a similar uniform with a fur cap. The uhlans wore the Polish *czapka* in black leather, a blue tail-coat with collar and red or yellow frogging, and the blue-grey trousers worn throughout the cavalry and mounted artillery. The hussars had a red dolman with yellow frogging, a white sealskin fur and yellow braid, Hungarian-style trousers, dark blue with yellow stripe, a sealskin kolback with a red badge for the emperor's regiment, and a green dolman and fur with red trousers for the Grodno Hussars.

The Guard also included artillery units, a sapper battalion and a regiment of His Majesty's railwaymen, whose responsibility it was to run the imperial train and guard the line. All the Guard Regiments were commanded by generals and the battalions by colonels. The best officers were assigned to these units. The Guard Regiments participated valiantly in all the campaigns until the First World War.

Trumpeter of the Mounted Life Guard in dress uniform. In accordance with the custom common to cuirassier units throughout Europe the trumpeter did not wear the cuirass as his brothers-in-arms did. The uniform is very similar to that of the German Garde du Corps.

The Cossacks

There is little that can be added to the vast quantity of writings about the Cossacks, the horsemen who ride without spurs. It is not known how they first came into being, but it is possible that the first Cossacks were Polish or Russian refugees who settled in the territories along the banks of the great rivers of southern Russia, where they established free villages and communities. The 'Little Russian' or Ukrainian Cossacks would have settled along the Dnieper, while the 'Great Russian' Cossacks occupied the territories along the River Don, the Volga and the Ural. In the sixteenth century a Cossack chief, Ermak Timofeevich, started the Russian movement into Siberia, while the Terek Cossacks opened the Caucasus to Russian expansion.

The Cossacks were, and still are, extremely intrepid horsemen. Traditionally they are armed lightly, with a lance, sabre, knife, musket and pistol. The first rather regularly organised units were created in 1575 by Stephen Bathory, king of Poland. He established ten regiments of two thousand men each, commanded by a hetman. In 1654 there were fifteen Cossack regiments.

The Russian Cossacks remained faithful to the tsar until 1708, when, on the eve of the battle of Poltava, they went over to the side of Charles XII of Sweden. Later they returned to their allegiance and were dissolved by Peter the Great. Many of them went into the service of the Khan of Crimea. Both Peter the Great and Catherine II had to face perilous Cossack uprisings.

At the beginning of the twentieth century, the Cossack nuclei were the Don Cossacks, the Zaporozhian Cossacks, the Volga Cossacks, the Siberian Cossacks, and those of Transbaikal, Amur and Ussari.

Until the fall of the tsar, the Cossacks were the backbone of the imperial cavalry, of which they constituted three-sevenths in peacetime and nine-thirteenths in wartime, with some nine hundred *sotnie* or squadrons. Their hetman-general was the hereditary prince.

There were fifty-four Cossack regiments in the regular army. Three of these were assigned to the guard, in addition to the imperial escort, which consisted of two *sotnie* of Kuban Cossacks and two of Terek Cossacks. Of the peacetime regiments, seventeen were Don Cossacks, six were Orenburg Cossacks, three were Ural Cossacks, two were Kuban Cossacks, four were Terek Cossacks and nine were Siberian.

The uniform of the Cossacks has always been characteristic despite its simplicity. The Don Cossacks wore a long blue kaftan, with a diagonal fastening on the chest, ample blue trousers with red bands and a tall sheepskin hat. The Caucasian Cossacks wore a dark grey Circassian costume with cartridge pipes on each breast, black trousers and a tall black hat. Those of the imperial escort wore a striking red uniform.

Some Cossack uniforms of the middle of the 19th century. The inclusion of the Cossacks in the regular army was the work of Catherine the Great. In 1770, the Empress formed the regiments and sotnie (centuries) that were to become famous as the Cossacks of the Don, Volga, Jaisk, Oremburg, Astrakan, Kisilar, Mosdok, Tobolsk, Tschuguschev, St. Demetrios, Azov, and Taganrog. The Cossacks already wore the long kaftan (like those grey ones worn by the fourth Cossack from the left, above, and the third from the last, below). Under Nicholas I, in 1831, they were admitted into the Imperial Guard. In 1899 the special regiments of the Emperor's Cossacks (in blue tunic) were formed of Don Cossacks and together formed the 3rd Brigade of the 1st Division of Cavalry Guards. In March 1917, the defection of the Cossacks marked the end of tsarism.

The Red Cavalry

The Red Cavalry, the title of a famous book by the Russian writer Isaac Babel, was an extremely important strategic unit in the Bolshevik army. It was formed to resist the counter-revolutionary forces of Generals Denikin, Wrangel and Judenic, and Admiral Kolchak.

Some of the cavalry units which had passed over to the new régime were organised in November 1918 into an army corps under the command of a former non-commissioned officer, Budenny, and a former metal-worker, Voroshilov. There was an immense amount of propaganda for recruiting enlistments. One of the many posters pasted on the walls of the cities and villages depicted a beautiful horse and a proletarian about to mount it. The caption read: 'Proletarians, mount up!' Many enlisted. Among the recruits of a unit formed in Moscow was the future Marshal Zhukov, then an ordinary non-commissioned officer of the 10th Imperial Dragoons. One brigade was commanded by Timoshenko, the future commander of the central-southern fronts in 1942. He had organised the mounted partisans of the 1st Revolutionary Regiment of Horse Guards.

In August 1919 Budenny defeated the 'White Cavalry' led by Mamontov, which had effected devastating raids behind the Bolshevik lines. A few months later, Budenny's cavalry corps became the First Cavalry Army, led by a council composed of Budenny, Voroshi-

Units of the 1st Cavalry Army in 1920, when this large strategic unit, the first of its kind in all military history, was transferred to the southern Ukraine to face the Polish army, which had entered deep into Russian territory. The Army consisted of 16,000 men with 300 machine guns and 50 cannons. Men like Zhukov and Timoschenko served in the Cavalry Army. The achievements of this army are among the final legendary episodes involving the cavalry.

lov and Scadenko - the commissar was one Joseph Stalin. Budenny's army then broke the front of the counter-revolutionary forces of General Denikin and in January 1920 took possession of the city of Rostov.

In the spring of 1920 the army was stationed in the Ukraine to meet the Polish army which had driven deeply into Soviet territory. The army then consisted of sixteen thousand men with three hundred and four machine-guns and forty-eight cannon. For a while the Poles managed to resist the attacks of Budenny's forces, but in the end they had to fall back and the Ukraine was liberated. Then began a counter-attack that would have taken the army into the heart of Poland but for an erroneous and over-audacious manoeuvre by General Tuachevsky, who took his divisions towards Lublin in the hope of drawing a tighter net around Warsaw and almost caused the Russians to be surrounded by the Polish forces. The negotiations opened between the Soviet Union and Poland put an end to the war and the army

was transferred to southern Russia, where it was employed against the 'White' forces of General Wrangel who continued to resist in the Crimea. When Wrangel had finally been suppressed, the army was moved to the Caucasus in 1921, to suppress anti-revolutionary activities there.

The great mobility and the speed of this legendary unit can in part be explained by the fact that Budenny's cavalrymen often changed their tired horses for others requisitioned on the spot. Moreover they were not slowed down by the problem of having to guard prisoners, because they shot all the enemy that fell into their hands. Nor did they have great problems of provisioning, because everything the army needed was forcibly requisitioned from the localities they rode through. Finally, one can say that the successes of the Red Cavalry were made possible by the nature of the terrain on which they operated: endless plains on a broken front and usually against ill-armed adversaries.

Fabbrica Nazionale d'Immagini.　DIVERSE UNIFORMI MILITARI DELL'IMPERATORE DI RUSSIA　N. 74.

Uniforme del Reggimento delle Guardie a cavallo
Deposée

Uniforme del reggimento degli Ussari di S. Maestá

Officine Grafiche E. DE-CASTIGLIONE & C. - Milano

Uniforme del reggimento degli Ussari del Grodno

Uniforme del reggimento Preobrajensky

Uniforme dei Cosacchi della scorta particolare di S. Maestá
Depositato

In distinct and symbolic contrast with the facing illustration is this early 20th-century print showing the last Tsar in one of the handsomest uniforms of that army which was to abandon him in 1917. From left on right: the uniform of the cuirassiers, His Majesty's Hussars, the Grodno Hussars, and the two favourites, the old 'plaything' of Peter the Great, the Preobzhenski, and the Cossacks of his personal escort. All the members of the imperial family, including the women, wore these uniforms.

Austria and Hungary

The Crown Guards

Because of the many nations that formed their empire, the Habsburg emperors never had guards of the kind that the kings of Prussia, Napoleon and the tsars did, and as British sovereigns still do. Nevertheless the Habsburgs did have various guard units which almost seemed to represent the various nationalities of the empire. And there was also a special unit assigned to the protection of the crown (a relic and symbol of Hungarian royalty), a unit known as the Guards of the Crown of St Stephen.

The oldest of these units was that of the bowmen, formed by the Emperor Ferdinand II in 1637, known as the *Arcieren Leibgarde*. It was entirely composed of officers, ninety-one to be exact, and a number of civil servants. The members of this aristocratic corps had to be at least fifty-five years old and to have won distinction through service at court or in the army, and of course they had to have particular physical endowments. Their uniform underwent many changes from the beginning until the fall of the monarchy. At first they had a hat with gold braid and white feathers, a black uniform with gold ornaments; their arms consisted of a sabre and a particular kind of halberd with a broad blade known as a *cause*. Later they were given a red coat with blac collar and braid, gold epaulets, white trousers and tall thigh boots. And the plumed hat was replaced by a white metal helmet with a plume.

The *Traibanten Leibgarde* was created by Leopold I in 1668, and this unit was also numerically small: eleven officers and eighty-two non-commissioned officers,

none under forty-five years old. At first they had a Swiss-type uniform with a halberd, but the design of the uniform underwent several changes, although the colours red and black remained essential. The *Traibanten Leibgarde* was responsible for mounting the guard at the imperial residences of Hofburg and Schönbrunn. When the last Habsburg emperor, Charles I, left Schönbrunn Palace in 1918, he forgot to change the non-commissioned officer guard in the Hall of Mirrors. The guard remained at his post until overcome by fatigue and drowsiness he fell asleep on the shiny floor. He was found the next morning lying next to his white-crested helmet.

A *Leibgarde Infanterie Kompanie* was formed in 1802. It numbered three hundred picked men who were assigned to the exterior guard of the imperial palaces. Their uniform, too, was altered several times. Their last uniform (1890) consisted of a black helmet with a hanging white plume, a green double-breasted coat with tails and a red collar, gold braid and epaulets and grey trousers with red stripes. Finally there was a *Leibgarde Reiter Eskadron*, composed of thirteen officers and two hundred picked non-commissioned cavalry officers who were assigned to mounted escort duty.

Among the various 'national' guards, mention should be made of the *Königliche ungarische adelige Leibgarde* (Hungarian Noble Life Guards,) who served in the imperial residences of the kingdom of Hungary. The men of this unit wore the Hungarian national costume, with a panther fur, a feathered kolback, a tailed

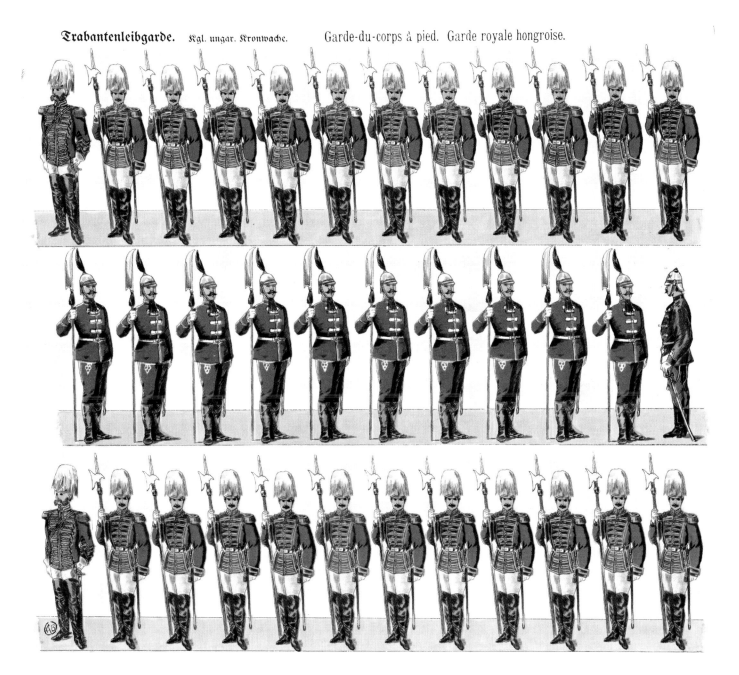

Trabantenleibgarde. Kgl. ungar. Kronwache. Garde-du-corps à pied. Garde royale hongroise.

Opposite: *The Habsburg crest. Above, in a German print, two rows of the* Traibanten Leibgarde *and, in the middle, a row of men of the Hungarian Royal Guard. The Traibanten Leibgard was created by Leopold I in 1668, with eleven officers and eighty-two non-commissioned officers. The habit of excluding ordinary soldiers from the life guards is still in use, for example in Belgium.*

coat known as an *attila,* Hungarian trousers with silver embroidery and soft leather boots with red cuffs. The unit was formed in 1740 and survived as long as the empire did.

The *Polnische Leibgarde,* or Polish Guards, founded in 1782 had a very short life, being dissolved after nine years. The *Bömische Adelsgard*e (Noble Bohemian Guards), created in 1812, had an equally short life. It was formed to serve at the imperial castle in Prague.

Finally in 1638 Ferdinand I created a Lombard-Venetian Noble Guard (*Lombardische-venetianische Leibgarde*) which was dissolved in 1848. It was formed to serve the emperor during his visits to his Italian possessions, but in fact it was almost totally inactive.

The last unit of the Habsburg guards was the Royal Guard of the Hungarian crown (*Königliche ungarische Kronwache*), which served as an honour guard at the royal castle in Budapest, where the Crown of St Stephen was kept. The uniform of this unit consisted of a silver helmet with a yellow plume, a red *attila* with silver braid, red Hungarian trousers and a large white cape. Their weapons were the sabre and a broad-bladed halberd. Curiously enough, this unit survived the fall of the empire, and when Hungary became an independent republic it continued to serve as an honour guard at the royal castle, which had meanwhile become the residence of the regent. The unit was suppressed only at the end of the Second World War.

The Hungarian Hussars

The origin of the word 'hussar' is debatable. Some maintain that it is derived from the Hungarian *husz* ('twenty') and *ar* ('equal'), referring to an order issued by Matthew Corvinus, king of Hungary, according to which every lay or ecclesiastical 'landowner' was obliged to provide twenty men in time of war. Others argue that the word comes from the obligation, during the time of the wars with the Turks, of every village to provide one man from every twenty: *huszar*, then, would mean 'twentieth'.

Mounted soldiers called hussars already existed in Hungary in the fifteenth and sixteenth centuries. They were equipped with a lance and a cuirass. By the time of the Thirty Years War, the hussars were employed as a kind of irregular cavalry, armed with sabres, pistols or carbines. The first regular hussar regiment was founded in 1688. The all but permanent state of war at the time gave the mounted soldiery a permanent character, and the hussars represented the backbone of the Hungarian army.

Mounted on small fast horses and highly skilled in the use of arms and firearms, the hussars were particularly effective in raids, patrols and scouting missions, especially in wooded areas.

During the Hungarian revolt against the Habsburgs, led by Ferenc Rakoczy, the hussars performed some brilliant deeds, penetrating deep into Austrian territory with their rapid raids. They even managed to capture the Austrian general, Stahremberg, after penetrating more than fifty miles into Austrian territory in midwinter. But the most famous feat of the Austro-Hungarian hussars was the attack on Berlin, led by Marshal Andreas Hadick in 1757, during the Seven Years War. Although sizeable Prussian forces were stationed in the environs of the capital, the city praesidium was undermanned, and this gave the hussars the bold idea of occupying Berlin with a surprise attack. Hadick achieved this remarkable feat with three hussar regiments - a total force of five thousand men. He fooled the Prussians by pretending to head for Frankfurt-on-Oder and only later turned toward Berlin. He succeeded in making the praesidium surrender before a proper defence could be organised. The hussars also achieved brilliant success in the war that saw the Habsburg empire take on Bismarck's Prussia in 1866.

The hussars in the Habsburg army wore a shako, the colour of which varied from regiment to regiment. Their uniform consisted of the *attila* and the traditional Hungarian trousers with soft leather boots. The *pelisse*, which usually hung loose and blew in the wind, was the same colour as the *attila*.

The Hungarian territorial army, the Landwehr of Honved, also had hussars: ten regiments ordered in three brigades. They wore the same uniform as the imperial hussars, but the *pelisse* was trimmed in white rather than black and the braid was red instead of yellow.

In the Habsburg army, generals who had commanded hussar regiments or who had served long periods of time with them were granted the privilege of a special uniform, similar to that of the hussars. It consisted of a fur kolback, with a red badge and a white kingfisher feather, a red dolman with gilt braid and embroidery, a red and gold belt, a white fur, red Hungarian trousers, white gold stripes and hitches and patent leather boots. In these splendid uniforms the hussar regiments appeared at the beginning of the First World War, when they won great distinction in their rapid raids during the first encounters on the Serbian and Russian fronts.

Above: *A lieutenant and sergeant (right) of the Hungarian Hussars of the regiment of Count Radetzky, which served in Italy in 1848-49. Opposite: an engraving by Martin Engelbrecht, depicting a colonel of the Queen of Hungary's Hussars. The hussars are a cavalry speciality of Hungarian origin. The word itself is derived from* husz, *which means 'twenty' in Hungarian, and* ar, *'equal'. Thus the name commemorates the ordinance of Matthias Corvinus according to which every lay or ecclesiastic 'holding' had to provide twenty men in case of war. Napoleon made the hussars the Light Cavalry par excellence.*

Austrian cuirassiers in the uniforms of 1825. During the Thirty Years War the Dampierre Cuirassier Regiment (later the 8th Dragoons) was created. Because of its behaviour during a revolt that threatened the life of Ferdinand II, it was granted the privilege of passing in front of the imperial palace playing fifes and drums. Its commanding officer could be received by the Emperor upon requesting an audience.

The Battery of the Dead and the Child Dragoons

A print of the Remondini of Bassano depicts the musicians of the Austrian uhlans. As the hussars all came from Hungary, so the uhlans all came from Galicia. After the conquest of Galicia a Polish uhlan corps was assimilated into the Austrian army in 1784. In the second half of the 18th century Austria-Hungary also had a Cossack corps.

One of the most brilliant episodes in artillery history is the one which gave birth to the legend of the Battery of the Dead. It happened during the Austro-Prussian War of 1866 in the orchards of Chlum. The Prussian infantry suddenly appeared nearby and with its new needle-guns attacked the Austrian cannon positions commanded by Captain Von Groeben. At a certain point the situation seemed hopeless. While the other batteries were ordered to retreat, Von Groeben's battery performed a rearguard action. The captain left a minimum number to man the cannon and led the others in a bayonet charge, supported and covered by the cannon as much as was possible. But they were sadly outnumbered and the Prussian rifles did not miss a shot. Von Groeben was killed and so were all his men, except for a Lieutenant Merkel and a soldier named Schunk, who managed to get back to the Austrian lines.

During the campaign of 1866, not only the artillery but the cavalry as well found itself in close combat, instead of making their traditional charges. On the Italian front, on 24 June, the uhlans of the 12th regiment, named after Francis II, king of the Two Sicilies, had to face the famous quadrilateral defence of Villafranca drawn up by the Fourth Battalion of the 49th Italian infantry regiment around Humbert of Savoy, the future king of Italy.

As the hussars were all Hungarian, so the uhlans were all Galicinian. As we observed when discussing the German cavalry, the name uhlan comes from the

One of the most outstanding episodes of the war that saw Austria-Hungary oppose Prussia in 1866 was that of the 'Battery of the Dead'. This unit was so called because it was wiped out under the command of Captain Von Groeben as it covered the retreat of the other batteries. Only one officer and a soldier survived.

former Polish cavalry, and the first uhlan corps of the Habsburg army was formed of Poles. That occurred in 1784, but the first independent regiment was only created in 1791. Other regiments were formed later.

The classic uhlan uniform consisted of the *czapka*, the flat-topped Polish helmet, a short light-blue tunic with fur, and red trousers.

Unique in the history of the Austrian cavalry is the case of the 14th Dragoons, known as the 'Child Dragoons'. The men of that regiment had been granted by Maria Theresa the privilege, rare in those days, of not wearing moustaches and beards. This clean-shaven regiment fought heroically at Zölln in 1757, during the Seven Years War. It was commanded by Colonel Thiennes, who saw that the Saxon cavalry was being driven back by the Prussians and asked Marshal Traun to let him lead his dragoons in a charge. The marshal consented, but added an aside which revealed that he had little hope in their success. 'There's little can be done,' he said, 'with your smooth-faced children.' But Colonel Thiennes, who knew the stuff of his men, addressed them with these words: 'Little shavers, show them how you can die even if you don't have moustaches and whiskers!' The impetuous charge of the Child Dragoons forced the Prussians to turn back after suffering serious losses.

Another distinguished dragoon regiment was the Dampierre Regiment, which, formed in 1619 as a cuirassier unit, was the oldest regiment in the entire Habsburg cavalry.

In 1867 there were twelve cuirassier regiments. Their uniform consisted of a white tunic, a light-blue pelisse, red trousers, a metal helmet with crest and a white metal cuirass. Later they abandoned the cuirass and became dragoons. The 8th Regiment kept the old Dampierre Regiment. It enjoyed several special privileges, including that of being allowed to pass before the imperial palaces playing pipes and drums, and the commander of the regiment could be received by the emperor without requesting an audience, as the Dampierre Regiment had saved the life of Emperor Ferdinand II during an insurrection.

The Tyrolean Chasseurs

The regiment of Tiroler Kaiserjäger, or the Emperor's Tyrolean Chasseurs, was in 1816 composed for four battalions. The number of battalions increased as the Tyrolean population grew, and there were ten in 1881, twelve in 1891 and sixteen in 1893. In 1895 four new regiments of four battalions each were formed. When these regiments were formed, chasseur battalions 3, 14, 15, 18, 26 and 27 were absorbed, so that these numbers were missing in the ordering of the other twenty-six chasseur battalions, numbered from 1 to 32.

Parallel to these regiments of the regular army (called in the Double Monarchy the 'common army', for it was composed of units recruited in the countries of the Austrian crown and in those of the Hungarian crown) there were, in the Landwehr, or second-line army, two regiments of Landesschützen or national sharpshooters. Later the Landesschützen regiments became three. The 1st was garrisoned in the Innsbruck area and the Voralberg; the 2nd in the Venosta and Pustheria valleys, with headquarters at Bolzano; and the 3rd in the Trentino area with headquarters at Trent.

These units continued the tradition of the war of 1866, when the Tiroler Kaiserjäger battalions with various companies of provincial Tyrolean sharpshooters, not yet organised in regiments, had comprised the

The Tiroler Kaiserjäger *were mountain troops particularly devoted to the Habsburg monarchy. After three years service the men spent seven years in reserve. Their plume of cock feathers on the black felt hat was typical.*

bulk of the small army (about twenty thousand men) with which Major General Kuhn had faced Garibaldi's volunteers in the Upper Valtelline and at Bezzeca, and the Fifteenth Medici Division in the Sugana Valley.

While the infantry regiments wore an elegant white coat, the chasseurs had a grey uniform with yellow buttons and green stripes, braid and frogging. Their characteristic hat was black felt with a green feather.

Until 1913, by virtue of an historic privilege, the military forces of Tyrol and Voralberg were autonomous within the Austrian state. They were supported by civil groups of marksmen under the command of the highest military authority in the Tyrol, the commandant of the Fourteenth Army Corps, quartered at Innsbruck, who also served as territorial commandant and commander of the Landwehr units, the second-line army, and of the Landsturm, or territorial army.

These civilian associations were responsible for training the civilian population in the use of arms, in military exercises and with developing in them a patriotic spirit and devotion to the emperor. They still function in those Alpine regions which have remained subject to Austria. In those days, however, citizens had to be over seventeen to be admitted and had to possess certain physical and moral qualities.

When their military training was complete, they were called *Standschützen*. Sixteen-year-olds could be admitted to the *Jungschützenschulen*, the school for young sharpshooters, where they familiarised themselves with the handling of the rifle and studied tactical exercises. These associations assembled almost all able-bodied men, and organised ceremonies and demonstrations of devotion to the emperor during manoeuvres and on imperial visits.

In 1913 these associations came under the control of the Defence Ministry, which was responsible for the Landwehr of the countries of the Austrian crown, and a special commission was established to coordinate and direct their activities. This gave new impetus to the Standschützen organisations, which continued to develop, taking on an even more militaristic character and instilling in its members a highly combatitive spirit. In the summer of 1914 many units were assimilated into the regular army.

At first these units were only relatively efficient. But in the winter of 1914-5, the men who were not suited for the fatigues of wars - those over forty-five or under eighteen - were eliminated, and their efficiency rapidly improved. On 24 May 1915, they held the positions on the Italian border alongside the battalions of Tiroler Kaiserjäger. These latter, together with several infantry battalions which had been trained in mountain warfare, were organised into mountain brigades, while

Tyrolean military uniforms of the early 19th century, from a contemporary print. From left to right, a non-commissioned officer, an officer, and a soldier. The famous Regiment of Tyrolean Chasseurs was founded by the Emperor in 1816. It was preceded and followed by the creation of units of local Jäger and Schützen, with special formations and privileges typical of mountain troops. The common fundamental characteristic was marksmanship. (Schütze, in fact, means marksman and is also eloquently applied to Sagittarius of the Zodiac.) The Tyrolean Chasseurs also had mounted units (Tiroler Verittene Landesschützen).

the volunteers were organised in demi-brigades. Six Standschützen battalions constituted the Tyrol group reserve, stationed at Trent, and twelve other battalions were stationed in Carnia.

In such other Alpine regions as Carinthia, Styria, the Salzburg area and Upper Austria, where the institution of the Standschützen did not exist, units of Freiwillige Schützen, or volunteer riflemen, were formed.

Standschützen battalions together with the Kaiserjäger and the Landesschützen formed the mountain brigades, while volunteer rifle companies, directly commanded by the various sectors, formed 'sector flying co-

lumns' assigned to reconnaissance, advanced positions, night attacks and to the recovery of certain localities lost during the first months of the war.

The Strafexpedition of May 1916 saw all the units of the Kaiserjäger and Landesschützen incorporated into the armies of the Arch-Duke Eugene, which also included eighteen battalions of Standschützen. In the battle of November 1917, Kaiserjäger and Landesschützen fought in the uplands under the command of Conrad, and three regiments, the 2nd, 3rd and 4th, were in Krauss's army corps on the Grappa. This army corps also included a Schützen division.

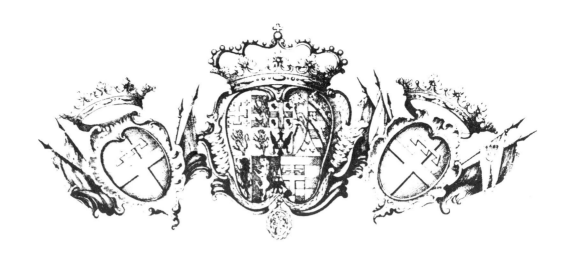

Italy

To Me the Guards!

The Italian grenadiers, like those of every other European army of the past, were ordered in special companies assigned to infantry battalions and regiments. The Italian grenadiers have a long history. In 1659 Charles Emmanuel II, duke of Savoy, organised a Guard Regiment. This regiment, consisting of three battalions, was distinguished by its red uniform and silver braid, which characterises the grenadiers of today. The colour red was first limited to the collar and to the red square on which the white or silver braid is applied. The Guards Regiment fought in 1748 on the Cold de l'Assiette, when it faced the French troops which were attempting to descend the Chisone Valley. The French losses were heavy and included their commander-in-chief.

In 1796 they faced Bonaparte's troops at Cosseria. The campaigns in which the Guards Regiments took part in the seventeenth and eighteenth centuries include that of 1672, those of 1690-6, that of 1701, with the battles of Luzzara and Chiari, those of 1703-12, with the battle of Turin, that of 1733-5, with the famous battle of Parma, and the campaign of 1742-8, with the already mentioned battle of Assiette. When the king of Sardinia was forced to cede the mainland states to Napoleon, the Guards Regiment was dissolved, but was reformed in 1814 and took part in the campaign of Dauphiné in 1815. In 1816 Victor Emmanuel I joined all the army grenadiers together in the regiment that came to be called the Grenadier Guards Brigade.

The red uniform was replaced by the dark blue infantry uniform, though the red collar and cuffs were kept along with the braid. The traditional fur hat was also resumed, and thus garbed the grenadiers fought in the 1848 campaign at Pastrengo, Santa Lucia, Goito and Sommacampagna, as part of the reserve division commanded by Victor Emmanuel, then duke of Savoy. It was at the Battle of Goito, on 29 May, that fearing for the outcome Victor Emmanuel shouted to the guards brigade: 'To me, the guards, for the honour of the House of Savoy!' The guards swung the balance.

The Grenadier Guards Brigade was later reorganised into two regiments of grenadiers and one of Sardinian chasseurs. During the reorganisation of the Piedmontese army which was carried out in 1852, the Sardinian chasseurs regiment was incorporated into the Grenadier Regiments, which were subsequently called 'Sardinian Grenadiers'. It was then that the grenadiers gave up their fur hats for the infantry kepi. They distinguished themselves at San Martino in the campaign of 1859 and at Perugia and Gaeta the following year.

With the unification of Italy six other Grenadier Regiments were formed and organised in the Grenadier Brigades of Lombardy (3rd and 4th regiments), Naples (5th and 6th) and Tuscany (7th and 8th). A fifth brigade, known as the Savoy Grenadiers (9th and 10th regiments), was formed for the campaign of 1866, but it was dissolved after the Peace of Vienna. In 1871 the six Grenadier Regiments formed after the unification were transformed into infantry line regiments. The Grenadiers, organised in battalions, took part in all the colonial campaigns.

From left to right: *carpenter, drummer, drum major and musician of the Grenadier Guards Brigade, 1821. After the reform of Victor Emmanuel I, the original red uniform was replaced by infantry blue, but the bearskin resisted the advance of the shako, the felt hat with brass scale chin strap worn by the two musicians. The drum major wears a tall cocked hat. One can also note the silver facings that still distinguish the grenadiers. The carpenter's apron is of white leather. The typical beard, according to regulations, had to be 'long and flowing'.*

The famous plate of Quinto Cenni illustrating the evolution of the grenadier uniforms from the end of the 17th century to the last years of the 19th century. It seems that in the 18th century the grenadiers had the most beautiful marches in all of the Piedmontese army and that they were preferred by other corps to the regulation marches. Note, in the third group, the kepi covered in red cloth that came into use in 1848 and spread throughout the infantry.

The Red Shirts

The white cross was the badge of several volunteer units that took part in the first war of Italian independence, 1848-49. They were called Crusaders and were largely Venetian, as the names of their units indicate: Belluno, Piove di Sacco, Cologna Veneta, Buia, etc.

The red shirts which Garibaldi's volunteers wore in South America and in the campaigns of the Italian *Risorgimento* were the symbol of voluntary service in the years between 1848 and 1870. The Italian volunteer spirit was very strong in 1848. Some two hundred and eighty volunteer corps were formed, comprising all branches - infantry, cavalry, artillery and engineers - with the most varied names, from chasseurs to death volunteers, from bersaglieri to crusaders, and so on.

Giuseppe Garibaldi landed in Italy when he learned of the revolutionary activity of the spring and was made a major-general by the provisional government of Milan. He organised a 'Lombard legion', in which Giuseppe Mazzini served as an ensign. The campaign was so successful that the legion had no chance to take part. But other volunteer units fought with distinction, such as those from Reggio, which fought at Governolo and Borgoforte, those from Piacenza which fought on the Adige, and the Po bersaglieri, who were at Cornuda. The defence of Rome in 1849 saw Garibaldi commanding the Medici volunteers from Lombardy, the Masina lancers, the Lombard bersaglieri of Luciano Manara, and other famous units. The glory of these

units were the victory over the Neapolitan troops at Velletri, the defence of the so-called Villa 'Il Vascello' in Rome and finally, the retreat through the midst of enemy troops made by the volunteers who followed Garibaldi even after the fall of Rome.

At the first signs of war in 1859, thousands of volunteers from all parts of Italy flocked to Piedmont. Many were incorporated into the regular army, but several thousands were sent to the bersaglieri depot in Cuneo, where General Cialdini, then commandant, was to organise a corps to be known as the *Alpine Chasseurs*. The command of the entire corps was entrusted to Giuseppe Garibaldi, major-general in the royal army. Three infantry regiments of two battalions each, numbering five hundred or six hundred men, were formed under the command of Enrico Cosenz, Giacomo Medici and Nicola Ardoino. In addition to a headquarters and administrative unit, the corps included a guide squadron made up of sixty young men armed, equipped and mounted at their own expense. They wore a picturesque uniform with a red tail-coat with black braid, grey trousers and a red hat. The chasseurs wore a red tunic.

A regiment of Apennine Chasseurs was also created, and they wore dark blue tunics with light blue badges. The regiment consisted of four battalions, Tuscans for the most part, who were joined to the Alpine Chasseurs. In June a battalion of Valtelline bersaglieri was formed in Sondrio which resumed the traditions of the corps of the same name, created in 1848.

The Alpine Chasseurs fought in Upper Lombardy at Varese, Malnate and San Fermo, on 22, 26 and 27 May, and defeated Urban's Austrians. In the guide squadron, which was commanded by the Lombard nobleman Francesco Simonetta, was the writer Ippolito Nievo. The Alpine Chasseurs liberated Como and Bergamo, entered Brescia, fought at Tre Ponti and Salò and reached the Stelvio, where they were when the Villafranca armistice was declared. Part of them formed the Alps Brigade (51st and 52nd Infantry), which had green insignia and a red tie as a memento of the chasseur tunic.

The name of the Alpine Chasseurs was resumed by Garibaldi when on 5 May 1860 he left Quarto for Sicily with the Thousand. They were organised in eight companies, an artillery squad, an engineer squad, a guide squadron and a unit of Genoese carabineers. With subsequent arrivals and local recruitment, the volunteers, who now called themselves the Southern Army, formed four divisions as well as several irregular cavalry, carabineer and chasseur units. After the siege of Capua and the battle of the Volturno, this army was disbanded, some of its commanders, like Sirtori, Bixio, Medici and Cosenz joining the regular army.

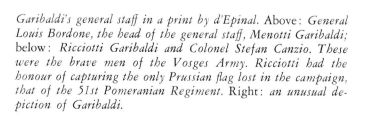

Garibaldi's general staff in a print by d'Epinal. Above: *General Louis Bordone, the head of the general staff, Menotti Garibaldi;* below: *Ricciotti Garibaldi and Colonel Stefan Canzio. These were the brave men of the Vosges Army. Ricciotti had the honour of capturing the only Prussian flag lost in the campaign, that of the 51st Pomeranian Regiment.* Right: *an unusual depiction of Garibaldi.*

Général Garibaldi.

The Faithful Branch

A vivid drawing of a mounted carabiniere by Quinto Cenni, the painter from Imola (1845-1917) whose fundamental work had great influence on the evolution of Italian uniforms. When they were founded (13 July 1814) the carabinieri were considered to be a cavalry unit. Actually they were modelled after the Napoleonic gendarmerie.

The carabinieri were formed by Victor Emmanuel I, king of Sardinia, on 13 July 1814. They were to serve as the king's guards in wartime and to assure civil order in peacetime. Furthermore the carabinieri were at the top of the army hierarchy, immediately after the Life Guards, which were disbanded in the years of the Italian Risorgimento. The uniform of the carabinieri drew inspiration from the fashions of the day, consisting of a tall bicorn hat with a blue plume, a blue tailcoat lined in red, with blue badges and a white bandoleer.

The carabinieri had their baptism of fire at Grenoble in June 1815, where a horse unit charged. Scattered throughout the kingdom, they had a chance to demonstrate their loyalty to established institutions and to the crown as early as 1821, when the Carbonari organised the revolt of Turin. Obeying the orders of the regent, Charles Albert, the carabinieri joined the forces that had remained loyal to the king at Novara. During the invasion of Savoy, led by Giuseppe Mazzini and Ramorino, a horse carabiniere, Giovambattista Scapaccino was captured by the rebels at Les Echelles. He refused to shout 'Long live the republic' and was killed, thus earning the first gold medal of military valour for the branch.

Meanwhile the carabinieri cadets were instituted for the purpose of training men who wished to serve in that branch of the army. In fact, since 1861 the carabinieri have, unlike their opposite numbers in other European armies, been considered a branch of the army. The cadets had a uniform similar to that of the carabinieri, but without the red ornaments and without epaulets or silver braid on the collar. In those years the carabinieri were also assigned to Sardinia, which until then had had its own special police corps.

In 1848, during the first War of Independence, the carabinieri had, in addition to their normal responsibilities of a military police, the task of providing three squadrons and won the day at Pastrengo, on 30 April 1848. They won distinction again at Santa Lucia on 26 May, and at Custoza, where in July they covered the infantry retreat to Valeggio with the help of the Savoy and Aosta cavalry regiments.

When Italy was unified, the carabinieri, who in 1859 had been organised in seven divisions or groups and nineteen companies, extended their activities to all the provinces which joined the kingdom of Italy, enlisting into their ranks selected police forces from the individual states. In 1861 the corps was made a branch of the army and organised into thirteen territorial legions and one cadet legion. The number varied, however, over the years and according to the structure of the army as a whole, and now consists of twenty-five legions and two cadet legions.

Immediately after the unification of Italy, the carabinieri had the difficult task of combatting, together with units of the army and the national guard, brigandage in the southern provinces, and of assuring respect and observance of the law.

Naturally they took part in the campaigns of 1866 in the Veneto region and in the Roman campaign of 1870. They fought against the Palermo rebels in 1866 and functioned in other regions as one of the finest police forces that has ever existed. It is worth mentioning that the carabinieri have never become conventional policemen, but have always preserved their special military character. They took part in colonial operations and enrolled local members, known as *zaptiè*, both in the colonies of East Africa and in those of North Africa, where in the years between 1936 and 1940, special 'guard' units were formed of carabinieri and *zaptiè* dressed in picturesque uniforms suited to their functions and geographical locations.

At the beginning of the First World War a carabi-

niere regiment of three battalions was formed to serve at Podgora. Thirty-eight per cent of these troops were lost. Later, in view of the fact that the carabinieri had so many difficult tasks to perform on the front and at home, this regiment was dissolved and the carabinieri took up once again their normal tasks. Nevertheless, on 28 October 1917, a platoon of two carabinieri who had been delayed at Udine, killed General Von Berrer, the commandant of a German army corps, who thought that the city was completely free of enemy soldiers.

Carabinieri units were formed for the war in Ethiopia, where their armoured units on the southern front won distinction at Negelli. In 1941 the carabinieri won glory in the defence of Gondar and at Culquaber. They wrote pages of glory after the armistice as well, with the sacrifice of Brigadiere d'Acquisto at Palo Laziale, who took the blame for a raid on the Germans in order to save twenty-three hostages, and with the loss of five carabinieri at Fiesole, who offered themselves in exchange for hostages that were to be shot.

Carabinieri and Cuirassiers in a plate by Cenni, 1880. From left to right: vice-brigadier on foot, mounted carabinieri cuirassier officers in ceremonial uniform, a carabiniere officer in high dress, and, behind him, a cuirassier. Far right, a mounted cuirassier officer in high dress. The term carabiniere *originally indicated a soldier, foot or mounted, armed with a carbine, a firearm shorter than the harquebus and rifle, with a grooved and hence more accurate and effective barrel. The carabinieri have taken part in all the wars fought by the Italian army and distinguished themselves in such famous enterprises as the Charge of Pastrengo (30 April 1848) and the defence of the Culquaber Pass (21 November 1941), near Gondar, Ethiopia.*

Italian Cavalry

The Piedmontese cavalry units, from which the Italian cavalry derives, were formed by Emmanuel Philibert. They were divided into a heavy cavalry for combat, a light cavalry for surprise actions, and harquebusiers (later called dragoons), for combat on foot. In 1683 Victor Amadeus II formed two regiments of dragoons and one of 'cuirasses', the name that had been assigned to the heavy cavalry. These regiments were increased to five in 1695; three of dragoons (those of His Royal Highness were called 'Blues', those of the Genevois were called 'Greens' and those of Piedmont 'Yellows' and two of cavalry (Royal Piedmont and Savoy).

During the Napoleonic period there were Italian cavalry regiments in the French army, in that of the Regno Italico and in that of the kingdom of Naples. With the restoration in Piedmont, six regiments were formed, two consisting of the King's and the Queen's dragoons, two of light cavalry (the King's and Piedmont) as well as the two already mentioned, the Royal Piedmont and Savoy.

After various developments due to the events of 1821 the Piedmontese cavalry was reorganised in 1835 into six regiments, each with its own name - Nice, Royal Piedmont, Savoy, Genoa, Novara and Aosta - and these were divided among brigades. In 1840 all the regiments adopted the crested helmet known as the 'Minerva', designed by Palagio Palagi, Charles Albert's court painter. In 1845 all the men were given a lance with a blue swallow-tailed pennant, a curved sabre, and a musket known as a *pistolone*.

The cavalry took part in all the battles of the campaign of 1848. And several volunteer regiments were formed - the 'Lombard Dragoons' and the 'Horse Chasseurs' in Lombardy, as well as squadrons in Tuscany, Rome and in the Veneto. In 1850 the Piedmontese cavalry was divided between nine regiments, so that a light cavalry regiment could be assigned to each infantry division. The original cavalry division continued to be composed of the first four regiments - Nice, Royal Piedmont, Savoy and Genoa - the only ones to keep

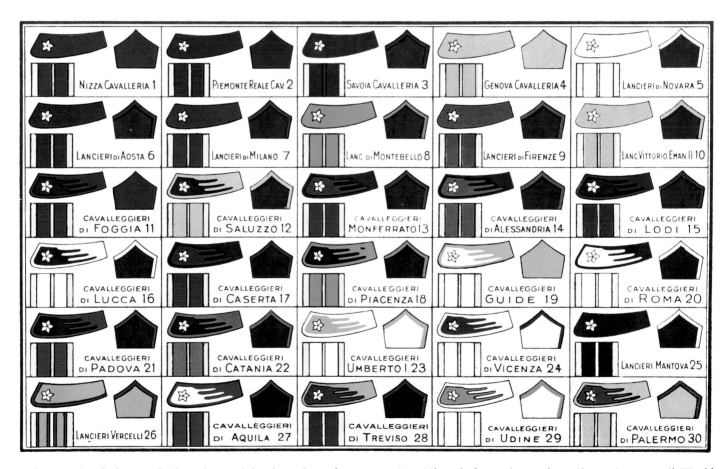

Italian cavalry badges with the colours of lapels, cuffs, and trouser stripes. These badges refer to the uniforms in use until World War I. Later only the lapels were kept and, for the officers, a coloured badge. The trouser stripes were black as they were in other branches. In 1940 the coloured lapels were also abolished. A badge the same colour as the lapels was substituted. Those regiments which already wore badges on the coloured lapel reduced the lapel to a rectangle on which they desplayed the badges. These are the only distinguishing features on the lapels used today by all the units. The three-pointed badge is used only by the cavalry. The other branches have one- or two-pointed badges.

the helmet and lance. The other five regiments - Novara, Aosta, Saluzzo, Monferrato and Alessandria - became light cavalry and their helmet was replaced with a kepi which matched the jacket collar in colour. The Piedmontese cavalry fought at Montebello. In that battle the French cavalry, mounted on heavy horses, could not charge on the damp ground. The French general, Forey, asked General De Sonnaz, who commanded the Novara, Aosta and Monferrato regiments, if his regiments could charge. De Sonnaz replied in Piedmontese dialect: 'We always charge!' They won the day with a series of bloody charges.

After the war, with the annexation of the various provinces, several regiments were formed, so that on the eve of the war in the Veneto (1866) the Italian cavalry numbered four line regiments - Nice, Royal Piedmont, Savoy and Genoa - who had briefly worn the cuirass and been called cuirassiers, seven lancer regiments, six light cavalry, one of hussars and one of guides. Later the cavalry, which had taken part in the operations against the brigands, in the 1866 campaign, and in all the colonial campaigns, reached a total of thirty regiments, including twelve lancer regiments (the first four being of this number and maintaining the helmet), and eighteen light cavalry who, like eight of the lancer regiments, wore the kolback. The lancers

had a solid-colour collar with three-pointed flames of different colours as their badge.

Italy entered the First World War with four cavalry divisions and a regiment for each army corps. The trench war forced the cavalry to dismount and fight in the trenches, some to form machine-gun units, while other officers and men were assigned to the infantry and artillery as bombardier units; about one thousand officers and thirteen thousand men were so employed. The mounted cavalry was employed against the Austrian offensive in the uplands, in May 1916, at Gorizia, and in the following August, and more notably still in the autumn of 1917, after the Caporetto break-through.

The count of Turin, cousin of the king, then commanding-general of the cavalry, said on that occasion: 'The cavalry is not only the branch of success but also the branch of sacrifice.' At Pozzuolo del Fiuli, the Second Cavalry Brigade, together with the Genoa and Novara regiments resisted enemy attacks for hours, while the First Brigade with the Monferrato and Rome regiments sacrificed itself at Pasian Schiavonesco. In June 1918 the Milan lancers opposed the enemy infantry on the Piave both on foot and on horseback. At the battle of Vittorio Veneto, cavalry units attacked the enemy and penetrated the Trent and Udine areas.

After the war the cavalry was reduced to twelve

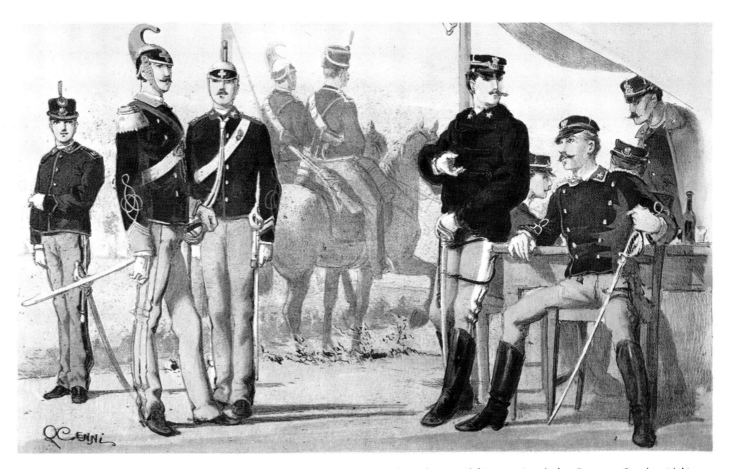

Italian line cavalry and light cavalry about 1880. From left to right: *Aosta lancer (6th), captain of the Genoese Cavalry (4th), sergeant of the Royal Piedmontese Cavalry (2nd); mounted in the rear, soldiers of the Savoy Cavalry (3rd) and a Novara lance (5th) in dress uniform; a Milan lancer officer (7th), adjutant major of the Nizza Cavalry (1st). Behind is an officer wearing a cloak. The Milanese lancer officer wears the spencer, a typical garment of the hussars, which was widely adopted abroad during the Napoleonic period. The Piedmont introduced it in 1848 and its use was extended to cavalry officers in 1849. It was very ample so that it could be worn over the tunic. Trim and cuffs were covered with astrakhan fur or Persian lamb.*

regiments and almost all of those formed after the unification were dissolved. Six were joined into three rapid-attack divisions together with bersaglieri and artillery. On the eve of the Second World War the Milan Lancer Regiment was reorganised, while three 'mechanised'

regiments had already been organised. There was one per division and they were called St George, St Mark and St Justus. During the course of the war other mechanised regiments were also formed - they were called Lodi, Montebello and Lucca.

Another fine plate by Quinto Cenni illustrates the evolution of the uniforms of one of the most brilliant Italian cavalry regiments, the Royal Piedmont. The painter inserted it in a special number published at his own expense in Milan, 2 June 1892, on the occasion of the regiment's second centenary. The armament of the Piedmontese cavalry under Victor Amadeus II, i.e. at the time in which the Royal Piedmont Regiment was established, comprised a short rifle, sabre with a shoulder strap, bandolier with cartridge case and a pistol kept in a holster called a cappelletto *next to the saddle. Giovanni Battista Scapaccino, the first winner of the Gold Star of the Italian army, served in the Royal Piedmont before being transferred to the* carabinieri.

The Foot Soldiers

The term 'foot soldier' conjures up the humility and the glory of the infantry, the queen of battle, the branch that in all wars has always represented the greatest contribution of sacrifice and the highest example of an undemonstrative heroism, in short, the branch of the people, without privilege and title.

The Italian infantry was formed from the guard regiments - Savoy, Aosta, Monferrato, Piedmont and Nice - which had been created by Charles Emmanuel, duke of Savoy, in 1664. A little more than a century later the infantry regiments of the Sabaudian duchy numbered ten. After the Napoleonic wars the regiments were called 'brigades' and comprised two battalions in peacetime, four in war. In 1831, when Charles Albert ascended the throne, the brigades were again divided into regiments, numbered from one to eighteen and comprising the Savoy, Piedmont, Aosta, Cuneo, Regina, Casale, Pinerolo, Savona and Acqui brigades.

The strength of the infantry of the kingdom of

Piedmont remained unchanged until the second War of Independence. In the famous battle of San Martino the Aosta Brigade encountered the king, Victor Emmanuel II, on its way to battle. The battle was severe and there seemed little chance of victory. The Aosta infantry cried 'Long live the King!' And the king replied in Piedmontese dialect: 'Boys, either we take San Martino or they'll have us doing the St. Martin!' (He was alluding to the Piedmontese habit of moving house on St. Martin's Day.) The attack of the Aosta and Pinerolo brigades won the day for the Italians. After the proclamation of the kingdom of Italy, the infantry brigades were increased to thirty-six. The foot soldier of 1865 wore a cloth tunic, dark blue in colour and with two tails, grey trousers with scarlet facings and a leather kepi covered in blue cloth with badge and pom pom.

The First World War saw the Italian army begin operations with one hundred and twenty infantry brigades, four hundred thousand infantrymen and as a result of this holocaust the branch was called 'the holy infantry. Of the 125,472 men decorated for bravery, 82,507 were infantrymen, an average of three decorations for every hundred men. The war in fixed positions, the loss of life in the trenches and the attacks with the bayonet all demonstrated the bravery of the infantry. Noteworthy were the 'Death Volunteers', men armed with helmet and cuirass who faced the barbed wire and entrenched fields as pioneers and sappers. At the end of the war the flags of all the regiments were decorated with the Cross of Knights of the Military Order of Savoy. Gold medals were awarded to the following brigades: Tuscany, Avellino, Casals, Sassari, which received two for each regiment, and Lombardy, Liguria, Regina, Ferrara, Pinerolo, Arezzo, Pisa and Aosta. The First World War, as in all the armies, saw the end of brightly coloured uniforms. In the words of D'Annunzio, the foot soldier was 'offered up in grey clothes'. Grey-green became the colour of Italian uniforms.

After the First World War the Italian infantry was at first reduced to fifty-one brigades, then to thirty, each consisting of two regiments. In 1933 an infantry inspectorate was created; some time later several regiments of motorised infantry were formed, anticipating the mechanised warfare of modern times. A new speciality, created in 1936, was the motorised infantry.

Two romantic illustrations of the Italian infantry. Left: The uniform is that of 1908, the first to be made of grey-green cloth. Overleaf: A drawing by Quinto Cenni of officers, non-commissioned officers and soldiers of the 'Cremona' in the uniforms of 1880.

Cenni
1880

The Sons of La Marmora

A
BERSAGLIERE

A bersagliere in the uniform of the years before World War I, in a drawing by the American artist Henry A. Ogden (1856-1936). He made the bersaglieri famous in America as the Black Devils. The bersaglieri had their baptism of fire at Goito, in 1848, during the First War of Italian Independence.

Since the Piedmontese army did not have chasseurs, in 1835 Alessandro Evasio Ferrero, marquis of La Marmora, then regimental captain of the grenadier guards, proposed the creation of a corps of *bersaglieri* (sharpshooters), an infantry group with modern arms to be used in rapid actions. In 1836 La Marmora (as he has come to be known in history) presented to King Charles Albert, Grenadier Sergeant Giuseppe Vayra in the new unit uniform he had designed, and by the decree of 18 June 1836 the new unit of bersaglieri was founded. They wore the classical round hat with a plume of rooster feathers, black for the troops and green for officers, and the uniform was dark blue with crimson frogging and piping, lapels and badges. (La Marmora had wanted them light blue). Insignia and rank badges were made of gold or yellow wool depending on rank.

The modern weapon used by the bersaglieri was a rapid-action needle-gun designed by La Marmora himself. The first official appearance of the bersaglieri was on 1 July 1836. The first company went out that day with La Marmora (then a major) leading them at a rapid pace, new at that time, marked by a lively fanfare on twelve instruments.

In 1848 at Goito, they had their baptism of fire. They crossed the bridge on the Mincio along the parapets, because the arches had collapsed, and demonstra-

ted at once the value of their athletic training. At Governolo the second company performed a dazzling feat. They surprised the enemy troops at the drawbridge on the Mincio and with a great din of trumpet and drum suggesting the presence of a large contingent put the Austrians to flight. Their brilliant achievements resulted in 1849 in their numbers being increased to five battalions. All five took part in that famous Italian expeditionary corps that went to the Crimea in 1855. In the battle of the Chernaya, where victory was due to them, the bersaglieri allowed the Russians to approach extremely close before striking with well aimed rifle fire. In one manoeuvre they gave a demonstration of their training by surrounding the English general leading the manoeuvre before he was aware of what had happened. It was in the Crimea that Alessandro La Marmora, founder of the bersaglieri, met his death.

In 1859, during the second War of Independence, there were already ten bersaglieri battalions. Their finest hour was at Palestron, where they rivalled the Zouaves in daring and bravery.

At the proclamation of the kingdom of Italy, there were twenty-seven, and then thirty-six bersaglieri battalions divided between six regiments. At first successfully employed in putting down the brigands in the southern provinces, it was the bersaglieris' task to face Garibaldi's volunteers at Aspromonte and to wound 'the hero of two worlds'.

In the third War of Independence, in 1866, a seventh regiment was created. In that unfortunate campaign, the bersaglieri distinguished themselves at Borgoforte, a fortified position on the Po, which they occupied after a brilliant attack. And in 1870 their twelfth battalion was the first to enter Rome through the breach of the Porta Pia.

The original thirty-six battalions were later organised into ten and then into twelve regiments. Bersaglieri units took part in the colonial campaigns. An entire battalion was wiped out in the battle of Adua, while in the Libyan campaign, the 11th regiment won glory by resisting overwhelming Turkish forces and repulsing them at the famous battle of Shara Shat. The 3rd, the deciding element in the conquest of Gondar, took part in the Ethiopian campaign of 1935-6.

Bersaglieri of the Italian National Guard in the uniform adopted by the provisional government of Milan in 1849. In the ordinary uniform the plumed hat was replaced by a low cap with visor; the bottom of the trousers had a black leather covering.

The Long Black Feather

A country like Italy, whose land boundary is formed by the most impressive mountain chain in Europe, had to have a special corps to protect it. These were the Alpine troops, a unit 'invented' in 1872 by the Captain of His Majesty, Giuseppe Perrucchetti. At first they were divided beween fifteen companies which were then assigned to the military districts of the various zones. Later they were joined into four battalions, but after only ten years the corps already had six regiments. The uniform was the normal infantry one, but with a truncated cone hat of black felt decorated with an eagle feather for the officers and a crow feather for the men. The first badge they wore was a white star. The eagle badge on the hat came in 1879 and the green insignia in 1883. The present hat, traditional now, was formally established in 1905.

The battalions were named after the mountains and valleys they defended, and the name also indicated the zone in which the men were recruited. In later provisions the *Alpini* were organised in three brigades, with a total of eight regiments, twenty-six battalions and seventy-eight companies. This was their total strength at the outbreak of the First World War, but new territorial battalions were also formed then. The regiments remained only as formal units, while for tactical purposes 'Alpine groups' were formed, each with its own headquarters, gun companies and mountain artillery batteries. In fact, these units corresponded in strength to regiments. They were organised in groups similar to brigades and these, in turn, formed Alpine divisions.

The Alpineers' mountaineering made it possible for them to be assigned to heights that would have been beyond the capabilities of normal infantry troops. The Tonale, the Pasubio, the Cadore and Carnian mountains were garrisoned by Alpineers, who had to defend themselves from avalanches as well as face the enemy, and they had to provision themselves under extremely difficult conditions. They won glory for themselves on Monte Nero, on the Laguzoi, on the Adamello and on the Ortler. In the summer of 1917 they sacrificed themselves in the attempt to open the road to Trent. One Alpine officer, Cesare Battisti, was captured and condemned to death by the Austrians in the counter-offensive of June 1916. After their sacrifices on the Ortigara there followed the days of the twelfth battle of the Isonzo and the disaster at Caporetto. In perfect order the troops withdrew, remaining in column as they marched through their hometown. They fought in the Asiago uplands to defend their homes and succeeded in halting the enemy. The Aosta battalion won a gold medal, twenty-three battalions were awarded a silver medal and three were given a bronze medal. After the First World War the Alpineers were organised in nine regiments with twenty-seven battalions. In 1935 five Alpine divisions with ten regiments were formed.

There were six divisions at the outbreak of the Second World War, and the Alpine divisions took part in operations on all fronts. The Albanian campaign, because of the difficult nature of the terrain and the lack of roads, required extensive use of Alpine troops. Thus the Tridentina, Pusteria, Cuneense and Julia divisions were employed in this region, and the Julia lost almost all its men in the Voyjussa valley. The sacrifice of the Julia inspired one of the most beautiful and saddest of Alpine songs, a song that was born from the suffering and heroism of these mountain troops.

In 1942 one army corps, comprising three divisions (Tridentina, Cuneense and Julia) was sent to Russia. After taking part at Seramivovich in the defence of the right bank of the Don, the Alpineers achieved a remarkable feat at Nicolajevka, where they held off the Russian troops allowing a large contingent of Italians, Germans, Rumanians and Hungarians to withdraw. The Tirano, Edolo and Vestone battalions won particular distinction. After the armistice an Alpine battalion, the Piedmont, was formed in southern Italy which, with the Legnano division, took part in the liberation.

An Alpine soldier with a mule in a French sheet of paper soldiers. Opposite: *Another imaginative French interpretation (signed 'A. Ferdinandus, 1886') of the Italian Alpine uniforms as they were at the end of the 19th century, with the black felt hat that was still in use in the first years of the 20th century.*

The Cayman of the Piave

In 1914, when Italy's entry into the war was imminent, special units had been formed in every infantry regiment for surprise attacks and actions against enemy outposts and behind the enemy's front lines. These were known as 'explorers'. Trench warfare and barbed-wire barriers soon made it necessary to form 'wire-cutting' units. They were organised in small squads with steel helmets and face protectors, a cuirass of small metal plates, boots and knee pads. These units were called 'explorer volunteers'; among the soldiers they were known as 'death companies'.

Later, in 1916, it was decided that soldiers who had distinguished themselves in dangerous missions, like cutting enemy barbed wire or laying explosives, exposing themselves to the enemy trenches and carrying out reconnaissance missions by day or night, should be entitled to a special title, *'militare ardiot'* (bold soldier).

In 1917 the *arditi* were organised into assault units by Major Giuseppe Alberto Bassi, who obtained a special uniform for them. It consisted of an open coat, with black insignia on the turned-down collar, a grey-green pullover (later replaced by a shirt with black tie), a fez like that of the bersaglieri but black, and alpine-style trousers. The equipment was reduced to a total of 15,580 kilogrammes for the infantry. The Arditi, as they liked to be called, carried as personal arms a knife and twelve hand grenades. The haversack was replaced by a knapsack. Among the assault units, one merits particular attention, the so-called 'Caymans of the Piave'.

After Caporetto it was decided to resist at the River Piave, but the problem of communication between the banks immediately arose. Communications were assigned to the Arditi Swimmers under Captain Remo Pontecorvo Bacci. These men were incredibly skilled in silently swimming the icy waters of the river. They were trained to remain up to sixteen consecutive hours in the water, wearing only their helmets and rope belts on which they kept a knife and a waterproof pouch with two hand grenades. The Caymans of the Piave numbered eighty-two in all, selected from four hundred volunteers. Fifty of them died in the river carrying out their captain's orders.

On 15 June 1918, at Zenzon di Piave, Lieutenant Piero Fadigati made two platoons of Arditi *stand at attention for two minutes under Austrian artillery fire in order to avoid disorder in the ranks and delay an attack. The water colour is by Italo Cenni, the son of Quinto.*

The Garibaldini of the Sea

Until the second half of the nineteenth century warships had infantry units aboard for service in close-range naval combat. In the Sardinian army there was a 'Royal Navy' battalion which did the same job, but by the time of the campaign of 1848 this battalion was used on land as a normal infantry unit. The naval infantry - or marines - played an important role in the battle of Lissa in 1866, when the ships were drawn up for close combat. These soldiers wore a plumed hat like the bersaglieri. Naval infantry units also served aboard the *Re d'Italia* and the *Palestro*, the two ships that were sunk in that engagement.

With the later reorganisation of the navy, the infantry units were abolished and 'landing companies' were formed to serve on battleships and cruisers. In actual fact, these units were very often composed of crew members who were armed and used as infantrymen. They were supported by artillery units armed with small, 'landing' cannons (as they were called) with wheeled gun carriages that could be handled and moved by two or three men.

The first time fairly large landing companies were employed was in the Libyan campaign of 1911. On 5 October a company of sailors from the naval division composed of the battleships *Sicilia, Sardegna* and *Umberto I* landed and occupied Fort Sultania in Tripoli. Later in order to occcupy the city and its oasis, some two thousand sailors landed, organised in about ten landing companies with cannon and machine guns.

The company that guarded the wells of Bu Meliana, which provided water for the entire city, was attacked on 19 October. It put up a successful resistance and won the name for all the landing companies of the Garibaldini of the Sea. On 4 October the landing companies of the battleship divisions *Vittorio Emanuele, Regina Elena, Roma* and *Napoli,* together with those from some heavy cruisers, occupied Tobruk and held it until 10 October, when they were replaced by infantry, artillery and engineer units. On 20 October, these same companies together with normal infantry units landed at Benghazi and suffered notable losses. In April 1912, the landing companies served in the Aegean, occupying Stampalia, Leros, and other islands.

The First World War saw few landing actions and those only at the beginning. On 11 July 1915 a small mixed unit, with seven cannons, occupied the island of Pelgosa and held it for about a month and half, but the sailors fought on all fronts as infantry or artillery men. At first it was the survivors of the cruiser *Amalfi* and other ships that had been sunk who joined army infantry and artillery units. Later there were batteries which manned ninety-seven cannons, six of large calibre, as well as twenty-five barges, veritable floating batteries which were armed with cannons of a calibre that exceeded one hundred and fifty millimetres.

The first units of naval infantry were formed in the autumn of 1917 for the defence of Venice. At first these consisted of the Grado and Monfalcone defence units, which constituted the naval battalions Monfalcone, Grado and Caorle. A fourth battalion was later added, composed of volunteers from various maritime stations. These battalions formed the San Marco regiment, one of the most popular in Italy, which was dressed in grey-green uniforms with beaded bands on the trousers. On the blouse cuff the sailors had a red patch with the lion of St Mark embroidered in yellow. The regiment, which numbered one hundred and fifteen officers and two thousand six hundred men, held the Coltellazzo area in November and resisted the enemy attacks on the isle. During the battle of Vittorio Veneto, the San Marco crossed the Piave on 30 November and advanced as far as Cervignano. With demobilisation, the San Marco was reduced to one battalion stationed in Venice. One unit was sent to occupy the Italian concession of Tien Tsi in China.

In the Second World War, the San Marco battalion was transformed into a regiment, the several battalions being named after First World War heroes and the overseas territories.

Above and opposite: two Italian sheets of paper soldiers show the marine infantry in two periods of its history. Above: seamen during the period immediately after Lissa practise pistol fire. Opposite: the 'Garibaldini of the Sea' land in Libya and conquer Tripoli.

Spain

The Alabarderos

The kings of Spain had a halberdier guards corps that served within and without the royal palaces. This force consisted of forty officers and two hundred and fifty men. In the eighteenth century, until the Napoleonic invasion, the Spanish kings had a *Maison du Roi*, units assigned to the king. In addition to the sovereign's adjutants, there were six battalions of Spanish Guards and six of Walloon Guards, a total of six thousand three hundred and sixty men. The alabarderos kept the same uniform from the eighteenth century right up to 1931. It comprised a white jacket with blue tails and red lapels, white trousers, tall black gaiters, silver sword and halberd, and bicorn hat with silver braid. For official functions the kings of Spain also had a royal horse escort dressed in a helmet with spike and a hanging white plume, a blue tail-coat with crimson lapels, skin trousers, high black boots and a metal cuirass.

The halberdiers also escorted the king outside the palace for certain ceremonies, such as the procession of 2 May, when in honour of the men of Madrid who died in the revolt against Napoleon in 1808, the king walked on foot. At one time the halberdiers replaced their two-pointed hat with a tall black fur hat, like the Napoleonic grenadiers', but they eventually returned to their original, eminently Spanish headgear.

When the republic was proclaimed in April 1931, the halberdiers continued to serve at the gates of the royal palace, the East Palace, as well as inside the palace, even after the departure of the king. They stayed in service until the next day, 15 April, when the queen and princes departed, notwithstanding the immense republican demonstration that was being held in front of the palace. The halberdiers were disbanded immediately after the institution of the republic. They were never reorganised and were replaced, in the function of guard and escort to the head of state, first by a Moroccan guard of two hundred men, known as the Moorish Guard, and then by a special unit with colourful uniforms modelled after those of the nineteenth-century dragoons. The members of this unit were known as the Prado Guards, as they guarded the Caudillo's residence, the Prado.

The Spanish army had other regiments with extremely old traditions. In the eighteenth century there were also foreign regiments - two Italian, called the Naples and the Milanese in memory of lost Spanish possessions, three Walloon (Brabant, Brussels and Flanders), three Swiss and three Irish, known as Ireland, Hibernia and Ulster. Several Spanish regiments, including the Lombardy, Galizia, Savoy and La Coruña, were founded in 1537; the Zamora regiment was founded in 1580 and the Soria in 1587.

Above: *A 19th-century Spanish decoration for 'military merit'.*
Opposite: *Halberdiers of Queen Isabella II in a sheet of paper soldiers published in Spain about 1845. Isabella reigned from 1843 to 1868.*

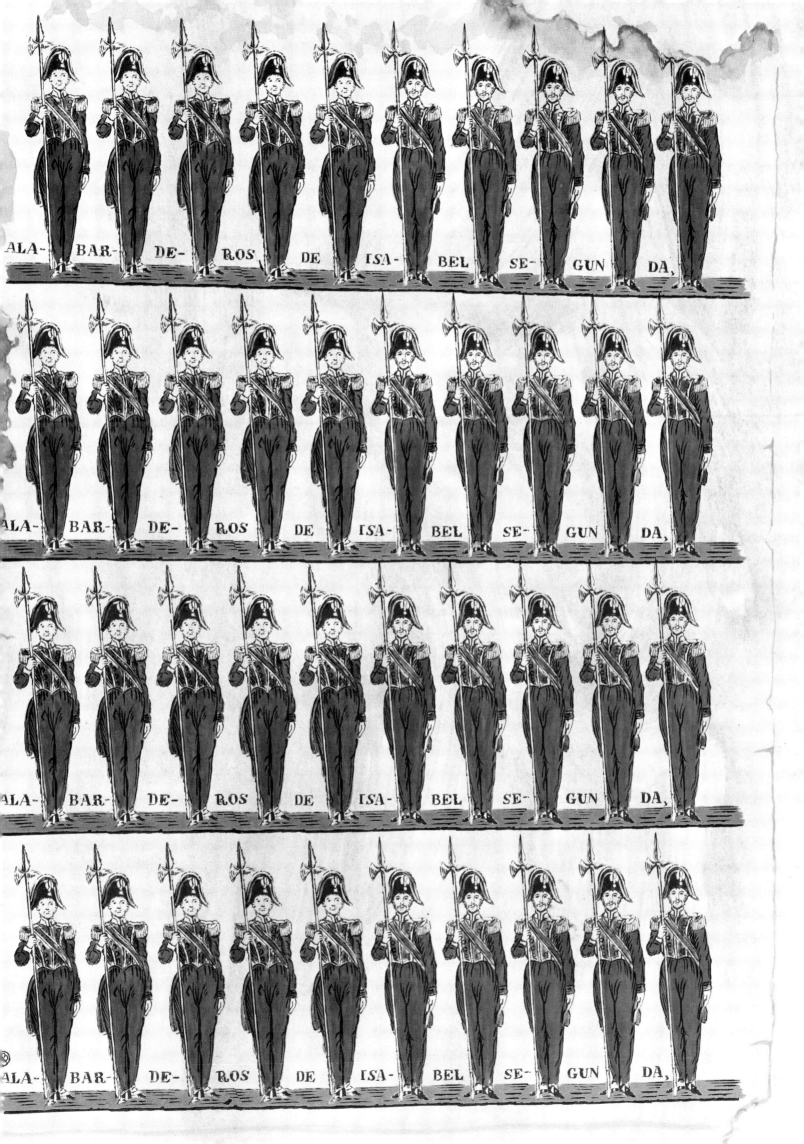

ALA- BAR- DE- ROS DE ISA- BEL SE- GUN DA,

ALA- BAR- DE- ROS DE ISA- BEL SE- GUN DA,

ALA- BAR- DE- ROS DE ISA- BEL SE- GUN DA,

ALA- BAR- DE- ROS DE ISA- BEL SE- GUN DA,

The Civil Guard

The Civil Guard performs the functions of keeping public order in Spain and its dependencies today. Its history goes back to the times of King Alphonso VI of Castille, who in the eleventh century employed the *Hermandades*, or brotherhoods, to defend him from the attacks of unruly nobles and the raids of Moslems and bandits. But the more immediate predecessors of the Civil Guard go back only to the *Santa Hermandad Nueva*, founded by the Catholic Kings, who issued the relevant order in 1476 at Duenas in the province of Valencia. The Santa Hermandad did much for the safety of the road and for the punishment of delinquents, but its functions were limited and many of these were assumed by the *Quadrilleros*. Its political functions were taken over by Municipal Guards, and as the army was used ever more frequently in activities concerned with public order, the Guard was dissolved in 1834.

Its remaining functions were assumed by regional public safety units and by other special corps, which (particularly after the War of Independece and, more notably, after the first Carlist War) turned out to be insufficient for their purposes, both for maintaining public order and combatting banditry. Because of the gravity of the situation, the modern Civil Guard was founded by a decree of 28 March 1844. This decree had several defects, however, for the Guard was dependent on too many higher authorities, there was no commander-in-chief of the entire corps who could function as an intermediary between civil and military authorities, and the pay in the unit was extremely low. To rectify these defects the duke of Ahumada was entrusted with the reorganisation of the corps, and he made provisions that were sanctioned in a decree of 13 May 1844, the real date of the foundation of the corps.

This corps was under the War Ministry in matters of organisation, personnel and discipline, and under the Ministry of the Interior in matters concerned with maintaining public order. The corps was organised in thirteen *tercios*, with thirty-four companies and nine squadrons. There were fourteen commanders, two hundred and thirty-two officers and five thousand seven hundred and sixty-nine men. It was so successful in its functions that the government made provision to increase the number of men to seven thousand, then to eleven thousand and, in 1858, to fifteen thousand, with excellent results in public order. In fact, by about 1870 the traditional banditry in Andalusia had been brought to an end, and soon after the Guardia Civil managed to eliminate the organisation known as the Black Hand, which operated in the province of Jerez. Thanks to the Guardia Civil, the reign of Alphonso XVI and the subsequent regency were marked by remarkable calm throughout Spain.

With the new century, the Guardia Civil found itself faced with political demonstrations on a large scale and in 1909 intervened in defence of established institutions and public order in the famous *Semana tragica* of Barcelona. Under the government of General Primo de Rivera, the corps was increased to twenty-six thousand men, subdivided into twenty-eight *tercios*, sixty-three *commanderias*, one hundred and seventy-four companies, thirty-nine squadrons and 3,134 posts or stations. Of the Guards, twenty-one thousand were foot and five thousand were mounted. Similar duties were performed by other units, such as the Barcelona squadrons, the *miñones* of the provinces of Avila and Biscay, and the *miqueletes* of the province of Guipozcoa, the capital of which is Bilbao.

A sheet of Knötel illustrates the uniforms of the division of the Marquis de la Romana, seen in Hamburg in 1807-08. From left to right: *grenadiers and sappers of the Princess' infantry regiment and an officer and men of the Catalogna Regiment.* Opposite: *uniforms of the mounted* Guardia Civil.

BARCELONA, LIT DE PALUZIE, DIPUTACION, 421

EJERCITO ESPAÑOL. GUARDIA CIVIL.

N.° 238.

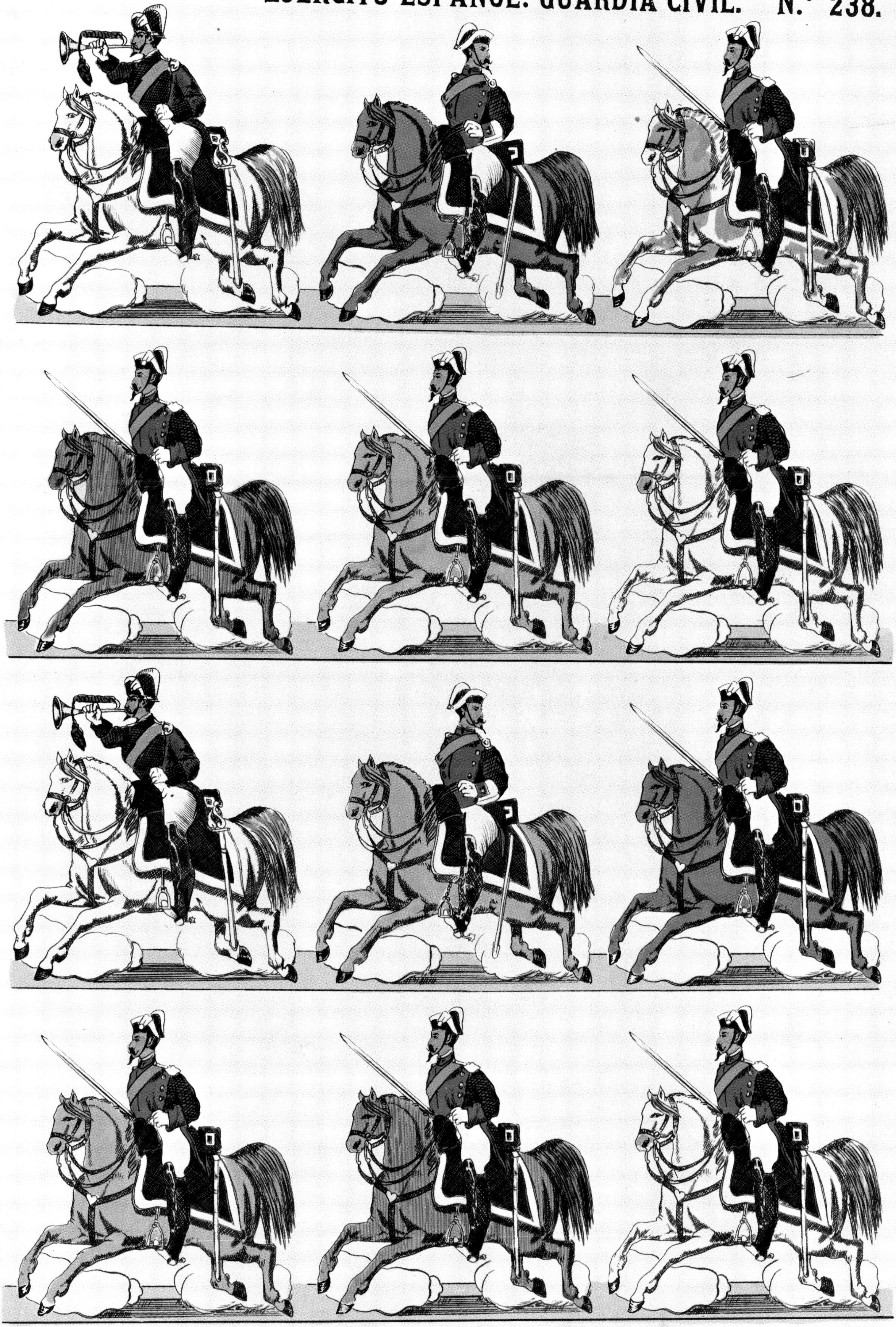

Cavalry and Caçadores

Chasseurs of the Spanish Royal Guard during the first half of the 19th century. The caçadores *were employed overseas; three regiments took part in the war against the United States.*

Although the Spanish infantry won especial fame in the centuries from the Renaissance until the eighteenth century, the cavalry also had regiments which could boast of glorious traditions. The cavalry was founded by King Ferdinand the Catholic, who as soon as he had conquered Granada decided to create a national army to replace the feudal army which had served him in the 'reconquest' of territories held by the Arabs. After the manner of Charles VII of France, Ferdinand at first obliged noblemen who had a certain income to maintain a horse per man. Later, in 1495, he formed twenty-five heavy cavalry companies of one hundred lances each, and seventeen companies of light cavalry called *estradios*. The armament of these men, who owned their own weapons, was extremely varied. Theoretically recruitment was by conscription.

The ordinance of Valladolid of 22 February 1496 provided that among Spaniards between the ages of twenty and forty-five, one man in ten should be enrolled. In the event that a city failed to provide the required contingents, provision would be made for compulsory enrolment. The troops of an army so constituted could not be permanent. In fact they were paid only in the event of mobilisation according to a custom that had been introduced in Spain in the ninth century by the emir of Cordoba, Hakem I. The Spanish cavalry won distinction in all the wars. At Rocroi it was represented by one hundred and twenty-five flags (platoons) of cavalry.

In the eighteenth century Spain had twenty-eight

cavalry regiments, each with its own name, with more than twenty-eight thousand men. The specialities into which it was divided were the line cavalry, which until the late eighteenth century included cuirassiers, carabineers, dragoons, hussars, horse chasseurs and lancers. In the first half of the nineteenth century these specialities were still in existence, and the cuirassiers wore a uniform reminiscent of that of Napoleonic cuirassiers. Likewise the dragoons wore a crested helmet with a flat plume, a coat covered with braid and frogging, white skin trousers and top-boots. In fact the entire Spanish cavalry, whose regiments were all numbered in progression, had particularly elegant and colourful uniforms. The lancers, like the dragoons and cuirassers, had a helmet, while the hussars wore the kolback and the horse chasseurs the shako.

In the course of the nineteenth century several specialities were suppressed. All that remained were the lancers, the dragoons, the horse chasseurs and the hussars. The regiments were numbered from 1 to 8 for the lancers, from 9 to 11 for the dragoons, from 12 to 18 and from 21 to 30 for the chasseurs, the hussars being assigned the numbers 19 and 20 and the titles of Princess' Hussars and Pavia Hussars. These were the most colourful regiments of the Spanish army. The Princess' Regiment wore a light-blue dolman with yellow galloons and fur, and a black fur kolback. The Pavia Hussars had a dolman and white fur with yellow braid. Both regiments wore Hungarian trousers, a badge of the same colour as the dolman and a kolback with a white plume. The lancers kept the spiked helmet with a hanging plume for their dress uniform.

The cavalry units stationed in the American and Asian colonies belonged to the speciality known as *caçadores*. The three regiments 'Fernando Cortes', 'Pizarro' and 'Tacan' were stationed in Cuba. These three regiments took part in the ill-fated campaign against the United States in 1898.

À propos of the caçadores, it is worth mentioning that the Spanish army also had foot chasseurs, organised in eighteen battalions, which had a very long tradition going back to the *Infanteria lijera* of the old kingdom of Spain. Included were several 'volunteer' regiments from the various regions of Spain and a battalion of Caçadores de Barbastro.

Opposite: Spanish mounted artillery uniform of the first half of the 19th century. Note the large trousers and the similarity of the headgear to the busby of the British Royal Horse Artillery. The latter, however, wear the plume on the right. The loose plume was typical of the hussars.

The Papal Forces

The Swiss Guard

Of the existing pontifical armed units, the Swiss Guard can boast the longest history. In fact, as soon as Julius II ascended the papal throne, in 1503, he created a special unit assigned to the protection of the apostolic palaces and the person of the pope. In those days, all European sovereigns recruited their personal guards among the Swiss, and Pope Julius was no exception. On 22 January 1506, a company of one hundred and fifty soldiers, recruited from the canton of Zurich and under the command of Gaspard de Silen, made its entry into Rome. The Swiss Guards, whose numbers were subsequently increased, took part in various battles. They fought with such bravery at Ravenna in 1512 that Pope Julius II called them the 'defenders of the freedom of the Church'. In 1517, during the papacy of Leo X, they faced the forces of Francesco della Rovere, who had formed an alliance with the Spanish but were overwhelmed by the numbers of their adversary. In 1521 Swiss units succeeded in maintaining the pope's sovereignty over the duchies of Parma and Piacenza.

A glorious moment in the history of the Swiss Guards came during the Sack of Rome, when on 6 May 1527 the soldiers of the high constable of Bourbon occupied Rome and the Apostolic Palace. The tenacious resistance of the Swiss Guards before the Church of St Peter's gave Pope Clement VII time to escape along the famous corridor of the Borgo to Castel Sant'Angelo.

The Swiss Guards faced the Spanish again in 1548, and at Lepanto in 1571, a squad of twenty-five guards, sent as a personal escort for John of Austria, succeeded in capturing two enemy centuries but the Swiss Guard saw no war action. Dissolved in 1798, it was reconstituted in 1814 as a unit of about two hundred men. The Swiss Guard arrayed itself to defend the pope once again on 16 December 1848, when the Quirinal Palace was attacked. Dissolved once again on the pope's departure from Rome, the guard was again reconstituted in 1850, when Pius IX returned to the city.

On 20 September 1870 the Swiss Guard, which was part of 'the military household of His Holiness the Pope', remained in the Vatican to guard the outer gates. The Swiss Guard was maintained even after the Church's temporal power had come to an end. It was reorganised in 1914, when Pope Pius X fixed their number at one hundred soldiers and six officers, including the commandant, with the rank of colonel, and the chaplain.

In 1919 the reigning pope, Benedict XV, established the precedence of the Swiss Guard over the Palatine Guard. Nowadays the tasks of the Swiss Guard are the custody of the entrances to the apostolic palaces and of the dividing line of the Vatican City. The Swiss Guard also serve at the pope's residence at Castelgandolfo, and they function as the pope's escort. They serve within the basilicas when the pope is present at functions

Opposite: a popular illustration reproduced about half actual size shows the papal court and the pontifical soldiers before the year 1906. After 1906 the Swiss Guards wore a crested hat instead of the plumed one in which they are shown here.

Corte e Milizie Pontificie (3)

Cour et Milices Pontificales - Pontifical Court and Militia.
Côrte y Milicias Pontificales - Paepstlicher Hofstaat und Heer.

N. 15.

The capotari *or* capotori, *whose uniform is shown here as it was in the early 19th century, were the urban militia of papal Rome. They were founded on 23 June 1580 by Gregory XIII. They wore a gilded helmet, hence their name. During the French occupation they served as Honour Guard to Pius VII. In 1850 they were assimilated into the Palace Guard.*

and also guard the papal antechambers and other areas. The guards must be bachelors and cannot engage in any activities outside the Vatican City. The oath of the guards is renewed every May, in commemoration of their sacrifice in defence of the pope during the Sack of Rome in 1527.

The Swiss Guard is the best known of the armed units that serve the pope, in part because of the uniform which is said to have been designed by Raphael (although that artist only designed the ample sleeve) and by Michelangelo (who in fact had no hand in the design at all). The original uniform of the Swiss Guard is preserved in a miniature which illustrated the manuscript of a poem in honour of Julius II. It consisted of a simple gown over which was worn a greatcoat. It was when the gown was abandoned, in 1548 that the greatcoat acquired its ample sleeve. The uniform was completed by the typical metal helmet over which was placed a cap woven of silk and gold. The cap was the classic headgear throughout the sixteenth century. On ceremonial occasions it was decorated with a metal badge, a plume and embroidery. The officers wore a red uniform, and when on military duty a cuirass like the soldiers'. In the nineteenth century the uniform lost much of its original beauty; it was divided in two parts, the left side yellow, the right blue and black. A casque with a white crested plume like that of the Prussians was adopted. In 1906 the casque was replaced in the dress uniform by the morion with crest. There was then a gradual evolution, until 1914, towards the revival of the traditional uniform.

Nowadays the Swiss Guard has a ceremonial uniform (decked with yellow, red and blue stripes, cuirass, steel helmet, white collar and gloves) a dress uniform (like that for the ceremonial but without cuirass and with a plumed helmet) and a daily uniform. This everyday uniform is striped like the ceremonial one but the helmet is of black aluminium. The fatigue uniform is adorned with a red feather, and this uniform is worn by the guards at some secondary entrances of the Vatican City (dark-blue jerkin, short trousers of the same colour, black stockings and the so-called 'Raphael hat').

The officers' ceremonial uniform consists of a cuirass, red velvet trousers, and a white steel helmet with a white plume for the commandant, red for the other officers. The collar and gloves are white. The dress uniform is that of the sixteenth century, of red and green velvet, with a black plumed helmet and white gloves and collar. The daily uniform consists of a black tailcoat, a pointed hat, a sabre, sash and epaulets. The weapons of the men are the halberd and the broadsword; the officers carry a sabre. In papal processions some non-commissioned officers carry the broadsword with undulating blade, symbolising the loyalty of the Catholic cantons. On night guard, and during the day at the Arco delle Campane, the guards carry a rifle. There are two guard posts. The one inside serves the three sentinels who guard the papal apartments; the one at the

The Swiss Guard at the entrance to the Quirinale Palace, now the residence of the president of the Italian republic. The print is 19th century but earlier than the adoption of the uniform depicted on p. 175, which was yellow on the left and blue and black on the right. Here the colours are those still in use, alternate blue and orange stripes.

Bronze Gate (Portone di Bronzo) provides the guards for the entrances.

When the pope is not in residence, the Swiss Guard serves the cardinal chamberlain, who is responsible for temporal order. The guard has its own flag, a silk banner divided into four fields by a white cross. In two fields appear the coats-of-arms of the founding pope, Julius II, and that of the reigning pontiff. The other two fields bear the guard's colours, one yellow and the other red and blue. At the centre of the cross is the coat-of-arms of the commandant *pro tempore*.

Another famous pontifical unit is the Noble Guard of His Holiness. It was founded by Pius VII by a *motu proprio* of 11 May 1801. It was to replace both the old Knights of the Guard of Our Lord (commonly called the 'Broken Lances') and the papal cavalry, both of which were dissolved with the constitution of the Roman republic in 1798. When Pius VII went into exile, the Noble Guard was imprisoned in Castel Sant'Angelo

by the French. Re-established in 1814, it never took part in combat. On 20 September 1870, when the troops of the Italian army occupied Rome the Noble Guard was assembled in dress uniform in the pope's antechamber. The members of the Noble Guard must have a noble title that goes back at least one hundred years, and they are selected from among the aristocratic families of the former provinces of the papal state. The commandant has the rank of lieutenant-general and is the 'standard-bearer of the Holy Roman Church'. The Noble Guard has the function of 'direct protection of the Sacred Person of His Holiness'. Every day there is a cadet and six guards on duty. Two at a time are assigned to the entry to the throne room and the secret antechamber. The Noble Guard serves to protect the corpse of a dead pope until he is buried. It serves at the opening of conclaves and is at the disposition of the cardinals, in token of the fact that the power of the pope is represented by the princes of the Church.

From Holland to the Balkans

The Mariniers

The Dutch like to trace the origin of their military traditions to ancient times, boasting of the undertakings of the Frisians and the Batavians against the Roman legions, and the feats of Civilis, the Dutch Vercingetorix, against the troops of Vespasian. They commemorate the tenacity with which their civil militias fought for the liberty of their homeland in the Middle Ages, and the long struggle of William (the Silent) of Nassau, count of Orange, against the Spanish, when the Dutch 'beggars' (as they were slightingly termed by a member of the court) held off the imperial troops.

Certainly the Dutch can boast corps and specialities of outstanding military prestige. For example, among landing forces there is no unit in the world older than their mariniers. Their feats go back to the first period of colonial conquest in the far east and America. The mariniers were founded on 10 December 1665. Holland was then at war with England, and although England succeeded in occupying the Dutch colonies of Africa and America, including New Amsterdam (which then became New York), the Dutch fleet under the command of Admiral Van Ruyter resisted the English fleet and maintained its predominance at sea.

The mariniers were always employed in colonial operations. As early as the beginning of the seventeenth century the Dutch had reached Java and by 1602 the Dutch East India Company had been founded. The mariniers had garrisons in the major islands of the Pacific; at the same time they were landing in the West Indies, and succeeded in challenging the Portuguese domination of Brazil.

At the time of the Napoleonic wars Holland was transformed into the Batavian republic, and the mariniers in the distant Dutch colonies were the only troops to represent symbolically the independence of the homeland and avoid Napoleonic domination.

When conditions required it, in more recent times, the mariniers were employed in Europe. In 1935 they were part of the international contingent in the Saar, at the time of the plebescite. At beginning of the Second World War, when Hitler's troops invaded Holland, the mariniers fought in the Rotterdam area and in Zeeland, and the units stationed in the colonies resisted overwhelming Japanese forces. Later, when the German and Japanese defeat seemed imminent, the mariniers, as part of the First Netherlands Brigade organised in Britain, fought on the Rhine front in 1945, while the units in the East Indies were reorganised by the Americans and landed on the islands they had formerly garrisoned and defended.

Nowadays, in addition to garrisoning Dutch possessions in the West Indies, the mariniers also serve in metropolitan units to provide coast guards and are still specially trained for landing operations.

Above: *The crest of the Dutch* mariniers. Opposite: *a recruiting poster of 1900. Various uniforms are shown; left are metropolitan uniforms; right are colonial ones. The* mariniers *of the Netherlands were founded on 10 December 1665.*

KORPS MARINIERS.
VRIJWILLIGE DIENSTNEMING.

Tot nadere aankondiging kunnen bij het Korps Mariniers als Vrijwilliger in dienst treden, op de onderstaande voorwaarden, ongehuwde personen van een goed gedrag, die lust hebben hun land aan den wal en aan boord te dienen, en wat van de wereld willen zien.

HANDGELD.

I. Personen boven de 19 doch beneden de 34 jaren oud, ontvangen een HANDGELD van ƒ150.—

II. Personen boven de 18 doch beneden de 19 jaren oud, ontvangen een HANDGELD van ƒ120.—

III. Jongelingen boven de 16 doch beneden de 18 jaren oud, ontvangen een HANDGELD van ƒ100.—

IV. Personen boven de 34 doch beneden de 40 jaren oud, ontvangen voor ieder jaar, dat tot het volbrengen van het 40e levensjaar nog verloopen moet, 1/8 van ƒ150.— als Handgeld.

Aan ieder aangenomen Marinier wordt verlof toegekend, onmiddellijk nadat hij in Uniform gekleed is, en vóór hij met verlof gaat wordt hem bovengenoemd handgeld ten volle zonder eenige korting uitbetaald.

De duur der verbintenis is:

6 jaren voor personen van 19—40 jaren oud.   10 jaren voor personen van 16—18 jaren oud.
8 „ „ „ „ 18—19 „ „

DE AANBRENGPREMIE bedraagt:
ƒ 20.— voor personen van 19—40 jaren oud.
„ 15.— „ „ „ 18—19 „ „
„ 5.— „ „ „ 16—18 „ „

WAAR MEN ZICH TOT DIENSTNEMING AANMELDT.

Indien er garnizoen in de plaats is, dan kan men zich tot dienstneming aanmelden op het Garnizoensbureau, aan alle Kazernes en bij elk Militair. Indien er geen garnizoen in de plaats is, dan moet men zich naar het Raadhuis begeven, waar men de noodige inlichtingen kan verkrijgen hoe men verder heeft te handelen.

De personen die geneeskundig geschikt zijn bevonden worden op Kosten van het Rijk door de Garnizoens-Commandanten naar Amsterdam gezonden, en keeren insgelijks op 's Rijks kosten terug indien zij aldaar afgekeurd mochten worden.

OVER TE LEGGEN BEWIJSSTUKKEN:

1. Extract Geboorte-register.
2. Bewijs van goed gedrag van af het 12e levensjaar, af te geven door den Burgemeester.
Zij die vroeger gediend hebben, en niet langer dan 3 maanden den dienst verlaten hebben, kunnen in plaats van dit Bewijs hun paspoort vertoonen.
3. Bewijs van voldoening aan de Wet op de Nationale Militie (zoo noodig).
4. Bevolkingskaart.
5. Miliciens met groot verlof, bovendien hun verlofpas.
6. Minderjarigen, bovendien een gelegaliseerd bewijs van toestemming om bij het Korps Mariniers in dienst te treden, afgegeven door dengene die het ouderlijk gezag uitoefent.

N.B. Deze bewijsstukken worden voor den Militairen Dienst ten Raadhuize kosteloos opgemaakt.

De Mariniers zijn in garnizoen te Amsterdam, te Rotterdam of te Willemsoord, (gemeente Helder) en dienen bij afwisseling aan boord van alle soorten van Schepen en Vaartuigen van Oorlog.

Hij die in dienst komt met het ernstige plan om een flink en braaf militair te worden, kan verzekerd zijn dat het hem bij het Korps Mariniers goed zal gaan.

Men komt in dienst als Marinier 3e klasse, en kan bevorderd worden tot Marinier 2e klasse en tot Marinier 1e klasse, indien men geschikt en bekwaam is en zich goed gedraagt. Deze bevorderingen gaan met verhooging van soldij gepaard. Bovendien heeft men de gelegenheid om Korporaal, Sergeant of Fourier, Sergeant-Majoor en Adjudant-Onderofficier te worden.

Na 2 jaren dienst kan men bij goed gedrag een Certificaat krijgen, waaraan het recht verbonden is om op de jas een Koninklijke Kroon te mogen dragen, en waarvoor een geldelijke toelage wordt gegeven. Verder kan men zich toelagen verzekeren door zich te bekwamen in het Schieten zoowel met het geweer als met geschut. Bij verblijf aan boord wordt een hoogere Soldij getrokken, die op nieuw verhoogd wordt wanneer het schip in de overzeesche gewesten verblijf houdt.

Tot belooning van langdurigen trouwen en eerlijken dienst zijn chevrons en medailles ingesteld waaraan geldelijke toelage verbonden zijn, en krijgt men wanneer men blijft doordienen aanspraak op Pensioen.

Nederland.   Oost- en West-Indiën.

LITH. SENEFELDER & Co. AMSTERDAM

Belgian Chasseurs and Carabineers

The kingdom of Belgium came into being in 1830 as a result of the rebellion that separated the Flemish and Walloon provinces from Holland. The king whom Parliament called to ascend the throne in Brussels, Leopold I, of the House of Saxe-Coburg-Gotha, then formed an army that in case of war could be increased to one hundred thousand men and whose first function was the defense of the country's neutrality.

This army was not called upon to fight until 1914. During the Franco-Prussian War of 1870-1, it had been mobilised but none of the combatants violated the frontiers of the small kingdom. Napoleon III preferred to let himself be captured with the army or Marshal MacMahon rather than enter the young kingdom. At that time the Belgian army included four territorial divisions - at Ghent, Mons, Liège and Brussels - with sixteen infantry regiments, of which one was carabineer, two were chasseur, one was grenadier and twelve were regular infantry. The cavalry had seven regiments, of which two were chasseurs, four lancers and one of guides. The artillery consisted of a regiment of horse artillery, two of field artillery and three of fortress artillery. There was also a regiment of engineers.

Later increases brought the number of these territorial divisions to six, stationed around Ghent, Antwerp, Liège, Namur, Mons and Brussels, in addition to two divisions of cavalry in Brussels.

The war formations of these units were, for each division, three or four mixed brigades, consisting of two infantry regiments, a group of three batteries, a company of machine-gunners and a provost platoon, as well as a regiment of field artillery, an engineer battalion and a transport corps. The cavalry division was composed of two brigades, with four horse regiments, a motorcycle battalion, an artillery group and an engineering company.

Belgium also had a special military unit, the Civic Guard, heir to that 'National Guard' which had represented the popular army or 'armed nation' of the nineteenth century. It was composed of all men between the ages of twenty-one and fifty who were not enrolled in the regular army. Its functions were to guard public order and to join in the defence of the country.

In August 1914 all these troops entered the campaign in their vari-coloured peacetime uniforms. The grenadier regiments, picked troops, were stationed at Brussels and had as part of their uniform a tall black hat with a red feather (later replaced by the kepi), blue cape and jacket with scarlet trim, grey trousers with scarlet seams and white accoutrements. King Albert, the 'Cavalier King', was a very tall man and always wore the grenadier uniform.

The line infantry had a similar uniform but wore the shako. The chasseurs and carabineers had a dark-green uniform and grey trousers. They were distinguished by their headgear - a green shako with a small plume of rooster feathers for the chasseurs, and a broad-brimmed hat, with hanging plume like that of the Italian bersaglieri for the carabineers.

The cavalry was distinguished by the colour of the dolman. The guides wore green with a magenta braid, trousers and a kolback with badge, while the lancers and chasseurs had a blue dolman with white or yellow braid and blue trousers with different coloured stripes. The lancers wore a czapka and the chasseurs the shako. The artillery had a blue jacket with grey trousers and scarlet stripes, the engineers an all-blue uniform.

Left: *A Flemish horse chasseur in an old wood engraving* Opposite: *Foot chasseurs and carabineers of the Belgian army in a print of Pellerin d'Epinal. Notice the carabineers headgear. Its form is similar to that of the Tyrolean chasseurs. The feather is similar to that of the Italian bersaglieri.*

LLERIN & Cⁱᵉ, imp.-édit. (Armée Belge) **CHASSEURS A PIED** IMAGERIE D'EPINAL, Nᵒ 526

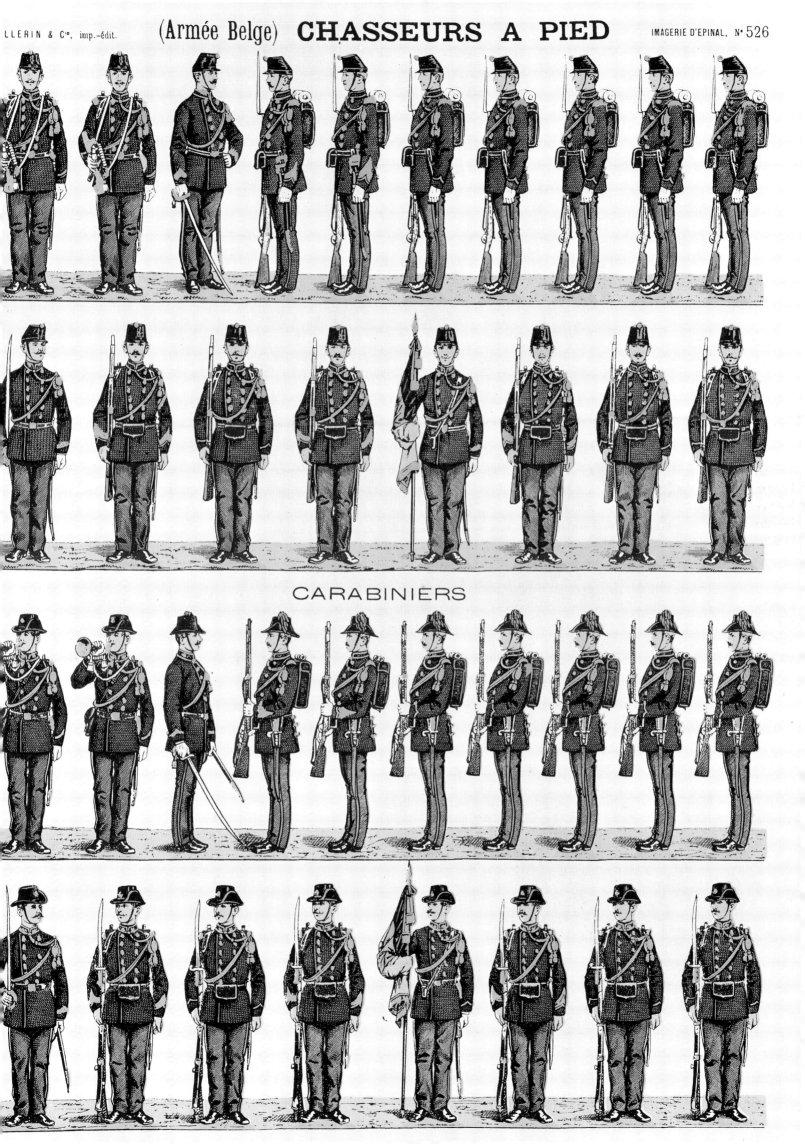

CARABINIERS

The Danish Guard

Private of the Royal Foot Guard of Denmark, from a sheet published by Jacobsen of Copenhagen. The bearskin hat has been in use since 1805. The red uniform is worn three times a year, on the King's birthday, the Queen's, and at New Year. On duty at the royal palace the Guard wears the field uniform of 1848. The normal uniform is khaki.

Every day the streets of Copenhagen enjoy the colourful spectacle of the Life Guards regiment marching to the Amalienborg Palace, the residence of the sovereigns, for the changing of the guard. This is the fourth of the Foot-Guard Regiments (twelve in all) of Denmark and the most popular among the Danes for its unchallenged tradition of valour.

A deep sense of fellow feeling unites those passersby who once served in the regiment. It was founded by Frederick III on 30 June 1958 with the name of Horse Guards. It was created as the sovereign's personal guard, to protect the crown against any attacks by the nobility, restless and uneasy because what had been an elective monarchy was now hereditary and absolute. Originally the Guards consisted of a detachment of five hundred men, foot and horse, who every day mounted the guard at the palace, at the city gates and at the residences of ministers and ambassadors. In 1684 the unit's name was changed from 'Body Guards' to 'Regiment of Foot Guards', and the king himself became its commandant. This name remained in use until 1867, when during the general reorganisation of the army after the War of the Duchies it took the simpler name of Guard Regiment. The loyalty of the guards never had occasion to be put to the test by any threat to the king's person until 1940, when after the German attack a detachment fought to defend the royal castle of Amalienborg.

But the corps had several occasions to fight against foreign enemies: against the Swedish armies during the first and second wars of the North, against the English in 1801 and 1807, against the Prussians in 1848-50 and in 1864. It always defended the honour of the nation and the sovereign, living up to its motto, *Pro Patria et Rege*. Famous dates and names of battles are recorded on ribbons on the regimental flags. The Guards also fought as mercenaries on the side of the English and William of Orange against James II. That was in 1692 in Flanders, during the War of the League of Augsburg. And they fought with the English under the command of Marlborough during the War of the Spanish Succession. More recently, in 1943, when the Germans decided to dissolve the Danish army, the Guard Regiment, barricaded in their barracks, resisted for several hours until they were overcome.

After the dissolution of the army, members of the Guards kept in contact and took an active part in the resistance until the end of the war.

An old discharge certificate of the Danish Life Guards, showing the evolution of the uniform from 1750 to 1894. In the centre, the standard bearer carries the colour with the royal crest, later replaced by the regimental colours. Together with its brother regiment of the Guard, namely the Royal Hussars, the Foot Guards wore the sovereign's initials on their uniforms. They had their baptism of fire almost as soon as they were formed, against the Swedish troops of Charles X who tried to take Copenhagen in 1658-59. They took part in many battles. There were two honorary colonels, King Charles XV and Tsar Alexander II of Russia. Preference among recruits is given to those whose ancestors have served in the regiment. The regiment's motto is Pro Patria et Rege.

The Swedes in Yellow

At Lützen in 1632, fighting against Wallenstein during the Thirty Years War, a great king died, Gustavus Adolphus of Sweden, the 'Lion of the North'.

A student of the great warriors of antiquity - Alexander, Hannibal and Caesar - he applied their methods and strategy and adapted them to his own campaigns.

A hardy and well-trained army, equipped with conventional weapons, was all he needed to face his many enemies - Danes, Poles and Germans - enemies he made chiefly through his expansionist policies.

Thus Gustavus Adolphus enrolled, in addition to mercenaries, the best Swedish subjects, rigorously selected, and achieved a highly efficient national infantry. Moreover, he reduced the size of the regiment from three to one thousand. This provision proved highly successful on the battlefield. Subsequently he lightened the armament and the army achieved a high degree of rapidity in manoeuvres. The pike was shortened and the musket was so lightened that it could be fired without a support. The artillery armament was also lightened and the cannons were mounted on wheels so that they could be drawn by two horses.

The cavalry was not neglected by Gustavus Adolphus, who made marvellous use of this branch against the imperial forces at the battle of Breitenfeld. But it was the unit created *ex novo* which may have been the dearest to the king's heart, because of the courage, tenacity and discipline it displayed. This was the Yellow Regiment, so called because yellow was the distinctive colour of the regimental uniform.

These had been called Royal Guards since their foundation in 1612 and wore a grenadier uniform consisting of blue coat and trousers with bright yellow collar, cuffs and lapels. They wore a yellow metal mitre-shaped hat from which hung a blue cloth pouch. Later the jacket became yellow and the mitre was replaced by a spiked helmet. Yellow was extensively used for certain badges and accessories of the Swedish uniform. It was the colour of the shoulder straps of fifteen of the twenty-six infantry regiments of the nineteenth century, and a pelisse of that colour was worn by the three hussar regiments, the Shonische Husaren, the Smålands Husarer and the Kronprinzen Husaren.

But to turn back to the 'Royal Guard', it should be noted that the regiment originally consisted of four companies of three hundred men each. In each company, thirty 'nobles' had the special task of mounting the king's guard. Later the regiment was composed of thirty companies of twenty-five men each.

The men of the Yellow Regiment fought for Gustavus Adolphus against Russia from 1613 to 1627, against the Poles in 1628 and against the imperial forces in the Thirty Years War. It was during this war that, as we noted above, Gustavus Adolphus was killed leading his cavalry at Lützen.

The king's direct opponent, the imperial general Pappenheim, was also killed in the engagement. The Swedish troops won, and the Yellow Regiment won distinction for the firmness with which it resisted the enemy. After the king's death, the Yellow Regiment continued to win distinction under the command of other generals in other battles, and particularly in the war with Denmark from 1655 to 1679. Later, during the reign of Charles XII, when the Danes, Poles and Russians formed a coalition against Sweden, the Yellow Regiment continued to fight courageously and take part in all the battles until the disastrous end of that war. At the battle of Narva and at the battle of Poltava, in July 1709, and at the siege of Freichshall in 1718 the regiment performed valourous service. Many years later, in 1788, it was employed in the war against Finland and in 1808 against the Russians. In the Napoleonic period Sweden took up arms against the emperor.

The Yellow Regiment took part in the 1813 campaign, facing Napoleon's army in Denmark and in France. It fought at Leipzig, under the command of Bernadotte.

THE "YELLOW" REGIMENT 1700

The mitred hat and the large grenadier cartridge bag were characteristic of the uniform of the Swedish Royal Guards. They were known as the 'Boys of the Yellow Regiment' because of the bright yellow facings of their blue tunics.

A Swedish general in parade uniform, first half of 19th century. In Sweden, too, the tall hat was characteristic of the hussars; the Swedes had three famous regiments of this type of cavalry. The most famous was that of the Smålands Husarer, founded in 1543. Its men came from the cantons of Kalmar and Kronberg. In 1801 they took on the title of Smålands lätta dragoner. In 1812 they were divided into two regiments, one of foot and one of horse.

Polish Halberds and Wings

A Polish uhlan of the Napoleonic period. Among Polish regiments in Napoleon's service, often mentioned for their valour, the Vistula Lancers were particularly noteworthy.

Among the various political and territorial changes effected by the congress of Vienna, one of the most important was the assignment to the Russian empire of much of Poland. Although Poland was granted a formal independence, it was actually held in complete subjection by Russia.

Thus in the period that followed the decisions of the congress, revolutionary movements were fermenting in Poland. The people wanted independence and the memory of the Napoleonic campaigns was still very much alive in many officers of the national army. It was within the Napoleonic army that the Poles created one of the finest cavalry specialities of all times: the light cavalry lancers. This corps consisted entirely of volunteers and were often referred to as 'explorer regiments'. Their uniform was extremely colourful.

The Polish cavalry always had outstanding traditions concerning their spectacular uniforms. Suffice it to mention the large feather-crested helmets worn by the famous hussars and other seventeenth-century units. The modern Polish army was born of the 1830 revolt when the National Guard was founded. It was designed to form the backbone of the army. Its uniform comprised a jacket with rows of white buttons, red collar and cuffs, dark-blue trousers and black accoutrements.

In Sandomir a corps of francs-tireurs was created bearing the city's name. They wore a fur hat with a

white eagle as ornament and a chinstrap of golden scales. They wore a green coat reaching to the knees, with black collar and cuffs and a red breastpiece; the trousers were green with red bands. They wore two pistols and a knife at the waist and a Circassian cartridge belt was worn across the chest.

There was another unit of the same type: the Podlasia francs-tireurs created by Colonel Kuzzell. They wore a green truncated - cone kepi trimmed in front with the characteristic skull and crossbones. The kepi was topped by a green and red plume. The long grey coat had green collar and cuffs; the grey trousers had green band. These soldiers were also armed with knives.

The Scythe-Bearers, a select unit formed in Kraków, were so called because of the long lance they bore, which ended in the shape of a scythe. They wore a long blue coat with carmine collar and lapels, false Tartar pockets on the chest, light blue trousers and black accoutrements.

There were also the free uhlans of Kalis, a cavalry unit which had a black uniform with blue lapels and stripes. Their headgear was the typical Polish czapka, the upper part of which was light blue. They bore lances with carmine and blue pennants.

All these units, together with their varied colourful uniforms, disappeared with the defeat and disbanding of the Polish national army. Subsequently various units were incorporated into Russian regiments.

The severe Russian repression of the revolution did not however extinguish the patriotic ardour of the Poles, who after a long period of waiting and conspiring rose up again in 1862 and fought for two years. The Russian strategy this time was to firmly occupy some of the larger cities with light columns of infantry, dragoons, Cossacks and artillery. On this occasion the Polish units were improvised, and ranks were granted to those who, like Miniewski, could advance the funds to equip and pay the soldiers.

It was under the command of Miniewski that the Italian Francesco Nullo, formerly an alpine chasseur, fought. Naturally a revolution was not a propitious time to reorganise an army and standardise its uniforms. This time, too, there was great variety in the kinds of units that were engaged.

Francesco Nullo had under his command a unit composed of Italians and Frenchmen who wore the red shirt of Garibaldi; he called them the 'foreign legion'.

Opposite: A 19th-century French print shows the Death Zouaves, with the cross on the chest, and the Scythe-Bearers, two famous military units. The Zouaves served under the Garibaldine Francesco Nullo in a unit that he formed with a varied group of recruits.

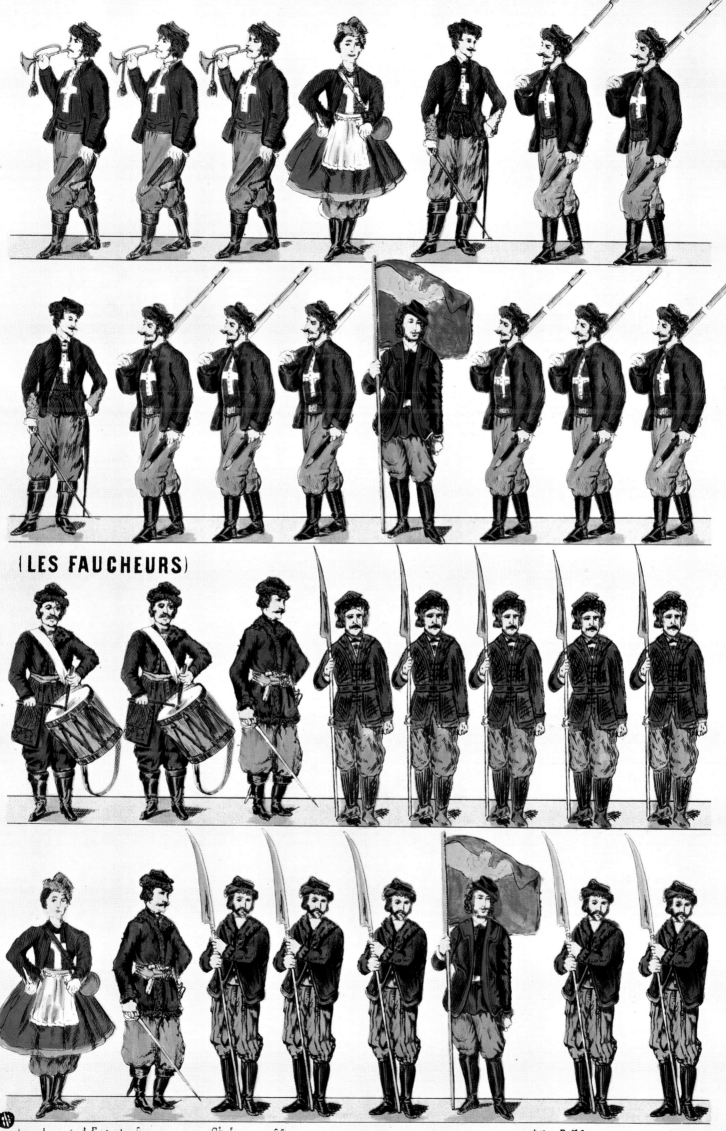

(LES FAUCHEURS)

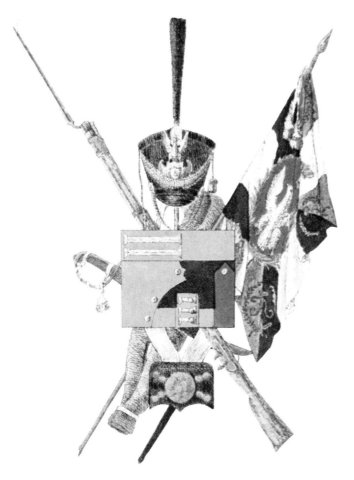

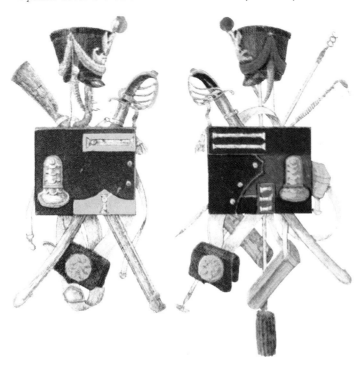

Symbols, weapons, trophies, and details of the uniforms of several Polish units of the early 19th century. The central squares show the colours and ornaments of the uniforms.

About five hundred Poles were placed under his command and he formed several companies of chasseurs and Death Zouaves. The latter were not successful. During a reconnaissance mission the unit was lost and only one Zouave returned. Nullo admitted him to his 'foreign legion'. The reconstituted battalions of scythe-bearers distinguished themselves, but the second Polish revolution failed.

A Polish winged lancer in a plate in Ludovic Menin's history of costume. It is a 19th-century interpretation of horsemen depicted in low relief in Kraków Cathedral. The winged hussars constituted the heavy cavalry that Jan III Sobieski, King of Poland, sent to help the Austrian army in 1683, at the time of his alliance with the Habsburgs against the Turks. The 'winged hussars', so called for the attachments on their backs, wore the helmets and cuirasses and were armed with lances, axes, swords and pistols. They wore large fur cloaks.

The Balkan Armies

AN EVZONE

The evzones wear a uniform inspired by the costumes of the mountain people of Epirus. The pleated skirt is characteristic. The officers' dress uniform includes red embroidered hose and they carry a curved sabre. Besides this traditional uniform, the evzones have three other uniforms.

It is not only among the armies of small countries with long traditions - countries like Holland, Belgium and Denmark - that one can find special corps which represent the pride and are to a certain extent the symbol of the armies themselves. One can find them as well in the armies of countries whose autonomy and independence are recent achievements.

For example, there are the Greek *Evzones*, the only soldiers in Europe (except the Scots) who wear a skirt as part of their official uniform. Recruited in the mountainous region of Epirus and outstanding in all the wars which that small Balkan country has fought in its struggle for independence, the Evzones can be said to have been born with the Greek army in the 1821 revolution against the Turks. In 1855 the Evzones already constituted about half the entire Greek infantry. Later they became picked units, rigorously and distinguished from other units of the army by their strong physique and typical uniform, inspired by the costume of Greek mountaineers.

In addition to their white wool skirt or kilt and the long woollen leg-guards, also white in colour, the Evzone uniform consists of a blue embroidered jerkin (called a *phermeli*) and a red fez (the *pharion*).

Six battalions of Evzones took part in the Balkan War of 1912-3, fighting valourously at the conquest of Salonika. Organised in regiments and divisions, the Evzones took part in the two world wars. Now there is only one regiment in service as a royal guard assigned to the royal palace in Athens and to the royal summer residence in Corfu.

On the borders of Greece, Yugoslavia comprises those populations of Slavic origin which, except for the small kingdom of Serbia, were under Habsburg or Turkish domination until the First World War. Noteworthy among the units of the monarchical period were the 'Royal Guard', composed exclusively of Serbian elements. It was organised in a large military unit the size of a division and included an infantry regiment, two cavalry regiments, an artillery regiment and an engineer unit. It did not have a special uniform but was considered a select unit as well as a prestigious group.

Special units of the Yugoslav army were the Border Guards. They were armed in the same manner as the infantry, and they wore the infantry uniform, but their hat was distinguished from that common to other units of the army by a black leather visor. The Border Guards too, were a special unit of the Rumanian army but their functions were more specifically those of customs guards and, in fact, they were under the administration of the Finance Ministry, though their enrolment was supervised by the War Ministry. Because of the extent of Rumania's border and the threat of neighbouring states, by 1933 the Border Guards had reached a total strength of twenty-five thousand men.

Named after Michael the Brave, the hero of the struggle against the Turks, was a regiment of the Royal Guard. It was created by King Karol, and its original nucleus was provided by the royal escort regiment and the chasseur brigade. Later other units were added to the Royal Guard, among others four battalions of Border Guards.

Noteworthy in the Rumanian army are the Mountain Chasseurs, alpine units recruited in the Transylvanian Alps. In the period preceding the First World War, the mountain chasseurs consisted of a few battalions assigned to the divisions stationed along the Austro-Hungarian border. After the war they constituted an entire army corps garrisoned in Transylvania.

Opposite: *A Morlacco from Zara, Dalmatia that belonged to one of the famous bands that served in the armies of the Venetian Republic and the Austrian Empire at the time of the struggles against the Turkish Empire. Croatia contributed similar troops, the Panduri, which were organised in a regiment in 1741. They were famous for their cruelty.*

Abbildung eines in das Feld gehenden und mit Waffen wohl versehenen
Morlacken oder Dalmatiners.

Deren Feld-Music Bestehet in einer türckischen Schalmey und einer messingenen Trommel, welche oben mit einem
Schlegel und unten mit einem Riegel gespielet wird.

Uns hat die Meeres Fluth an teutsche Gräntz getragen,   Ein scharffer Säbel muß das Leben uns beschützen,
    Wir seynd von rauher Art, genüssen grobe Speiß,   drey oder vier Gefchoß, die tragen wir am Leib,
Den Knoblauch lieben wir, der Zwibel stärckt den Magen,   darzu ein lange Flinth, die auf den Feind thut blitzen,
    Ein rauh Stück Brodt und Saltz behält bey uns den Preiß.   Das Fechten in dem Feld ist unser Heil-Vertreib.

C. P. S. H. S. V. Vicarius. a. C. P. S. V.   Elias Bäck s. H. sculps. et ex. A.V.

PART FOUR

Beyond
Europe's Frontiers

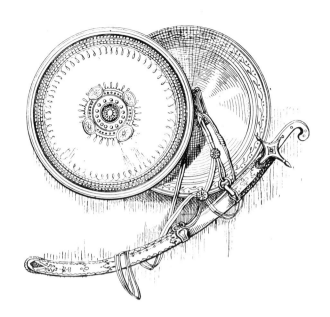

Asia, Africa and Oceania

The Janizaries

The famous chosen corps of the Turkish army, the janizaries, was originally formed of Christian slaves or, more precisely, of men captured in infancy during Turkish raids on the coasts of Christian countries and raised as Moslems.

Janizary, from the Turkish *yeñicheri*, means 'new troops'. The unit was created in 1632 by Sultan Murad I. Legend would have it that these troops were blessed by the Moslem holy man Hadji Bektashi. In reality there were close relations between the janizaries and the Bektashi dervishes, which had been founded by the holy man. In fact, when a new chief of the dervishes was elected, he went first to the headquarters of the janizaries and then to the grand vizier for 'recognition'.

The janizaries were foot troops and had garrisons in Constantinople and other cities of the empire. The entire corps was divided into four troops - one would call them divisions today - called *jema'at, bölük, segban* and *adjemi oghlan*. These in turn were divided into *orta*, or regiments, of varying strength. At the end of the seventeenth century the janizary corps consisted of about two hundred *orta* of two hundred men each. The orta were divided into *oda* or companies commanded by an officer.

At the time of Suleiman the Magnificent there were seventy-seven orta garrisoned in Constantinople, about one-third of the entire janizary force. They were housed in four large barracks and provided the guard for the sultan's palaces, embassies and government offices. Each orta had a number and a name, e.g., Zaghar-gi, Turnagi, Solaq and others. The Solaq were the sultan's personal escort. Each orta had its own flag with special badges and insignia. The janizaries wore a cloth uniform and a white woollen hat, and were armed with lance, sabre, hatchet and harquebus. They had a strange set of customs. The symbol of their solidarity and fraternity were the cauldrons (*Kazan*) in which their mess was cooked. They would overturn the cauldrons in protest when dissastified with their leaders. Selim II, who reigned from 1788 to 1807, tried to do away the janizaries, whose lack or discipline made them a constant danger, and created an infantry trained in the European fashion. But the janizaries, backed by the Bektashi confraternity, declared that the creation of such a unit was a violation of the laws of Islam.

An officer of the Janizaries, the most famous Turkish military unit. They were suppressed by Mahmud II in 1826 after five centuries of history marked by periods of glory and others of abuse and excess. Two energetic reorganisers of the Janizaries were the Viziers Mehemet and Ahmet Köprülü, father and son, under whose leadership the Turks reached Vienna (1683).

Turkish soldiers of the 17th and first half of the 18th century, of whom Raimondo Montecuccoli said: 'They are extremely obedient in the observation of their laws, in silence, in prayer in respect for their officers, and in their promptness to execute commands. I have seen them hurl themselves over into a river with sabres between their teeth in the attempt to swim across.'

The Wolves of Asia

It seems that one can trace the origin of the Ottoman cavalry to the passion for horses that marked the inhabitants of the Arab countries occupied by the Turks. The sultans took advantage of this predilection to form those skilled and hardy cavalry units which played such an important role in the Moslem adventure. It was horse troops, in fact, that fro mthe fourteenth century on, traversed the whole of the Balkan peninsula, first conquering Bulgaria and Macedonia, then Bosnia, Serbia and the Morea, carrying their terror to the very gates of Vienna. Nevertheless, despite their numbers and efficacy, the Turkish cavalry never matched such other mounted units as the Cossacks, for example, with which they were often compared.

It is interesting to note that although the Ottoman empire, at least until 1914, could boast some two million horses in its territory, it still often turned to foreign markets for horses for its cavalry and artillery.

As for the organisation of the Turkish cavalry, there were, in addition to the regular units, *spahis* as early as the seventeenth century. They were armed with the sabre, lance and musket and were distinguished by their yellow or red standards. There were also many special corps with typical costumes and names, most of which were of Kurd or Tartar origin.

The *djellis*, for example, were all volunteers assigned to guard the government and provincial governors. *Djellis* means 'crazy heads', and these horsemen lived up to their name. Their bizarre uniform included eagle feathers on the hat and panther skins for the pelisse. They wore pointed yellow boots with very long spurs and were armed with lance and shield. Another formation was that of the *Sieghans*, who resembled eighteenth-century dragoons. They were assigned to escort the army baggage and fought on foot. Then there were the *Acanzi*, armed with scimitar and bow, and the so-called 'Little Tartars', who were skilled bowmen. These units were chiefly employed by the Turks in reconnaissance and advance guard actions.

In the first decades of the nineteenth century, or, more exactly, after 1826, the year of the massacre of the Janizaries, the sultans decided to give the Ottoman army an organisation and dress that were more European. After this first reform the cavalry wore the typical red or yellow fez, green jackets with red or white braid, blue trousers and a red belt.

At the end of the century the jacket was replaced by a blue *attila* with black braiding, and the tall narrow fur hat known as the *talpac* came into use. There were twenty-four regiments at the time, and two of them were garrisoned at Constantinople. Nevertheless, notwithstanding the reforms in structure and the formal reorganisation of the army, there survived, alongside the regular cavalry, irregular units such as the Humidie Cavalry, consisting of twenty-four regiments 'from the tribes', the warlike eastern Kurd tribes. These men stayed at home looking after their own affairs, but between the ages of eighteen and forty-five they were obliged to present themselves at base as soon as they were called up, fully equipped with arms and horse and wearing the traditional tribal costume. Their commanders, however, belonged to the regular army.

There were also units mounted on camels, stationed in the hegiaz, and - perhaps unique in the history of the cavalry - units mounted on mules.

Late 18th-century Turkish lancer. Opposite, above: *a mounted bashibazouk;* below: *Circassian cavalry. The bashibazouks (crazy heads, in Turkish) were volunteer troops of the second half of the 18th Century. Italy also employed them in the Eritrean Campaign (1885-1888).*

Türkische Cavallerie (Baschi-Bozuks.)

Türkische Cavallerie (Tscherkessen.)

Turcos and Spahis

A local turco *lieutenant. The simulated red pocket known as the tombeau, indicates that he belonged to the first of four* turco *regiments. The tombeau was white for the 2nd Regiment, yellow for the 3rd, and the same colour as the tunic for the 4th.*

There were two colonial specialities integrated into the French army in North Africa: the Turcos and the Spahis. The former were infantry and the latter cavalry.

The name of Turcos was given in honour of the formal sovereignty which the Sublime Porte of the Turks exercised in Algeria even after the French occupation. Later, however, the official name of that unit of local infantry was changed to Algerian Tirailleurs. They were brought to Europe at the outbreak of the First World War, and were present at the battle of the Marne. Later they were incorporated into the metropolitan French army, eleven regiments being permanently garrisoned in France. The colourful uniform, with the beautiful blue bodice and the large white trousers gave way to khaki, and the customs and traditions of these units, by now Europeanised, preserved nothing of their colonial origin.

Employed in all the campaigns of France, the Turcos took part in the second war of Italian independence,

fighting at Magenta and Solferino side by side with the bersaglieri, who had been their brothers-in-arms in the Russo-Turkish war in the Crimea.

In the Second World War France made extensive use of colonial troops, although it would be more precise to say North African troops, for Algeria and Tunisia were considered metropolitan territories. Many of these tireur regiments fought in Corsica and in Italy with the American and British forces as well as in North Africa. The Spahis were originally part of mixed squadrons of forty Arab light cavalrymen and forty French. Later, by 1841, entirely local units were formed alongside regiments of African chasseurs, as the French cavalry units stationed in Africa were called.

An Italian, Giuseppe Vantini played a singularly important role in the formation and development of this colonial cavalry unit. A native of the island of Elba who was captured by Barbary pirates and taken to Tunis, Vantini entered the good graces of the Bey and because of his exceptional talents was made commander of the first Spahi units. He served thirty-four years in the army with the name of Yusuf and reached the rank of division general. With his Spahis he took part in the conquest and pacification of Algeria. The uniform and arms of the Spahis represented a mixture of Arab and European elements: a fez, a cloak, red on one side and white on the other, a red jacket, full blue trousers, short boots, an Arab rifle and a sabre.

During the First World War the Spahis adopted for the French front the typical combat technique used in the desert. They made their horses lie down and fired from behind their crouching bodies. The Spahis, like the Algerian tireurs, were part of the metropolitan French army. Two regiments were garrisoned in France, two were part of the Rhine Army and one was stationed in the east.

The Spahis were engaged in the Second World War and assigned to motorised units. They fought in North Africa, Italy, France and Germany. The last regiment of Moroccan Spahis was dissolved in 1965.

The French spahis *in a Thomas and Roy sheet, Metz. The* spahis, *like the* zaptié, *were typical Turkish cavalry. The Italian army also had such units among its colonial troops. They were called the 'desert knights', and were first organised in bands named after their commanding lieutenant.*

Metz. Imprimerie et Fabrique d'images de THOMAS et ROY.

From the Mamelukes to the Zouaves

The horse chasseur regiment of the Imperial Guard, Napoleon I's personal guard, was headed in reviews and parades by an extremely colourful unit. This was the Mameluke unit which Napoleon brought to France after the battle of the Pyramids.

Their uniform was extremely picturesque: large scarlet trousers which hung down over yellow leather boots and a short green, blue or yellow jacket. The Mamelukes wore a blue turban with a scarlet top and a black and white plume. Stuck into the narrow striped belt were the ivory and silver handles of pistols and knives. Their weapons also included the scimitar and a blunderbuss. The unit was preceded by its own insignia: a horse's tail set on a pole and topped by a copper ball and the half moon.

The Mamelukes paraded on magnificent Arab horses and were dazzling riders. They could trot and gallop in large groups and still bring their horse suddenly to a halt on all four hooves.

The Mamelukes were originally a mercenary troop of Turkish slaves (*mamàlik* in Arabic means 'slaves'), but as early as the thirteenth century they formed a genuine military caste. In 1217 they overthrew the Ayubbid dynasty, despite the fact that it had been

Napoleon's 'personal' Mameluke, the 'faithful' Roustam, in a drawing by Caran d'Ache. He disappeared as soon as the Emperor signed the Act of Abdication. He reappeared during the Restoration with a libellous publication of alleged memoires. On 2 December 1840 he tried to join the veterans honouring the Emperor's ashes but was forcibly driven away.

a member of that dynasty who had made the Mamelukes his personal guard. Meanwhile the original Turkish nucleus was augmented by heterogeneous elements, including Christian slaves and renegades and many Mongols. Because of their arrogant power and their political interference, they continued for centuries to exercise great influence in the life of Egypt, for they constituted almost the entire effective army. Thus Napoleon faced them in 1798 'in the shadow of the Pyramids' and soundly defeated them at that battle.

The emperor took about thirty of them back with him as a souvenir, but this first nucleus grew, until by 1813 it numbered two hundred and fifty men. Naturally, they could not be recruited in Egypt, so the new elements were for the most part hussars. The Mamelukes who remained in Egypt were exterminated in 1811 by the Turkish viceroy Mohammed Ali.

Of a different order was a unit of the French army created in Algeria in 1831 by General Clauzel - the Zouaves. They were first organised as overseas troops, but - as was the case with the Turcos as well - they were incorporated in the metropolitan French army when the local units were organised independently. The Zouaves in the French army were organised in battalions of four companies, three Algerian and one French.

At the beginning of the Second Empire they constituted three regiments. A guard regiment was added later, when the Imperial Guard was re-created.

The Zouaves were much liked and admired, and not only among the French, because of their dazzling uniform (red fez, open blue jacket with jonquil-yellow braids, blue waistcoat, red trousers and white leggings) and their valour in war. They took part in the Crimean campaign, rivalling the Italian bersaglieri in valour, and they fought in the Italian campaign of 1859. At Palestro, the 3rd regiment won a gold medal, and all the officers were decorated with the Military Order of Savoy. The Zouaves in turn, as if in exchange for this recognition, asked that Victor Emmanuel II, who had been among them during the battle, accept the rank of honour corporal and one of their uniforms. During the First World War, when it seemed that the German troops would reach Paris a brigade of Zouaves was employed by General Gallieni as a mobile reserve. They were launched against the German flank, and all the taxis in Paris were mobilised for their transport. This episode has become famous as the 'march of the taxis'.

In 1865, when the French troops abandoned the territory of the papal states, after the 'Convention of September', many French and Belgian volunteers, formed a battalion (later a regiment) to defend the pope.

The original two battalions of indigenous soldiers that comprised the Zouaves were soon replaced by wholly metropolitan units. As in the case of the turcos, the colour of the tombeau, the simulated pocket on the side of the 'tunic' served to distinguish the various Zouave regiments. The Royal Armoury in Turin preserves an honourary colonel's uniform of the 3rd Zouave Regiment. It was given to Victor Emmanuel II by Napoleon III after the second day of the Battle of Palestro (31 May 1859), when the King leapt to the head of the regiment which hesitated before fording the Sesietta. The popularity of the Zouaves was such that regiments of this type were also formed in the United States during the Civil War.

Rebels and Loyals

Among the military formations which resisted European penetration in Africa and Asia, worthy of mention are the troops of Abd-el-Kadir, the third son of Mahi-ed-Din, a highly respected *marabout* of the region of Mascara. The twenty-four-year-old Abd-el-Kadir quickly gathered round him those who wanted to resist the French. He organised a veritable regular army, consisting of infantry, artillery and a special cavalry unit known as the 'Red Riders'. It was their task to harass the French columns with rapid and decisive actions and then to withdraw to the Atlas mountains or the less accessible areas of the desert. At first Abd-el-Kadir seemed disposed to treat with the French, but exalted by his success in achieving a number of victories, he decided that he could create a kingdom which would include all the territories of North Africa.

But his troops were not sufficiently trained, particularly in matters of discipline. Thus, when a French column entered the La Macta pass on 28 June 1835 and was attacked by the Red Riders, it succeeded in averting disaster, both because of the successful resistance of a battalion of the 66th Infantry and because the Arabs stopped to sack the convoy and kill the wounded rather than pursue the enemy. Almost six months later Kasir's army fled before a French column, leaving behind them warehouses full of food, stores and arms. These troops were so unskilled in tactics that in five years of siege they did not succeed in overcoming the citadel of Tlemcen.

In 1836, during the withdrawal of the expeditionary corps from Constantine, the 2nd Light Battalion, under the command of Changarnier, resisted every attack of the Red Riders. Nevertheless Abd-el-Kadir fought on until 1847, when, having been abandoned by almost all his troops, he surrendered to the French.

Among the 'loyals', the African troops faithful to the colonists, mention should be made of the Somalian Dubat, the bands which guarded the frontiers of Italian Somalia. For the most part, they were native groups dressed in white trousers, which they carried rolled on the chest, *a futa*, a kind of white cloak, and a pure white turban. They were armed with rifles and a few machine-guns. Each band was commanded by an Italian officer, and the second-in-command was a non-commissioned officer. Until 1943 they were almost unknown, but on 5 December they were attacked at Uwal Uwal and repulsed that attack of the Ethiopian soldiers which triggered off the Italo-Abyssinian war.

The Dubat units, organised in six groups, with a commander-in-chief, distinguished themselves throughout the campaign. On 18 October 1935, the group of Dubat bands from Mustahil attacked and overwhelmed Dagnerei on the River Uebi Scebeli. In the Second World War they took part in the operations which led to the occupation of Somaliland, with two groups of bands. They took part in the defence of Italian Somalia and remained loyal to the end.

Other countries had similar units. In addition to local tireurs and spahis, France had special units of desert police. In Morocco there were Goums units organised in tabors and groups of tabors. There were Saharan groups, consisting of mixed units of mehara, on foot and mounted, which served as desert police.

The Zulu army existed from 1816 (when it was organised by King Chaka) until 4 July 1879 (when it was destroyed by the English at the Battle of Ulundi). A well-organised force, it never had cavalry or artillery. It was divided into regiments with picturesque names. Their uniforms were made of leopard and monkey skins and they wore varicoloured headdresses.

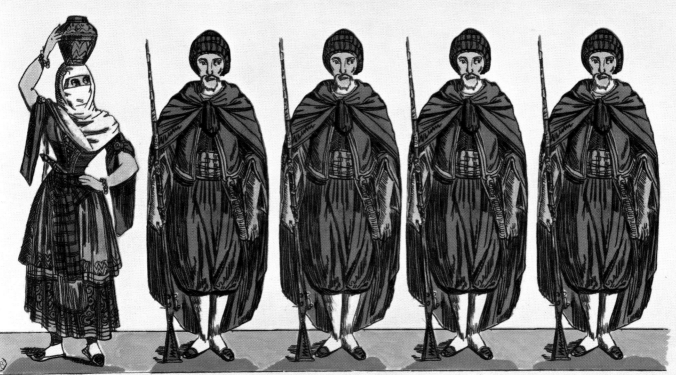

When the French first entered North Africa they had to face Abd-el-Kadir, who gathered together a considerable body of men who were determined to obstruct French occupation. He organised a veritable army with infantry, artillery and a special cavalry corps known as the 'Red Riders' shown above. They were employed in harassing actions and ambushes against the French columns on the march (which included the famous Chasseurs d'Afrique). After their attacks the Red Riders would retreat to the Atlas Mountains or the desert. Intoxicated with success, Abd-el-Kadir dreamt of becoming sovereign of all the territories of western North Africa. But because of the poor discipline of his troops he was forced to surrender in 1847.

The Boers and the Amazons of South Africa

The name Boers (lit. peasants) is commonly applied to descendants of those colonists, Dutch for the most part, who settled in the extreme south of Africa in increasing numbers in the seventeenth and eighteenth centuries. With the British occupation of the Cape Colony in 1814 these colonists were forced into the interior. By 1836 relations with the English had deteriorated greatly and the Boers were forced to move further into the interior, where they finally settled, establishing the Orange Free State and the Transvaal Republic.

Although the military forces of the two republics were small, the British were sorely tried in the war which broke out in 1899 (the Second Boer War). The

The nieces of Oom Paul Kruger, the president of Transvaal, in the uniforms of the Boer Amazons, the women's unit that fought against the English in the war in South Africa. They carried the typical Boer cartridge belt over the shoulder. This photograph was taken in Marseilles, in 1900, during one of the president's unsuccessful trips in search of aid.

Boers fought energetically under the vigorous leadership of President S. G. P. Kruger. We shall not consider here the events of that conflict, which ended with the defeat of the Boers after their desperate fight against a larger and better-armed enemy.

In 1899 the Orange Free State had only one artillery unit of twenty-one guns, three officers, thirteen non-commissioned officers and one hundred men. The artillery reserve numbered four hundred men, there were one hundred and eighty-one police. With the general mobilisation, the Orange Free State managed to increase its forces to a total of twenty thousand men, who had to provide their own horses, rifles, weapons and food for eight days.

The permanent forces of the Transvaal Republic were likewise limited to a single artillery unit of twenty-nine officers, eighty-three non-commissioned officers and two hundred and eighty-eight men. There was also a telegraph unit of one officer and fifteen soldiers. After mobilisation, the forces were increased to thirty thousand men. Thus the united forces of the Orange Free State and the Transvaal Republic, all white, did not exceed fifty thousand men. Nevertheless the hundred thousand English that faced them had no easy time.

From a strictly technical and military point of view, this conflict had many interesting aspects. In fact, it was during this war that many arms and methods were tried out which were to have wide application in the course of the two world wars.

Thus one first heard of barbed-wire barricades, trenches, communication trenches and fox-holes, not to mention machine-guns, though these were no longer new weapons. The British surrounded with barbed wire the blockhouses they had built to protect cities and roads and they made new use of the machine-guns which had first appeared in the war of 1870. The Boers turned to the use of defensive trenches and communication trenches so that supplies and ammunition could safely be brought to the front lines. Thus one has an example of the first use or final trials of means of offence and defence which European troops were to become extremely familiar with after 1914.

The Anglo-Boer War saw the first appearance of several generals who were to play important roles in later conflicts. There were Smuts and Botha on the Boer side; French and Kitchener on the British. The English discovered the particular utility of the new speciality of mounted infantry. These troops moved from place to place on horseback but fought on foot, as the seventeenth and eighteenth-century dragoons had done before them. This speciality was particularly effective in a country which had relatively few roads and railways.

The Boers won distinction by their courage and tenacity, and they were also notable for the simplicity of their uniforms, which, in effect, were developed naturally from their normal civilian clothes. Because of the common vicissitudes of their life in Africa, their individual clothing was anyway very similar. The broad-brimmed hat which kept off the sun was worn in battle too, and everyone wore stout leather boots, necessary to protect them against animals and insects in the grass. They wore light clothes because of the heat of the climate. Nevertheless the most distinctive features of the Boer uniform were the cartridge belts worn across the chest. They took the place of ammunition pouches and cartridge belts worn at the waist, which would have been inconvenient for men on horseback.

Another special feature of this war was the use of female units, the Amazons, the first modern example of women's military auxiliaries. The Amazons fought side by side with the men and won distinction in guerilla actions, when the Boers had been defeated in open field engagement. The women also looked after the kitchen, medical aid and other matters.

In addition to the technical innovations discussed, the use of female units constituted an anticipation of methods and means extensively employed in the wars of the twentieth century. This has been true of both world wars, and today women soldiers are regularly trained in the armies of Israel and other nations.

Mounted Boer soldiers in a print by Pellerin d'Epinal, at the time of the war in Transvaal. The name of Boer (from the Dutch boer, meaning 'peasant') was applied to the descendants of the Dutch who had colonised the region of the Cape of Good Hope in the middle of the 16th century. From the very beginning, the Boers had to perfect their military organisation to face the local populations, the Hottentots and Bushmen. England occupied the Cape Colony in 1795, returned it under the Treaty of Amiens, and occupied it once again in 1814. It was occupied for strategic reasons. Relations between the English and the Boers were difficult from the start and many Boers emigrated north and founded the Orange Free State and the Republic of Transvaal.

The Bengal Lancers and the Panjab Lions

There is a particular air of the romantic about the units of the Indian army, and in particular about the Bengal Lancers, who are probably the most famous of the many units.

Before considering them it would be worthwhile to look at the role they played in the immense panorama of India in arms. To do this we must go back to the time in which the country was administered by the East India Company, a commercial undertaking that, albeit under the sovereignty of the British government, exercised real political and military power.

The immense territory of India was subdivided into three districts, Bombay, Bengal and Madras, each of which had its own army. In addition there was the Punjab Frontier Force, the Hyderabad Contingent and many other regiments. India was never at rest. On the borders there was the constant peril of restless peoples like the Afghans and other frontier tribes. In 1845 British troops had to face a bloody war against the Sikhs, known as the Lions of the Punjab, one of the most efficient and warlike peoples of India. They were descended from those Bactrians who proved so resilient at Arbela when Darius faced Alexander of Macedonia in 320 BC.

Trained and enrolled in the regiments of the East India Company, the Sikhs formed an army of sixty thousand men organised and led by French and Italian officers. They wore red and blue uniforms and had a large artillery corps. But their leaders did not possess outstanding military qualities, and in 1845 at Ferogeshah, the 3rd Light Dragoon Regiment routed them with a charge. The following day General Grough carried out a bold action and succeeded in surprising the Sikhs when they were reorganising their forces. The English defeated them again and captured cannons and supplies. The next year, at the battle of Aliwal, the war came to an end and the Sikhs entered the service of England with such regiments as the 20th Punjab (Duke of Cambridge's Own) and the Punjab Pioneers; they were reputed to be fine soldiers.

From several points of view the East India Company army left much to be desired. Many of the officers were old, and were kept in service only so that pensions would not have to be paid. The soldiers lived in family cantonments and passed long periods of the year in conditions which were not strictly military. Some of the regiments had been in India for more than twenty years and those who left the service found local employment in administrative posts.

This was the situation when, in 1857, the Sepoys rebellion broke out. This revolt was provoked by a rumour which the local princes had spread throughout the company's units that the waxed cartridges

for the Enfield rifles with which the troops were armed had been lubricated with the grease of pigs, an untouchable animal for Moslems, and cows, the Hindu sacred animal. The real causes for grievance were so deep that this spark was sufficient. The revolt spread rapidly and the British found themselves face to face with a force numerically four or five times superior. By the end of the year, however, the mutiny had been quelled.

The East India Company was dissolved; India became first a crown colony and then (in 1870) an empire. The army was reformed and reinforced with British troops. Moslems and Hindus, who at first had refu-

sed to be part of the same units, finally reached agreement and together performed valuable services. Careful selection saw to it that only the best suited troops were incorporated into the Anglo-Indian army. Among these, special mention must be made of the Bengal Lancers. The name is extremely broad in meaning. Bengal had some twenty cavalry regiments, which counted for half the units which went to make up the new army. Some of these Bengal troops were properly called lancers. Particularly noteworthy was the 1st Regiment, which was known as Skinner's Horse after the name of its founder. These troops were dressed in

The camp of the 13th Bengal Lancers in Egypt, 1882. The regiment then numbered eight officers and five hundred men. The 13th Lancers, founded in 1805, is now part of an armoured regiment of the Pakistan army. In 1917, it had its 'Balaclava' at Instabulat, Iraq. It won glory in a tactically useless charge that cost the lives of all its officers and most of its men. The junior officers of the Indian regiments were usually natives, while the senior officers were English. The parade uniforms of the Indian cavalry have always been of great interest to students because of their beauty and the subtle differences between regiments. And this interest still survives. Suffice it to mention the use of the sabretache *by the President's body guard.*

Madras, the third largest city of India after Bombay and Calcutta, was the capital of Madras State, which was much smaller during English rule than the modern administrative district of Madras. There were three Madras regiments (in addition to the Governor's guard regiment). One of these was a lancer regiment. The plate reproduced here, one of L. Vallet's (1893) famous Croquis de cavalerie, represents a light cavalry officer. The Indian uniform consisted of certain basic elements, including the turban or puggree, a length of silk or cloth whose design varied according to the race and religion of the wearer, the tunic known as a kurtali, and the broad silk waistband known as a cummerband. The trousers either had bands or hung loose.

yellow with white trousers, and they were consequently referred to as the Yellow Devils Regiment or Riders of the Sun.

About 1900 the English regimental officers wore a short jacket and a white spiked metal helmet with a band of red, white and blue stripes. The Indian officers wore the classical tunic with black embroidery and braid, silver and red braid on the chest, a red cummerbund at the waist, and a red turban with black and yellow stripes, white trousers and gloves and black boots. As in all the Indian units, the turbans were worn in different fashions according to race and religion. The Mohammedans, for example, wound the turban around a pointed hat. The regiment is still in existence today and still dresses in red for official ceremonies.

Besides the lancers, Bengal boasted a famous infantry formed of the mountain people of Nepal, the Gurkhas. They were armed with their typical hunting knife, the *Kukri*. This broad blade is still typical of the Gurkhas. Each Gurkha regiment, like certain other Indian army units, had bagpipes.

Today the Gurkhas, together with mounted troops, comprise the army of the king of Nepal, the Maharajaha Mahandra Bir Bikram. The horsemen wear a red tunic with gold braiding and tall black turbans. Their lances are decorated with red and blue two-pointed pennants.

During the Sikh War, the 3rd Bengal Irregular Cavalry won distinction. It was armed with bamboo lances about twelve feet long (which cost less than the ash lances imported from England) and with *tulwars*, sabres made from blades provided by the government and hilts made in India. This made them more easily handled by the cavalrymen (or *sowars*), who kept the blades razor sharp. To make them last as long as possible, leather sheaths were used instead of the regulation steel sheaths provided by the government. The regiment was born at Bareilly in 1815 and was called the 1st Corps of Rohillah Cavalry. In 1823 the name was changed to the 3rd Local Horse and, finally, in 1840 it was called the 3rd Bengal Irregular Cavalry. The uniform included a red tunic with a blue cummerband.

As for the equipment in the golden age of the Indian cavalry, i.e., the years around 1900, it is worth mentioning that in most of the regiments, except for the light cavalry of Madras, the 'Sillidar' system was in effect: men were recruited already equipped with their own horses, weapons and gear. Later the government provided on payment a horse and a rifle, while the rest of the uniform and equipment were provided by the regiment in direct negotiation with the soldier. Thus one cannot discuss the general characteristics of regimental arms. The sabre of the Bengal cavalry, for example, varied from regiment to regiment, because the style was determined by regimental preferences. This situation existed until the First World War and was general throughout the forty regiments of Indian cavalry.

We have already mentioned the turbans and their styles, which corresponded to the national usage of the

Rissaldar Abdul Majd Khan, an officer of the Bahawalpur Lancers (now part of the Pakistan army) in the uniform of 1897. He wears loose trousers. A. H. Bowling's drawing is taken from a contemporary photograph.

individual soldiers. The Madras Light Cavalry was exceptional in this regard too. Since the trumpeters and farriers were traditionally Christian, they wore European headgear, as did the British officers.

One modern expert on military uniforms, Lieutenant-Colonel Nicholson, recently wrote that as well as the air of romance that hung about the Indian army, there was also an air of mosquitoes, dust, heat, malaria, cholera and other eastern delights. This does not detract from the colourful element that has survived and seems likely to continue to endure. And it is the romance which continues to live in people's imaginations.

This famous illustration by A. C. Lovett shows the uniforms of important Indian regiments towards the end of the 19th century. The men on horse are Bengal Lancers of the 13th and 19th regiments. Other lancers are the last man on the right (1st Bengal Cavalry), the penultimate (15th Mooltanel Cavalry) and the fourth-from-last, with a lance (the Viceroy's Body Guard). In the centre is a soldier of the 1st Punjab Cavalry and a 'bagpiper' of the 1st Sikh Infantry.

The Eight Chinese Flags

Until the end of the nineteenth century the Chinese army had a unique kind of organisation. It was composed of two corps: the troops of the so-called 'Eight Flags', descendants of the Manchus, Chinese and Mongols who had dethroned the Ming dynasty in the seventeenth century, and the provincial troops, who were known as the 'Green Flag'. In addition to these units, which formed the imperial army, there were also small contingents of irregular troops, called Young, who were recruited when needed.

The troops of the 'Eight Flags' were organised in twenty-four regiments and never exceeded forty thousand men. They were garrisoned in Peking and in twenty-five other cities near the capital as well as in fortresses in Mongolia and Turkestan. They belonged to a particular caste and had nothing to do with the populations of the localities in which they were stationed.

The 'Green Flag' troops formed the provincial army, which was at the disposal of local governors. Each province was obliged to provide a contingent of thirty-five thousand men. They functioned like territorial militias and were composed of men almost totally lacking in military training. In fact, at the beginning of the twentieth century, China had only one hundred and fif-

ty thousand men ready to enter the field, and these were pitifully armed with harquebuses, matchlock muskets and even with bows and arrows. The Mongol cavalry was also part of the Chinese army. Badly armed, its total strength did not exceed thirty thousand men. But they were descendants of the invincible hordes of Genghis Khan and his 'leather cuirasses', the mounted archers who brought the Mongol empire to the very gates of Trieste and Twassan.

In 1850 the revolt of the T'ai-P'ing broke out in China, a religious sect which unleashed an iconoclastic war against idolatry. The government was able to oppose this war only in 1860, when the 'Ever Victorious Army' was created by the English colonel, Charles G. ('Chinese') Gordon. He usually led the attack unarmed except for a baton in his hand, which the Chinese soldiers believed was a magic wand.

After the Boxer rebellion (1900-1) the Chinese and Manchu war ministries were united, and China attempted to create a modern army. The 'Green Flag' troops were suppressed, and the provincial soldiery was reorganised. Although the army was to have been formed of conscripted troops, it was in fact composed exclusively of volunteers. Thirty-six divisions had been planned, but only thirteen were actually created. All branches wore the same uniform of dark-blue material and were distinguished from each other by the colour of the shoulder straps.

After the creation of the republic, the Kuomintang succeeded in creating a fairly solid army, which fought from 1927 to 1932 and then from 1937 to 1945 against the Japanese. Meanwhile, after the October Revolution in Russia, Communist thought had soon entered China. The long war against the Japanese and the reactionary elements in the country helped create that revolutionary peasant army which was eventually to bring the Communists to power.

The illustrations on these two pages show two different aspects of old military China. Above: *the so-called 'Green Turbans', who were active in the second half of the 19th century and owed their efficiency to European instructors.* Opposite: *Chinese garrison soldiers, in an English print of 1796. Note the archaic style of arms and dress.*

From Samurai to Kamikaze

Until the middle of the nineteenth century Japan was an all but unknown nation. Its warriors, particularly the famous Samurai, all came from the aristocracy. These warriors wore the national costume and were armed with scimitars, knives and lances. After the United States ships opened Japan's ports, the whole country was quickly modernised and the army was organised along European lines. At that time the Mikado had purely religious functions; he resided at Mjako protected by his own guard. This guard provided the nucleus of the imperial guard which until the Second World War constituted a genuinely élite fighting division, after the Napoleonic or Prussian manner. Civil powers were exercised by a Shogun, who lived at Iedo (mod. Tokyo) and had at his disposal a permanent army of one hundred thousand foot and twenty thousand horsemen. The feudal lords were obliged to provide twenty foot and two horse for every thousand thalers of their income. These forces formed an army of three hundred and eighty-six thousand foot and thirty-eight thousand horsemen.

In 1870 the Mikado deposed the Shogunate and assumed all powers. At the same time the modern Japanese army was born, with a corps of twelve thousand men trained and organised in European fashion by German officers. The feudal army was not immediately dissolved but gradually transformed. In 1885, the Japanese army was finally reorganised on the basis of European systems. At first it consisted of only sixty thousand men, organised in seven divisions, one of which was the Imperial Guard. Unlike western armies, the Japanese army had extremely simple uniforms.

With its limited military organisation, Japan faced

Japanese officer uniforms, 1886. From left to right: *Infantry lieutenant in march dress; lieutenant-colonel of the medical corps; infantry officer in summer uniform; infantry colonel (staff), and general. The uniforms are all French style. Note the extensive use of facings.*

Japanese uniform, 1890. From left to right: *Infantry second-lieutenant of the Imperial Guard; infantry officer in summer uniform; supply officer, second class; infantry line adjutant; Junior* NCO *soldier of guard cavalry in dress uniform. The Imperial Guard consisted of four infantry regiments, a cavalry formation, and engineer units at this time.*

China in 1894 and defeated the mammoth but inefficient Chinese army.

Russia deprived Japan of most of the fruits of that victory. To meet the new threat of Russia, the Japanese army was reorganised again in 1896, and military service was extended to men between the ages of seventeen and forty. The regular army was organised into twelve divisions in addition to the Imperial Guard. Because Japan is an island, a strong territorial army was needed to protect the country from landing operations. The regular army divisions were considered as an overseas expeditionary corps and kept this character until the Second World War. In the war with Russia which broke out in 1903, the new Japanese army showed its skill. Among the regiments that distinguished themselves in the siege of Port Arthur were the 25th, 26th, 27th and 28th, all part of the Seventh Division. A characteristic that the Japanese army borrowed from the Russians at this time was the ordering of regiments in divisions according to ordinal numbers. Thus the First Division was composed of the 1st, 2nd, 3rd and 4th regiments, the Second Division of the 5th, 6th, 7th and 8th, and so on.

In any case, it was the 25th, 26th, 27th and 28th regiments that made particular use of methods which were to be employed everywhere in the First World War, such as the use of barbed-wire barricades, and explosive laid by Death Volunteers, who were often blown up along with the barbed-wire obstacles.

In January 1905 the regiments (29th, 30th, 31st and 32nd) of the Eighth Division, recruited in the northern part of the island of Nippon, fought the Siberian troops at Sumapu, while the Guard Division, together with the 3rd and 4th regiments charged in serried ranks at Mukden on 3 March. The loss of life was great but they succeeded in getting through the barbed wire entanglements, trenches and other obstacles, such as fallen trees to win the heights of Tokatonsehishan from superior enemy forces.

After the Russo-Japanese War, Japan created four more divisions, two of which were stationed in Korea and two in Manchuria. Two Guards Brigades were formed with men from the warlike tribes of headhunters from Formosa. They were garrisoned on Formosa. They gained particular notoriety in the winter of 1942, when in Borneo they fought the Dutch and British forces which were defending Indonesia.

From 1932 Japan fought for thirteen years in China, and although the peacetime army of seventeen divisions was maintained, Japan had twenty-four divisions serving in China. In the Second World War Japan mobilised about eight million men, who fought throughout eastern Asia and conquered vast territories, from Burma to New Guinea, from the immense Chinese territories of Nankin China to the Philippines. They had already occupied Manchuria, and an empire had been established which was only formally autonomous.

看護長　二等　武裝　步兵卒　曹長　憲兵　要塞砲兵曹長

Japanese uniforms, 1890. From left to right: medical corps sergeant; foot soldier with full pack in march uniform; sergeant-major of military police; second-class sergeant of fortress artillery. These uniforms were worn during the war against the Chinese Empire. The colour illustrations are taken from water colours in the Imperial Military Museum, Tokyo.

武裝　中尉　步兵　大尉　騎兵　佐官　夏衣　明治三十七八年戰役

Japanese uniforms of the early 20th century. From left to right: second-lieutenant of infantry in march uniform with full pack; line cavalry captain in duty uniform; infantry officer in summer campaign uniform (1904-1905). Facings had already disappeared from service uniforms. Khaki came into general use during the Russo-Japanese War.

217

The Tonking Pavillons Noirs

During the struggles the French engaged in, first to defend their missions and then to assert their authority in Indo-China, there appeared formations of Chinese pirates known as *Pavillons Noirs* because of the black silk flags covered with gold writings which they raised in battle. In 1860 the French were restricted to a few points along the coast, while the Annamites supported by the Pavillons Noirs were masters of the rest of the country and even managed to besiege Saigon. After the war conducted by France and Great Britain against China in 1861, an expeditionary force of marine fusiliers and colonial infantry together with a battalion of Algerian Turcos and a chasseur battalion overwhelmed the Annamites. Thus, before the fall of the Second Em-

A Chinese musician from an Oliver-Pinot d'Epinal print. Opposite: A famous Pellerin d'Epinal sheet showing troops engaged during the Indochinese War-Annamites, Pavillons Noirs, and the French expeditionary force. Below: the death of Captain Rivière, killed on 19 May 1883 by the Pavillons Noirs. The Pavillons Noirs, so called because of their black silk flags with gold inscriptions, were pirate bands.

pire France had occupied a great part of Indo-China.

But the Pavillons noirs had found refuge in Tonkin, which was still independent, and it was in vain that Annam requested Chinese help in suppressing them. In 1873 a small French expeditionary corps, commanded by Naval Lieutenant Garnier, was ambushed by the Pavillons Noirs and the commanding officer killed. This small expeditionary corps of seven officers and one hundred and seventy-five seamen had occupied Hanoi, which had been defended by seven thousand Annamites, but they now had to abandon the city.

However, French interests in the area were increasing, and in 1882, under the government of Jules Ferry, an expeditionary force of six hundred men, under the command of Commander De Rivière, was sent to the Delta. It took Hanoi, but De Rivière was ambushed as Garnier had been. De Rivière was so well known that Epinal produced a print of the commander's death. The Pavillons Noirs were actually bandits armed with huge two-handed swords, rifles, javelins and arrows and with modern rifles provided by China. They lived by extorting money and goods from the local populations that they terrorised. There is a description of their jungle guerilla warfare in Pierre Loti's novel, *les Pêcheurs d'Islande.*

The Treaty of Hué, which made Annam a French protectorate, was not recognised by China, which gave even greater support to the Pavillons Noirs. This action on the part of the Chinese government in favour of men who could be considered nothing more than bandits led to a war between China and France. This war was won by France thanks to a skilful move on the part of Admiral Coubert, who blocked the Gulf of Pechihli, cutting off northern China's rice supplies. But before China gave in and abandoned the Pavillons Noirs to their fate, they had laid siege to the city of Tuyen-Kuan, assisted by the Pavillons Noirs. Six hundred Frenchmen resisted valiantly, and when the situation seemed hopeless an engineer sergeant gave his life to blow up the powder magazine. At the end of the war against China, Jules Ferry effected a clever treaty, only a few days before his government was overthrown, which gave France the protectorates of Tonkin and Annam. France then turned to the pacification of the colony. It was the work of a few men, like Generals Servières and Pennequin and an officer who was to win fame in 1914, the then Colonel Gallieli. The Pavillons Noirs had no intention of abandoning the country, which they considered conquered territory. They continued to carry out guerilla actions, ambushes in particular, but never attacking openly. They lived on booty extracted from the populations which they terrorised and exploited racial hatred and religious solidarity.

FRANÇAIS, ANNAMITES & PAVILLONS-NOIRS

DÉPART DE LA COLONNE EXPÉDITIONNAIRE — marins et infanterie de marine

ARMÉE ANNAMITE — types divers

LES PAVILLONS NOIRS

ESCORTE D'UN GÉNÉRAL ANNAMITE

en tirailleurs — MARINS ET INFANTERIE DE MARINE — à la baïonnette

TIRAILLEURS ANNAMITES

ATTAQUE ET PRISE D'UNE FORTERESSE ENNEMIE

MORT DU COMMANDANT RIVIÈRE, DE LA MARINE FRANÇAISE
tué le 19 mai 1883 par les Pavillons Noirs dans une sortie hors des murs d'Ha-noï

The Two Wars of the Anzacs

Artillery of the State of Victoria, Australia, in the second half of the 19th century. Note the white helmet with spike. The origin of this headgear was Danish. It was then adopted by the Prussians and eventually used throughout the world.

Australia came to be considered a habitable land only after 1770, when Captain Cook explored its eastern coast and annexed it to Great Britain under the name of New South Wales. Later other states were formed, and in 1901 Australia became a dominion. New Zealand was discovered by the explorer Tasman in 1642. It was explored by Captain Cook in 1769, became a colony in 1840 and a dominion in 1907. The two dominions based their military organisation on the system of a voluntary militia. Thus during the Second World War their regular officers could perform all the functions of a general staff, though they could not command the large units (divisions and army corps).

During the First World War, units of the Dardanelles expedition and in the defence of the Suez Canal against Turko-German forces. There were two divisions.

The expeditionary corps took the name of Anzac, from the initials of the Australian and New Zealand Army Corps, and fought heroically in the Gallipoli peninsula at the battle of Suvla Bay (1915). On Lone Pipe Peak the Australians lost two thousand men but

succeeded in taking the fort, digging tunnels and pits and eliminating the enemy in hand-to-hand combat. In the autumn of 1915 the Anzacs had to cover the re-embarkation of the Anglo-French forces and to do this resorted to the tricks of sappers and pioneers. Under cover of darkness the men slithered toward the embarkation planks, setting off rifle fire by means of candles which burned strings attached to the triggers. When they had left the trenches they covered the duck-boards, up which Australians, New Zealanders and Maoris had to pass, with sacks, so that the enemy would not hear the tread of their hob-nailed boots. They set off time bombs to create the impression of uninterrupted fire.

In the period between the two wars, Australia made good use of what it had learned in the First World War. It formed five infantry divisions, with seventeen brigades of four battalions each, in addition to artillery and other divisional units. Two cavalry divisions of eighteen regiments were also created. But all these units were part of the militia, and not a regular army. The regular forces consisted of field and garrison artillery units and engineers. New Zealand organised its forces similarly, with mounted infantry units as well as normal infantry ones.

During the Second World War the Anzacs were extensively engaged in Africa. A New Zealand division was stationed in Egypt in June 1940. In autumn 1941 the New Zealand division's front-line strength numbered three brigades of three battalions each, as well as the 2nd Motorised Cavalry Regiment, Maori units and various Australian units. Australian forces fought in Greece and Crete in the spring of 1941. Later these units, joined by the Second New Zealand Division, took part in the 'Crusader' battle, and three Australian divisions, the Sixth, Seventh and Ninth, were sent to the far east, where Japan had gone to war.

In the fortress of Tobruk an Australian battalion was stationed until November 1941. It was part of the Sixteenth Brigade, together with three British battalions. In the battles of Gazala and Mersa Matruh which brought the Axis troops to El Alamein, there were Australian units and the Second New Zealand Division, which included, among others, the 28th Maori battalion and the 19th to 26th battalions. The Sixth Australian Division, composed of the Sixteenth, Seventeenth and Nineteenth brigades, was in Syria together with the Seventh and Ninth Divisions. In Syria these troops had fought against the French troops who had remained faithful to the Vichy government and against Iraqi troops in Iraq. In the battle of El Alamein, the Second New Zealand Division and the Ninth Australian Division were part of the army.

An Australian mounted rifleman of about 50 years ago, with the typical broad-brimmed hat turned up at one side. The Australian field uniforms were always extremely practical. In 1915 at Suvla in the Gallipoli peninsula they wore the puggree *(a light scarf wrapped around the crown of a sun helmet and hanging behind to protect the back of the neck). The colour served to distinguish the various regiments. The Australians and the New Zealanders together formed a corps known as the Anzac (from the initial letters of the Australia New Zealand Army Corps), which also won distinction in World War II. A New Zealand brigade won honour at El Alamein. In the Pacific the IX Australian Division recaptured Borneo in 1945.*

PART FIVE

The
New World

The Three Americas

The Birth of the American Army

At the outbreak of revolution and the War of Independence, the thirteen American colonies had local militia units. Some of them were the Rangers, the Regulators and the Minute Men. The Massachussetts Minute Men are particularly famous because of their valour during the Lexington alarm. The Minute Men were formed in the county of Worcester, Massachussetts, just before the outbreak of hostilities. The first encounter with the English took place on 19 April 1775 at Concord and Lexington, and a monument to the Minute Men at Concord commemorates the event. The Minute Men were so called because they had to be ready for action within a minute after the call to arms was given. One month after Lexington, in May, Colonel Ethan Allen, with two hundred and thirty men known as the 'Green Mountain Boys' took Fort Ticonderoga on Lake Champlain. The fort was known as the 'American Gibraltar'.

On 14 June 1775, the Continental Congress in Philadelphia established the continental army so called in contrast to the English army, which was an overseas force. George Washington was made commander-in-chief. Among the units under his command were Daniel Morgan's Virginia Riflemen. They once covered six hundred miles in twenty-one days to reach Washington at Cambridge. They were rewarded with a handshake by Washington and a trust that they never betrayed. They were extremely skilled marksmen, and on the run could hit a target eight inches in diameter at a distance of six hun-

dred and fifty feet. They wore hunting shirts of jackets which Washington later suggested the entire army should wear. It was from Morgan's Riflemen that one of the most famous regiments of the American Army evolved, the 11th Virginia of the Continental army.

Another famous unit were the 'Macaronis' of the Smallwood's Maryland Battalion (2nd Maryland), which won distinction at the ill-fated battle of Long Island and later, as the Maryland Regiment, at the Guildford Court House, where on 15 March 1781 they were engaged in a memorable bayonet assault.

Among the Ranger regiments, noteworthy were Knowlton's Connecticut Rangers. Memorable too were Henry Knox's four artillery regiments. They had developed from the volunteer company known as the Train, which had been formed in Boston in 1763. Knox's artillery assured American victories on more than one occasion.

It is curious to note that the artillery were given a regulation uniform in 1777, at a time when the question of uniform was still being discussed by other units of the Continental army. The artillery uniform was blue with red lapels, and there were ten yellow buttons on each lapel. Particularly famous, too, was Francis Marion, the Swamp Fox, who continued the struggle in the South after the defeat at Camden. He led a few mounted volunteers in guerilla warfare against the English in the region between the Pee Dee and Savannah rivers.

An Odgen illustration showing (from left to right) *a member of the Virginia Riflemen; a Minute Man; one of the Connecticut Governor's Foot-Guard (in red uniform); and one of the City-troop of Philadelphia Dragoons (with a leather hat and raccoon tail). These were some of the independent units which in 1774-75 formed the first American military forces. The Philadelphia Dragoons and the Connecticut Guards are still in existence. Brown was the usual colour of uniforms at that time, since it was the easiest to produce with vegetable dyes even in country farms.*

The American Infantry

In the period of peace that followed the revolution, the regular army was reduced to less than one hundred men, and the difficulties with the Indians had to be faced by the militias of the individual states. The results were so unsatisfactory that America decided to reconstitute an army of some substance, and the command of

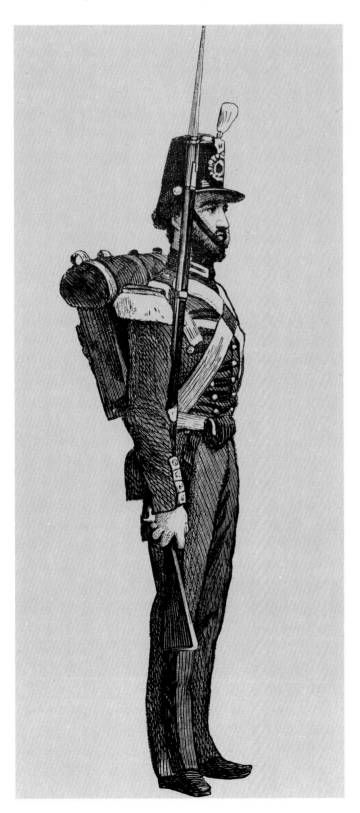

this army was given to General Anthony Wayne.

This army was called the Legion and was subdivided into four sub-legions. Each sub-legion was a fighting unit of infantry, riflemen, cavalry and artillery.

The legion infantry had a particularly colourful uniform. It was blue with red lapels, and plumes of various colours were worn on the hat. The uniform was designed to impress the Indian chiefs who visited the camps and to raise the morale of the troops. But when the infantry went out to fight the Indians they put on the revolutionary hunting jackets.

The War of 1812 against Great Britain made the creation of more military units necessary. Remarkable for the originality of its conception was the regiment of Artillerists, whose men served as infantry and artillery at the same time. The guns were drawn by rented horses led by civilians, and the artillerists marched alongside the weapons.

Among the infantry regiments that won distinction in the field, the 7th was particularly noteworthy. It was the 7th that founded the famous outpost of Fort Gibson in Cherokee territory. The regiment spent the first twenty years of its existence in that fort and played an important role in the struggles between Indians and Palefaces.

Another famous 7th Infantry was that of the New York Militia, one of the first to go into action when the Civil War broke out in 1861. This unit had already been in existence for fifty-five years and was nick-named the 'Silk Stockings'. It was the infantry that took the centre of the stage in the struggle between the North and the South. There were some one thousand four hundred regiments engaged in battle, and three hundred more that did not see combat.

Most regiments were organised in brigades, like the Vermont Brigade, which was put to the hardest tests in the war. Then there was the Iron Brigade of the West, another brigade which suffered terrible losses. It wore the black felt hats instead of caps, and came to be called the Black Hat Brigade.

The South also had distinguished units in the war. Garnett's Virginia Brigade entered the battle of Gettysburg with one thousand four hundred and twenty-seven men. At the end of the battle only four hundred and eighty-six were left standing.

A foot soldier of the 7th New York Regiment in marching uniform. Opposite: A Pellerin d'Epinal illustration of the American infantry. The uniform is that in use about 1900, the one that the Americans consider the least attractive of all the uniforms worn by their army.

IMAGERIE PELLERIN   INFANTERIE AMÉRICAINE   DANS UN CAMP D'INSTRUCTION

The Rangers: From Massachusetts to Normandy

Mention has already been made of the rangers in discussing the first American forces formed during the colonial period. They merit more than passing mention, and we shall consider some of the famous ranger units that have been formed in two centuries of history. The rangers' feats continued to the Second World War and have taken on an air of legend.

Among the first rangers, a scouting and raiding specialty typical of the American infantry, were those twenty-four men that Robert Rogers recruited from the Massachusetts militia in January 1755. This group gave birth to the corps of His Majesty's Independent Companies of Rangers or, more simply, Rogers' Rangers.

Rogers' Rangers won distinction in the Lake George Campaign (1755) during the French and Indian wars. Subsequently their numbers increased to six companies, each comprising one hundred soldiers, four sergeants, a colour sergeant, two lieutenants and a captain.

There were also 'seasonal' companies of Mohegan Indians. They were organised at the beginning of the year, employed in the summer and dissolved in the autumn, so that the Indians could return to their tribes for the winter hunting.

Robert Rogers was a curious figure and not at all American. Although he was born in the colonies, he remained faithful to the English on the outbreak of the revolution. He organised the Queen's Rangers and promised his men that they would have the 'rebels'' lands at the end of the war. Rogers died in London in 1795.

The regulations, training methods and aims of the unit, published by Robert Rogers in 1757, were reprinted in 1942 and adopted for the formation of the Infantry Rangers, whose six battalions were engaged on all fronts during the Second World War. They saw service throughout the world, from Africa to the Philippines, from France to New Guinea. Like their predecessors, the new rangers were used for assault and raiding actions, in the same fashion as the British commandos and the raiders of the United States Marine Corps.

Two ranger battalions, the 2nd and 5th, landed in Normandy on 6 June 1944. Their assignment was to neutralise and destroy a battery of large-calibre guns (including 381 mm. cannon) that the Germans were believed to have set up at Pointe du Hoc and which could have caused great harm to the invasion fleet. The Rangers attacked boldly, attempting to scale the sheer faced cliff with mortar-launched ladders and ropes. One hundred and thirty-five men were lost in this daring action. But the artillery battery had not been emplaced and the rangers came upon it, still unmounted, a few miles away with its ammunition intact. But between the time of Rogers' Rangers and those at Normandy, there were others that added remarkable chapters to the his-

tory of this speciality. Among the regiments that won fame for their part in the revolution were Knowlton's Rangers.

Thomas Knowlton recruited a few companies in Connecticut and led them to the battle of Bunker Hill and the siege of Boston. After the battle of Long Island, Knowlton organised his rangers into a regiment together with other Connecticut troops. One of the most famous episodes concerning these men is the story of Nathan Hale's sacrifice. He volunteered for a dangerous mission and was captured by the English. Sentenced to be hanged, his last words were: 'I only regret that I have but one life to give for my country.' The founder of these rangers, Thomas Knowlton, lost his life leading his men at the battle of Harlem Heights.

There were rangers in the army that General Taylor led against Mexico in 1846. That army, was a mixture of the most heterogeneous elements. Side by side on the road to Monterrey marched regular infantry units, in their sky-blue uniforms, field battery artillery men in the red and blue uniforms, and volunteers in improvised uniforms. Among these last there was a group of savage-looking men who always rode ahead of the column as advance scouts. These were the Texas Rangers, organised and led by Ben MacCulloch, a great soldier who was to die in the uniform of the Confederacy struck down by a sniper's bullet in 1862. The Texas Rangers were formidable in their skill at detecting the presence of Mexican units by the sun's reflection off a bayonet or lance. They wore rough shirts of red or blue or a fringed hunting jacket of animal skin. Almost all wore broad-brimmed hats to shade their eyes from the blazing sun. Each ranger had a heavy flintlock rifle, with a powder horn, a cartridge belt, a Bowie knife and sometimes a Colt pistol. Ropes, canteens and blankets were arranged around the saddle. Some of the rangers had Mexican-style equipment with star-shaped spurs and worked-leather saddles.

MacCulloch's Texas Rangers in action. Notice that the apparel varies from man to man. The speciality of the Rangers is typically American. Their duties were basically reconnaissance and assault. The latest descendants of the first rangers were the members of the Ranger Infantry, which was formed in 1942 in six battalions. They were engaged in 1944 in sabotage and behind-the-lines activities on various fronts. Their badge was a blue flash on the sleeve with the word 'Rangers' inscribed on it. They wore light equipment and carried a rifle and knife. The name of Texas Rangers is now borne by the Texas Mounted Police, which dates back to 1823. Canada has a comparable unit, the Queen's York Rangers Regiment, also known as the First American Regiment.

American Zouaves

We have already seen the success enjoyed by the first regiment of Zouaves recruited by the French among the Kabyle Berber tribes during the conquest of Algeria. Later there were mixed units of French and Algerians and finally there were entirely French Zouave units. The Zouaves became famous and confirmed their fame in the wars of the Crimea and Italy. The exotic flavour of the uniform - the ample loose red trousers, the scarlet fez, the blue jacket with its yellow or varicoloured embroidery and the broad sash at the waist - could not but appeal to volunteers. Such was the case in America as well, where Elmer Ephraim Ellsworth, who had learned of the Zouave, feats in the Crimea from a Frenchman, formed a volunteer cadet company in Chicago in 1860. In the picturesque confusion that then characterised the United States army, these men dressed and trained in the manner of the Zouaves found a perfect home. The zeal these volunteers put into their Zouave activities was such that, after a demonstration in New England, their fame spread throughout the states, and they are still remembered as the United States Zouave Cadets.

When the Civil War broke out hundreds of Zouave companies were formed in the north and south, and they were all modelled after Ellsworth's formation. One could almost say that every city, town and village made provision for such units, which were bolstered more by enthusiasm than by training. The Zouave units were attractive to those volunteers who longed for special risks and adventures. Thus one could see units dressed in red trousers and Algerian fezes in cities that had nothing of the exotic or tropical about them.

In March 1861, before the outbreak of hostilities, the first Zouave battalion of the state of Louisiana was formed in New Orleans. There were recruits of French, German, Irish, English and Italian descent. The uniform again copied the French original, with full red trousers, dark blue jacket and vest, red braid, blue sash, red fez and white hose. The officers, like their French counterparts, wore an open tunic and a red kepi. So closely was the French model followed that the commands were the same, and they were given in French.

There were many Zouave units in the army of the north as well. There were probably more Zouaves units in the state of New York than in the rest of the states put together. The most publicized of the New York Zouaves was the 11th regiment, Ellsworth's Rangers, commanded by Ellsworth himself. Ellsworth had followed Lincoln to the east after working in his legal office in the period before the election. He was made a colonel and put in command of the 11th, which was made up of men from the New York Firemen. They were given Zouave uniforms and training.

Member of the 11th New York Volunteers, or Ellsworth's Zouaves. The water colours are by George Woodbridge.

At the battle of Bull Run they sustained tragic losses as they withstood the charge of the famous Confederate Black Horse Cavalry. Shortly before that battle, Ellsworth was killed by a rifle shot while removing the Confederate flag from a hotel at Alexandria, Virginia. That was 24 May 1861. Ellsworth was the first Union officer to lose his life in Virginia. He was twenty-four years old.

Other New York Zouaves included those commanded by Hiram Duryea, the 5th regiment, one of the most famous regiments of the Civil War and one of the finest volunteer units in history. At the battle of Gaines's Mill they were decimated by enemy rifle fire but managed to reorganise in such a way that the unit could manoeuvre as if a third of its forces had not been lost. The uniform of Duryea's Zouaves was, more or less, that of the French Zouaves and, with slight variation that of the Confederate Zouaves. It must not have been easy to distinguish friend from foe on the battlefield. In fact, only small differences, such as less braiding and a softer fez, distinguished the New Orleans Zouaves from those of New York.

Member of the 14th Brooklyn New York State Militia with a Zouave-style uniform of evident French derivation.

A Zouave of the 5th New York Volunteers, a celebrated regiment of the period of the War Between the States.

On parade, the men wrapped a white turban around the fez and wore long white hose. The 44th New York Regiment also consisted of Zouaves. They took the name of Ellsworth's Avengers. Their uniform was slightly different, consisting of a dark-blue cap and open tunic, a red shirt and blue trousers with a red stripe. There were other distinctive features besides the name and uniform of this unit. It was composed exclusively of bachelors under the age of thirty who were at least five feet eight inches tall. On enrolment they had to provide proof of moral character. All these features made Ellsworth's Avengers a genuinely picked unit. The 44th's most famous action was the defence of the Little Round Top on the second day of the battle of Gettysburg.

With the end of the Civil War the Zouaves disappeared. The only Zouaves in existence after 1870 were French Zouaves. There was something of Zouave exoticism about the *Corps d'Afrique*, a coloured unit raised in Louisiana in 1862 and consisting of free and recently liberated slaves.

The question of a name for this unit was problematical for the Union authorities, who wished to give it a special distinction. Thus the French name of Corps d'Afrique was decided upon. This corps included an artillery regiment entrusted with the defence of the fortification of New Orleans. But the artillery was never called upon to open fire on the enemy. The artillery uniform was particularly handsome. It consisted of a plumed felt hat, a long dark blue tunic with metal epaulets (on the dress uniform only) and light blue trousers with a red stripe. Artillerymen wore a dagger at the side. The Corps d'Afrique also had a fine band, and the Negro soldiers were excellent musicians. The members of the brigade bands (individual regimental bands were abolished in 1862) played not only for parades but also in public concerts. They also played at dances for white officers.

The Cavalry

Officer of the 2nd US Cavalry in the uniform in use between 1855 and 1861. The black felt hat with the rim turned up on the right and trimmed with an ostrich feather was first introduced at this time and only in the cavalry. It was later adopted by other branches. Officers wore three feathers and the men wore one. This model was drawn by Frederick L. Todd.

The terrain on which the War of Independence was fought was not such as so to make it necessary for the Americans to organise a real cavalry, although there were situations in which mounted troops could have been employed to good advantage.

The difficulty of procuring horse and equipment settled the matter. Thus it was only at the end of 1776 that the Continental Congress authorised the formation of four cavalry regiments. They were called Light Dragoons after the British custom. Enrolment was based on several conditions. Since the cavalry functions were of the nature of military police, the dragoons had to demonstrate their loyalty to America and had to have unblemished moral records. Consequently the dragoons became a genuine élite corps. Thus it was in keeping with their reputation that the 3rd Regiment, created in 1777 with men from Maryland, Virginia and Pennsylvania, was given the name of the 'Lady Washington Dragoons'. It was a picked corps in the finest sense of the word and demonstrated its qualities in the field as well as in the personal behaviour of its members.

Until 1861 the dragoons were the only American cavalrymen. To secure the western territories from incursions of Plains Indians, who were extremely skilled riders, comparable military units were required. Thus the cavalry, which had been abolished for economic reasons in 1815, was reformed in 1832, when it became clear that the infantry was too slow to escort wagon-trains. A first battalion of mounted rangers, transformed the following year into the 1st Dragoon Regiment, was assigned to escort caravans and perform reconnaissance missions. This regiment, which was assigned to escort missions, frontier defence actions and the wars in Florida and Mexico, had little time to create a special uniform. It is said that its men looked more like bandits than soldiers. They had the unique privilege in the American army of wearing moustaches and long hair, earrings and pistols at their waists. They were typical frontier soldiers. When several Indian chiefs paid a visit to Fort Snelling, the camp of the 1st Dragoons, the soldiers put on light-blue uniforms with yellow stripes and braid to impress the Indians, and the trumpeters wore red jackets.

The 2nd Dragoon Regiment won distinction in the Mexican War. When General Zachary Taylor opened the campaign, it was a squadron of the 2nd regiment that attacked first on the banks of the Rio Grande. On 9 May 1846, at Resaca de la Palma, Captain Charles May's squadron was ordered to capture a Mexican Battery. May succeeded and captured General La Vega, the sole survivor, who was in the act of firing one of the guns. The name of dragoon was suppressed in 1861; all the mounted regiments came to be referred to as

Two Lady Washington Dragoons, the regiment also known as Baylor's 3rd Continental Dragoons, in an unpublished water colour by Fritz Kredel. The uniforms of the two dragoons date to 1778, the year after the regiment was founded by Colonel George Baylor. The reconstruction of the uniforms is the work of Frederick Todd. Baylor's Dragoons served as the Cavalry Guard of General Washington. They won distinction at Cowpens, where they faced the dragoons of Col. Banastre Tarleton.

cavalry. The former 2nd Dragoons took part in the Civil War and distinguished themselves at Beverly Ford, Brandy Station, Yellow Tavern and later at Winchester and Cedar Creek, as well as in other major battles.

In the Civil War, the Confederates started out with an advantage as far as cavalry was concerned. Local terrain and customs had fostered the formation of mounted units, even in the militias, and it was an easy matter for Jeb Stuart, commander of the Southern cavalry, to increase his force from three hundred sabres to the division that was to become a legend. Colonel Stuart's originality, and he was a warrior of infinite resource, was also reflected in the uniforms of his officers. They wore broad-brimmed hats decorated with ostrich feathers, tall boots, sashes at the waist and were armed with long pistols and heavy sabres. The remark that Stuart made when he lost his hat, in an engagement against a Union general, has become legendary. 'The

Yankees will pay for that', he said, and a week later he captured the general's entire equipment.

It took the Union two years to organise a cavalry that could face the Confederate cavalry, but from that moment on the Union cavalry created its own legends. The most famous name is certainly that of George A. Custer, known as the American Murat. A general during the Civil War and then a colonel in the regular army, he was in command of five troops of the 7th cavalry which the Sioux, Cheyenne and Arapaho Indians wiped out at the Little Big Horn on 25 June 1876.

At that time the dress uniform included a spiked helmet decorated with a hanging yellow plume; the dress uniform was covered with yellow braid and stripes, but the field uniform of the 7th Cavalry was much simpler. Custer himself preferred to wear the buckskin jacket of the rangers and scouts.

From the Rough Riders to the Marines

No discussion of the American cavalry would be complete without mention of the last 'personal' regiment in history, that First Volunteer Cavalry which Theodore Roosevelt himself raised for the Spanish-American War of 1898. He recruited these men among the farms and hunters of the Rocky Mountains. Roosevelt was then under-secretary of the navy and made himself second-in-command of the new unit; Colonel Leonard Wood was the commander.

Men from all walks of life enlisted in the ranks of the regiment, and they came to be called the Rough Riders, and thus they have taken their place in history. Their first brief campaign in Cuba is almost legendary. In only four short months they were transformed into veterans. So inexperienced had they been when they first embarked from Florida that many even left their horses behind.

There is another anecdote of the Cuban campaign of 1898 which has entered into history. On the evening of 15 February the battleship *Maine* was at anchor in the harbour of Havana when it was rocked by a terrific explosion that holed its steel plates and engulfed the ship in flame and smoke. Captain Sigsbee rushed from his cabin to the bridge and ran into his marine orderly, William Anthony. Anthony apologised and raising his right hand in the regulation salute said with total nonchalance, 'Captain, sir, allow me to in-

The Rough Riders were one of the first regiments to wear khaki. Their regimental insignia consisted of yellow epaulets and a pocket badge. (Yellow was the colour of the cavalry). During the Cuban Campaign of 1898, they abandoned their jackets and fought in blue shirts.

form you that your ship is sinking'.

This anecdote, one of hundreds in the history of the Marine Corps, may serve to introduce the subject of the marines, with which we will end this brief consideration of famous American military units.

At the time of the war in Cuba the American marines had already seen more than a century of service. Casual marine companies had been formed in the colonial period, but the official birth of the corps took place on 10 November 1775, when the Continental Congress decided to form two battalions of 'good seamen' to be known as the First and Second Battalions of American Marines.

In fact, the history of the marines, with certain exceptions, is that of the United States Navy. Their popularity, however, is a rather recent development. For more than one hundred years no particular mention was made of them except when they performed outstanding deeds. Early in the nineteenth century they fought the North African pirates, and in 1847 they faced the Mexicans at Chapultepec. Hence the Marines' song, 'From the halls of Montezuma, / To the shores of Tripoli, / We fight our country's battles, / On the land as on the sea...'.

During the Civil War they divided between North and South (which boasted a Confederate States Marine Corps) and took part in all the later 'official' wars of the United States. In the first years of the twentieth century, the following phrase became proverbial in the newspapers: 'The marines have landed, and the situation is well in hand.' But what won them a permanent place in history (despite all the attempts to suppress the corps made by such presidents as Jackson, Theodore Roosevelt, Taft and Hoover) was a question of censorship in the First World War. The war correspondent Floyd Gibbons was with the Fourth Brigade in the Belleau wood in France. He wrote a report of the battle named after that place and sent it to headquarters so that it could be transmitted to the United States. (It was at Belleau Wood that Sergeant Daly urged the Marines forward by shouting, 'Come on, boys! You don't want to live forever!') The censors forbade the mention of the names of corps and units in newspaper reports, but Gibbons wanted his fellow-citizens to know how heroically the marines had fought and mentioned them by name. The report was passed on, because it was accompanied as well by the news that Gibbons was dying. He had been shot in the head shortly after he had finished his report. The censor was a friend of his who forgot, or chose not to cross out the specific mention of the marines. This was the first and only time that a unit's name passed uncancelled through the censorship. Gibbons did not die, but lost an eye.

Private
(Marine Corps)—Full Dress

Drummer
(Marine Corps)
Full Dress

Warrant Officer
(Gunner)—Undress

Musician
(Navy)
Undress

Chief Petty Officer
(Chief Master-at-Arms)—Dress

Private
(Marine Corps)
Service

Corporal (Marine Corps)—Service
(Heavy Marching Order)

After the First World War the Marine Corps, whose motto is *Semper Fidelis*, was reduced in size. But in 1940, with rearmament, the strength of the corps was increased to thirty thousand men organised into two divisions, with three infantry regiments, a paratroop battalion, a light tank battalion, an amphibious battalion, four artillery groups and a unit of assault guns, as well as a group of dive bombers and landing craft. At the outbreak of war with Japan, several Marine units were stationed in the Philippines, Guam and other Pacific islands. Earlier a brigade, the First Provisional, had occupied Iceland. The units stationed in the Carolinas and on Wake Island fought heroically.

Throughout the Second World War the marines fought in the Pacific. They were raised to six divisions with a maximum strength of four hundred and eighty-five thousand, one hundred and thirteen men. They won distinction at Guadalcanal (2nd and 7th regiments of the Second Division) and at Tulagi in the Solomons. After the war, the strength of the corps was reduced to one hundred thousand men, but was later increased. Engaged in Korea were the First Marine Division, the First Provisional Brigade and later the Second Division. More recently the First and Second Divisions were sent to Vietnam.

Marine uniforms, 1899, dress (left) and field (right). The three men in the centre are in the navy. Below: An illustration from the Military Magazine *shows a lieutenant (seated) and a marine staff officer in the uniform of the years around 1830. The lieutenant is holding a shako in his hand. They have a remarkable esprit du corps and, with their particular armament and organisation, form a veritable independent army.*

Faithful Canada

The Canadian army is so clearly faithful to the British model that it has regiments named after British units. Thus, for example, there are the Black Watch of Canada, the Queen's Own Cameron Highlanders of Canada and Canadian Grenadier Guards, to mention only a few. The originals of these units are discussed in the chapter devoted to England and Scotland.

But Canada also has several units which are particularly its own, besides the famous Mounted Police, which has won universal fame because of an uninterrupted history of individual and collective bravery. They are usually referred to as the Mounties. They will have their first centennial celebration in 1973.

Among the regiments of the regular Canadian army, mention should be made of the Royal Canadian Dragoons, formed in 1883, which first won distinction in Canada in the 1885 campaign (the so-called 'Half-breed Revolt') and later in South Africa, in 1900, and in France in 1914 (where, in the tradition of the dragoons, they fought on foot and horse). In 1940 the regiment contributed a squadron to the formation of the 1st Canadian Motorcycle Regiment and then joined the Canadian Armoured Corps, with which it landed in Sicily on 22 October 1943.

During the Boer War Canadian dragoons repeated the daring Austrian feat of the Austro-Prussian conflict

The Halifax garrison artillery about 1880, in a lithograph by H. Burnett. The Canadian artillery was formed of volunteers corps recruited in 1855 and has taken part in all the wars in which Canada has been involved. Today the Canadian artillery is represented by the Royal Regiment of Canadian Artillery. It fought in Korea and in the Congo.

An officer of Lord Strathcona's Horse (Royal Canadian) in the dress uniform of 1930. One of the most outstanding regiments of the Canadian army, it started out in 1901 as Squadron A of the Canadian Mounted Rifles. The regimental motto is Perseverance.

of 1866. To cover the withdrawal of English batteries across the River Komati, a squadron of dragoons under the command of Lieutenant Cockburn fought to the last man, while a Sergeant Holland, single-handed, manned a mounted weapon. When the Boers were too near for him to remove the weapon, Sergeant Holland removed the band from its carriage and galloped away with it. A contribution to the 1st Canadian Motorcycle Regiment was made by another famous cavalry regiment, Lord Strathcona's Horse (Royal Canadians), which had been created at the time of the Boer War. It consisted of volunteers recruited by a celebrated Canadian politician, David Alexander Smith, First Lord Strathcona and Mount Royal. One of the four Victoria Crosses given to Canadians in that campaign was won by one of Strathcona's men, Sergeant Richardson.

Strathcona's Horse fought in Italy in the Second World War and took part in the Korean War. The heritage of France, which first colonised Canada, is represented by the 22nd Regiment, which is officially called the *Régiment Canadien Français* or *Royal 22ᵉ régiment*. The regiment's emblem is a beaver with the motto *'Je me souviens'*. French names are also borne by such units as *Les Voltigeurs de Québec*, a regiment founded on 7 March 1862 which now includes the *Régiment de Québec* (Mitrailleuses), originally established in 1869. Two distinguished Canadian units are the Royal Canadian Regiment and the Royal Regiment of Canada.

The first was founded on 21 December 1883 and consisted of Companies A, B and C as the Infantry School Corps. In 1899 it landed at Cape City to take part in the Boer War and was part of the famous Nineteenth Brigade commanded by General Smith-Dorrien together with the Gordon Highlanders and the Shropshire Light Infantry.

One day in February 1900 they attempted a surprise attack in the dark before dawn. An alarm device of iron wire and tin cans went off and aroused the Boers, who subjected them to terrific fire and drove them back. But one officer, Captain Stairs, nevertheless managed to reach a position and occupy it with seventy-three sappers and mine-layers. From that position he got the Boers in an enfilade and forced them to surrender though they had a strength of four thousand.

The Royal Regiment of Canada also goes back to the nineteenth century. It was founded in 1862 as the 10th Battalion of Volunteer Militia Rifles and was later called the Regiment of Toronto Volunteers and the Royal Regiment of Toronto Grenadiers. It was at Dieppe on 19 August 1942.

The dress uniform of the Royal Canadian Regiment consists of a red coat and a white spike-headed casque, as does that of another infantry regiment, Princess Patricia's Canadian Light Infantry, a unit organised in Ottawa in 1914 and named after the daughter of the governor-general of Canada.

The regiment of the Queen's Own Rifles of Canada. This uniform of about 1890 was drawn by Burnett. The regiment was founded in Toronto in 1860 as the Second Battalion of Volunteer Militia Rifles of Canada. In 1951 it provided a company of the 1st Canadian Rifles Battalion serving with NATO in Europe.

The Silver Sombreros

The South American armies are undoubtedly among the most colourful in the world. But behind the splendour of their uniforms is the history of desperate and bloody struggles and a painful and hard past.

Particularly noteworthy were the *Plateados* of General Santa Anna, the man who led the struggles for Mexican independence and the war against the United States in the stormy years between 1830 and 1850. These men were known as Plateados because of the silver, or *plata*, braid and saddle equipment they wore;

they were noted for their broad-brimmed sombreros.

Pancho Villa, the leader of the first revolution in contemporary history, had his own guard, known as *Dorados*. Another revolutionary force were fanatical *Cristeros*, who in the anticlerical fury of the revolution presented themselves as defenders of the clergy but actually indulged in endless atrocities.

Worthy of mention among Peruvian units are the Hussars of Junin, named for the cavalry battle between Perucian and Spanish forces that took place there in 1824. When in the first decade of the nineteenth century England began to attempt to establish naval bases in South American, the Spanish authorities of what is now Argentina began to form local military corps to reinforce the few metropolitan troops stationed there. These local forces were called *Milicias Civicas*.

It was from these forces that the Argentinian army was to be formed. Especially interesting were the *Husares del rey* (King's Hussars), a cavalry corps of five squadrons. The first squadron was called *Pueyrredón* after the name of its first commandant; the second squadron had the sombre name of *Infernales*. The other squadrons did not have names. Don Juan Martin de Pueyrredón contributed his own money to the equipping of his squadron, which wore a cyclindrical black hat with white tassels, a cockade and a red feather, a short dark-blue cloak with white braid and red lapels. The white braid also ornamented the dark-blue trousers. Tall grenadier boots completed the uniform. Another distinctive feature of these riders was their long hair tied with a silver ribbon at the line of the neck. Their horses were *criolla* bays. They had long manes and tails and were *reyunos*, that is, the left ear was partially lopped off.

The Infernales of the second squadron wore a similar uniform, but the feather on the hat was white and the cloak was green with yellow lapels, and their trousers were yellow. They, too, wore their hair long and mounted criollos, wolf-coloured rather than bay, with the right ear clipped. The black top hat is still worn with certain ceremonial uniforms of the Argentine army. Finally mention must be made of the Italian Legion under Garibaldi, which fought for the liberty of Uruguay and defeated the men of the Argentine dictator Juan Manuel de Rosas at the Battle of Sant'Antonio on 8 February 1846.

A water colour by Knötel shows an Argentinian officer from La Plata Province in the uniform of 1840. Opposite: a 19th-century French illustration of the Mexican Infantry. Notable Latin American units included the 4th Lancers of Paraguay, known as Aca-Caraya or 'Monkey heads', because of their monkey-skin trimmed helmets. They won distinction in the Chaco War (1932-35). The Latin American Republics have some extremely striking dress uniforms. The Brazilian Independence Dragoons, who serve as the Presidential Guard, have a 'Minerva-style' helmet topped by a dragon-shaped crest.

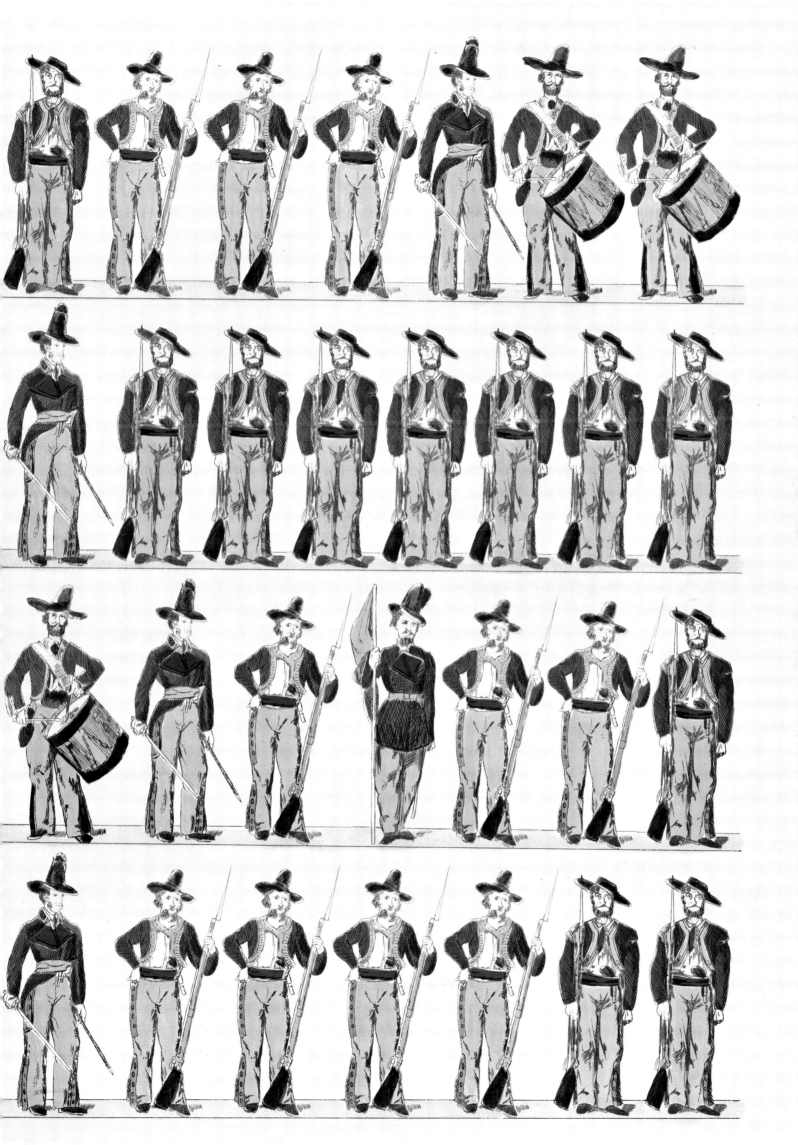

Catalogue of uniforms

On the following pages the uniforms of various corps and regiments which could not be described or illustrated in the text but which are of particular interest are illustrated. Pages 242 and 243 present a hasty review of particular and famous units of the ancient, medieval, Renaissance, and post-Renaissance periods, that is, the period of time extending to the threshold of the 17th century, when the regiment was born. Following pages illustrate modern uniforms nation by nation. Where no date is given the illustration is of a uniform still in use. The sources of illustrations or elements used to reconstruct the uniforms are indicated on p. 250 ff., in the appropriate index. The drawings were executed by Carlo Alberto Michelini.

Intrepid Guard of
King Gudea
(Mesopotamia, 2100 BC)

Sacred Battalion
(Thebes, 4th century BC)

Immortals
(Persia, 6th century BC)

Roman slinger
(Rome, 1st century BC)

Elephant-mounted Infantry
(Egypt, 15th century BC)

Shang Chariot
*(China, 13th cent. BC) Archer,
warrior armed with an ax-knife, and charioteer.*

Jezetere
(Macedonia, 4th century BC)

Heavy Infantry
(Byzantium, 7th-8th cent.)

Clovis' Guards
*(Kingdom
of the Franks, 482-511)*

Preux
*(The Valourous;
Carolingian Empire, 9th century)*

Soudiour
(Gall, 1st century BC)

Turkish Infantry
(17th century)

Samurai
(Japan, 17th century)

Poitiers Cameleers
(Moorish Army, 732)

Pikeman
(Spain, 16th century)

Mounted Gunner
(Italy, 14th century)

Cuirassier Captain
(Italy, 17th century)

Man at arms
of Charles Emmanuel I
(Italy, 17th century)

243

Dutch Foot Guards
(England, 17th century)

Scots Garde du Corps
(France, c. 1750)

Royal Scot Greys
(England, 1815)

The Buffs
(Royal East Kent)
(England, 1742)

1st Royal Dragoons
(England, 1939)

Royal Inniskilling
Fusiliers
(Great Britain)

Royal Tank Regiment
(Great Britain, 1917)

Horse Guard Artillery
(France, 1800-1815)

Lorraine Regiment
(France, 18th century)

Gardes-Françaises
(France, 17th century)

Gardes-Françaises Drum
(France, 17th century)

'Port-fanion' Soldier
(France, 1913)

2nd Chevaux-Légers
(France, First Empire)

Napoleon Guides
(France, 1799)

Chasseurs d'Afrique
(France, 1832)

Paratroops
(France, 1960)

244

Garde du Corps
(Hessen-Cassel, 1831)

Guard Grenadiers
(Prussia, 1813)

Guard Hussars
(Prussia, 1875)

Von Diesbach Regiment
(Switzerland)

Garde du Corps
(German Empire, 1890)

Belling Hussars
(Prussia, 1775)

Von Ziethen Hussars
(Prussia, 1745)

Marshal's Uhlans
(Saxony, 1745)

Hungarian Uhlans
(Austrian Empire, 1870)

Cuirassiers
(Austrian Empire, 1750)

6th Hussars
(Holland, 1823)

Afrika Korps
(Germany, 1942)

3rd Uhlans
(Poland, 1815)

Pavlov Regiment
(Russia, 1900)

Siberian Marksmen
(Russia, 1902)

Horse Guard Artillery
(Russia, 1906)

Women's Battalion
(Russia, 1917)

Trotskyite Infantry
(Russia, 1920)

Death's Head Battalion
(Roman Republic, 1849)

Death Volunteers
(Italy, 1915-1918)

Horse Artillery
(Italy, 1936)

Queen's Dragoons
(Spain, 1735)

Majorca Regiment
(Spain, 1807)

West Point Cadets
(USA, 1825)

Mexican Spy Company
(USA, 1847)

Confederate Infantry
(USA, 1863)

7th Cavalry
(USA, 1876)

Philippine Explorers
(USA, 1904)

Honour Guard
(Peru)

Carabineers
(Argentina, 1910)

Anti-guerilla Corps
(North Vietnam)

Gurkha Lancers
(Nepal)

Women's Battalions
(Israel)

Sheik
(Saudi Arabia)

Dervish
(Sudan, 1880)

Falcon Feathers
(Eritrea, 1930)

Paratroops
(Senegal)

Royal Guard
(Morocco)

INDEXES

INDEX OF NAMES

Note: Numbers printed in italics refer to picture captions

INDEX OF MILITARY UNITS

Note: Numbers printed in italics refer to picture captions